"Ensuring the full participation of women a[...] business of the twenty-first century. The stori[...] difference give me hope. We can use our powe[...] And once we do, we can fast-forward [...]
— *from the foreword by* **HILLARY** [...]

FAST

FORWARD

HOW
WOMEN CAN
ACHIEVE
POWER AND
PURPOSE

MELANNE VERVEER

KIM K. AZZARELLI

Praise for

FAST FORWARD

"We are all capable of great things, even world-changing things, if we take inspiration from others and join together to get it done. We are witnessing an awakening to the justice of civil rights for women in our time. You can feel it is imminent, and it will change the world when it is accomplished. Here are stories of a few women who have dared to imagine the day, and worked to make it happen. Let them inspire you." — Meryl Streep

"A life filled with purpose is the greatest gift we can give to ourselves — and to others. *Fast Forward* shows women how to lead lives of purpose and meaning, so that they, and our world, can thrive." — Arianna Huffington

"As I have traveled the world, I've seen the incredible strength and resilience of women everywhere, working at every level. If there was ever a doubt that our moment is now, this book dispels it. *Fast Forward* shows every woman how she can empower herself and her community, and why all of us will be better for it. Women are *the* growing force for progress in the twenty-first century." — Madeleine Albright

"What is life without a sense of purpose? Any woman who's asked herself this question must read *Fast Forward,* filled with inspiring stories of women who've achieved power in their own lives and used it to make a difference for others, especially other women and girls." — Maria Shriver

"I love this book. It tells the stories of ingenious women who took the circumstances around them and created successful companies and purpose in their lives, while at the same time recognizing their own power to lift other women up, supporting both economic growth and social progress all over the world. It's an inspiring wake-up call to action, and once you're fired up, longing to find your own power and potential, it gives you a toolkit of information as to how you can begin. Brilliant."

— Sally Field, actor and activist

"The stories of the remarkable women chronicled in *Fast Forward* are both inspiring and instructive, making it a must-read for anyone interested in leading successfully with purpose in the twenty-first century. *Fast Forward* is also a reminder that progress and gender parity are inextricably linked and that if we want a society that operates at its best, we have to work for both."
                                             — Ajay Banga, CEO, MasterCard

"The stories in this inspirational book serve as a powerful reminder that, with the right support, women can become an unstoppable force in their communities and economies. It is a rousing call to action for anyone who cares about creating a more equal world. Unleashing the full potential of women is not an option — it is an imperative."
— Cherie Blair, CBE, QC, and founder, Cherie Blair Foundation for Women

"In *Fast Forward*, we are reminded why Melanne Verveer and Kim Azzarelli are two leading 'sheroes' of the global women's movement. The book is chock-full of wise and clever advice for women *and men* committed to empowering women to reach their full potential. You will be inspired by their profiles of determined women of resilience, grit, and passion to change the world. Brava!"   — Darren Walker, president, Ford Foundation

"*Fast Forward* gives all of us hope through the inspiring examples of pioneering women in global leadership, public service, and the corporate world — a path forged by Melanne Verveer since she helped Hillary Clinton transform the concept of women's rights in Beijing in 1995. Verveer and co-author Kim Azzarelli share their practical experience with new insights into how we can all lean even further forward. A must-read for women — and men — who believe strong, educated women and girls are the key to advancing societies."   — Andrea Mitchell, NBC News

FAST FORWARD

FAST
FORWARD

How *WOMEN CAN ACHIEVE*
POWER and PURPOSE

Melanne Verveer
and
Kim K. Azzarelli

MARINER BOOKS
HOUGHTON MIFFLIN HARCOURT
Boston   New York

First Mariner Books edition 2016

For information about permission to reproduce selections from this book,
write to trade.permissions@hmhco.com or to Permissions,
Houghton Mifflin Harcourt Publishing Company, 3 Park Avenue,
19th Floor, New York, New York 10016.

www.hmhco.com

Library of Congress Cataloging-in-Publication Data
Verveer, Melanne.
Fast forward : how women can achieve power and purpose / Melanne Verveer
and Kim K. Azzarelli; foreword by Hillary Rodham Clinton.
pages cm
ISBN 978-0-544-52719-5 (hardback) —
ISBN 978-0-544-66435-7 (trade paper (international edition)) —
ISBN 978-0-544-52800-0 (ebook)
ISBN 978-0-544-81185-0 (pbk.)
1. Women in the professions. 2. Women executives. 3. Women in economic
development. 4. Success in business. I. Azzarelli, Kim K. II. Title.
HD6054.V47 2015
650.1082 — dc23   2015019683

Book design by Chrissy Kurpeski
Typeset in Minion Pro

Printed in the United States of America
DOC 10 9 8 7 6 5 4 3 2 1

"Silence" by Anasuya Sengupta, copyright © 1995 by Anasuya Sengupta,
is reprinted with the permission of Anasuya Sengupta.

To the women around the world who endlessly inspire us with their courage and commitment as they bring about change. We hope this book supports them in their efforts and inspires others to help contribute to advancing women and girls in ways large and small.

— *Melanne Verveer and Kim Azzarelli*

To my husband, Phil, who makes all things possible.
To my children, Michael, Alexa, and Elaina, and
my granddaughters, Leigh and Evan, who are
my pride and joy.

— *Melanne Verveer*

To my dear husband, my loving family, and all the women and men who have inspired me, often through quiet example, to focus on the power of perspective and to help me find my life's purpose.

— *Kim Azzarelli*

Contents

Foreword

by Hillary Rodham Clinton

ELEANOR ROOSEVELT ONCE SAID, "Many people will walk in and out of your life, but only true friends will leave footprints in your heart." For decades, Melanne Verveer has been that true friend to me and to countless women around the world she's never even met. She's devoted herself to helping women unlock their potential. That's been the story of much of her life — as an ambassador, advocate, and activist — and it's the theme of this book.

Fast Forward shows us how leaders at every level can use their power and purpose to help more and more women achieve their dreams for a better life. Melanne and Kim Azzarelli — an attorney and champion for women in her own right — explain how, in doing this, we strengthen communities, companies, and countries.

There were plenty of cynics in the lead-up to the 1995 United Nations' Fourth World Conference on Women in Beijing. Many in our own government thought the United States should not participate because of China's dismal human rights record, a concern we certainly appreciated. Others doubted that a conference on women would ever achieve much anyway. This one we didn't appreciate at all; in fact, it only served to deepen our determination to participate, speak out, and drive progress.

Melanne accompanied me to Beijing. There, together with leaders from across the world, I declared that "human rights are women's rights, and women's rights are human rights once and for all." For the first time in history, 189 nations came together and made a commitment to work toward the full participation of women and girls in every aspect of society.

Back at home, Melanne was determined to make good on that commitment and help me build on that momentum worldwide. While I was first lady, we worked to narrow the global gaps in girls' education and women's economic participation. We advocated for laws against domestic violence and human trafficking. We encouraged institutions like the United Nations, the World Bank, and others to underscore the importance of investing in women and girls.

After leaving the White House, Melanne spent eight years at Vital Voices, an organization that she and I started with Madeleine Albright, to support emerging women leaders around the world.

When I accepted President Barack Obama's offer to serve as secretary of state, I was determined to bring the progress of women and girls — progress that had too often been relegated to the margins — into the mainstream of American diplomacy. Naturally, Melanne was one of my first calls. I asked her to serve as our first-ever ambassador-at-large for global women's issues and help me craft a "full participation agenda" and weave it into the fabric of American foreign policy and national security.

It was then that Melanne introduced me to Kim, who shared her determination to unlock the potential of women and girls. Through her work at Avon, Kim focused on how to leverage public-private partnerships to enhance our efforts. She founded and chairs a center at Cornell Law School to support women judges in an effort to combat violence against women. Today, she also leads Seneca Women, which supports and connects women worldwide.

Together with activists around the world, we have worked to make the case, based on both evidence and morality, that our world cannot get ahead by leaving half the population behind. We have more data than ever before that confirms what we've always known intuitively: when women and girls have opportunities to participate, economies grow and nations prosper.

Over the past twenty years, women and girls have made important progress around the world. Access to health and education has improved markedly. The rate of maternal mortality has been cut in half. Girls now attend primary school at nearly the same rate as boys.

Yet significant gaps remain. Progress has been slow when it comes to economic opportunity for women. Globally, the gulf between men's and women's labor force participation hasn't narrowed that much, and equal pay remains out of reach. One in three women continues to experience violence. And not enough women have risen to the highest ranks of business and government.

Ensuring the full participation of women and girls is the great unfinished business of the twenty-first century. However, as Melanne and Kim often remind us, this isn't just a women's issue. It's a family issue and a men's issue too. These days, in the United States and elsewhere, many hardworking families depend on two incomes to make ends meet. When one paycheck is shortchanged, the entire family suffers.

The future of our global economy depends on more women participating in it. The evidence on this is overwhelming, and Melanne and Kim have worked tirelessly to gather it. If we close the global gap in workforce participation between men and women, gross domestic product worldwide would grow by nearly 12 percent by 2030. We cannot afford to leave that growth potential on the table.

A true friend, Melanne gives me hope. A rising star, Kim gives me hope. The stories in this book of people making a difference give me hope. No more rewinding the rights of women and girls. We can move fast and we can move forward. We can use our power and purpose to help all women achieve their own. And once we do, we can fast-forward to a better world for all.

1

Why Women, Why Now

IT WAS JUST ANOTHER APPOINTMENT on the calendar for both of us: 2 p.m. on a warm spring day, at Kim's office on the twenty-seventh floor of Avon's headquarters in midtown Manhattan. To Melanne, it was one more meeting on top of dozens she'd already taken to explore private-sector partnerships for Vital Voices, the women's leadership nonprofit she had cofounded eight years earlier and was always working to grow. As far as Kim knew, Vital Voices was just another worthy nonprofit that Avon might consider supporting.

Melanne by then had grown used to the standard corporate position: women were fine as a philanthropic gesture, but not as the active partners she knew they could be. But something was different about this particular meeting. Kim, who then served as vice president, corporate secretary, and associate general counsel, had just taken charge of public affairs at Avon and was ready to use her platform to go beyond traditional corporate social responsibility. As she saw it, companies could join forces with women to both do well and do good, contributing to a company's goals while also advancing the lives of women and girls.

So when Melanne started talking about a potential partnership, Kim jumped in. The traditional approach to corporate charity was often limited. Kim was interested in exploring what she called "next-generation corporate social responsibility" — weaving social impact directly into the business strategy. Melanne did a double take: this was exactly how she envisioned Vital Voices making its impact. She glanced at her deputy, Alyse Nelson (now the president and CEO of Vital Voices), who looked at Kim and said, "You're one of us."

In the near decade since that meeting, wherever we've sat, we have worked together on the basis of the shared conviction that progress for women and girls can fast-forward us to a better world.

The two of us are a generation apart and come from vastly different backgrounds. Melanne, the granddaughter of Ukrainian immigrants who settled in the Pennsylvania Coal Belt, has spent much of her professional life advocating for women from within the public sector — from the White House to the villages of India. Born and raised in New York City at a time when the women's movement was gaining a new foothold, Kim, an attorney, has spent much of her career advocating from the private sector, using her legal and deal-making skills to forge partnerships across sectors on behalf of women and girls.

But despite being from different worlds, we share a fundamental understanding: women are critical agents in creating economic growth and social progress. Yet in the circles in which we traveled, it often felt as if few others saw that potential in women.

In our own lifetimes, we have seen women's advocates win major battles, changing laws and putting issues like domestic violence and sexual harassment on the map. But in government and the private sector, where people puzzled endlessly over how to end conflicts and grow new markets, "women" was still, well, if not a taboo word, a largely unspoken one. In our experience, in those environments, arguments about the catalytic role of women did not get the traction they deserved.

Melanne witnessed this from the vantage point of international diplomacy and development, as Hillary Clinton's deputy and chief of staff during the Clinton administration, then as the cofounder of Vital Voices, and later as the first ambassador-at-large for global women's issues at the State Department. She knew how effective a force women could be, even in societies where their worth was devalued, their legal rights circumscribed. Despite these obstacles, women opened small businesses, invested in their children's health and education, and worked across religious and tribal divides to bring peace to conflict-riven nations. They leveraged what power they had for the greater good.

Kim witnessed the same phenomenon from a different vantage point.

In her work with female judges around the world, as cofounder of Cornell Law School's Avon Global Center for Women and Justice, she knew the impact women leaders could make, especially if they were supported and connected. In her corporate and legal career, Kim had also seen women entrepreneurs, often starting with the tiniest amounts of capital, build dynamic businesses. In 2005, she had listened to the economist C. K. Prahalad discuss his thesis that the world's poor were viable business partners, as he laid out in his now classic business book *The Fortune at the Bottom of the Pyramid*. "If we stop thinking of the poor as victims or as a burden and start recognizing them as resilient and creative entrepreneurs and value-conscious consumers, a whole new world of opportunity will open up," he wrote. In 2011, Harvard professors Michael Porter and Mark Kramer would coin the concept "creating shared value" to describe how some farsighted companies developed strategies to achieve both business goals and social benefits. Kim quickly saw how these models could apply specifically to women.

But in their rush to partner with those at the base of the pyramid or to create shared value, very few companies envisioned how women fit into the picture. It often seemed that the talent and contributions of women at all levels were being overlooked. This was true in diplomacy and international development as well. Women's potential as full economic participants and agents of change had been undervalued for too long.

In the years since we first met, we noticed a shift in perspective. One by one, leaders from around the globe are beginning to recognize the critical role women can and must play. While this shift is being driven by a number of factors, chief among them are (1) a growing body of empirical evidence demonstrating the impact of investing in women and girls, and (2) a historic and rising number of women in leadership positions.

Today the data is in. Institutions ranging from McKinsey & Company to the World Bank have published research showing that women are one of the most powerful demographic groups the world has ever seen. In 2012, a leading consultancy estimated that as many as a billion women were poised to enter the world economy over the next decade. Their impact could be as great as that of China or India. Women are also a fast-growing entrepreneurial force, creating jobs and fueling economic prosperity. From 1997 to 2014, women-owned businesses in the United States grew one and a half times faster than the national average. As of 2014, the nation had more than 9 million women-owned businesses, which employ almost 7.9 million people and boast over $1.4 trillion in revenues. Women own or lead more than a quarter of private businesses worldwide. Women also wield enormous purchasing power, controlling some $20 trillion in annual consumer spending globally. Muhtar Kent, the CEO of Coca-Cola, put it simply: "Women already are the most dynamic and fastest-growing economic force in the world today."

But this story is not just about how much money women have to spend, but how they spend it. Investing in women and girls creates a "double dividend," as women tend to reinvest their earnings in their communities and families, raising the gross domestic product and lowering illiteracy and mortality rates. This "multiplier effect" has made advancing women and girls a primary goal in global development. In 2012, the World Bank's annual *World Development Report* stressed the promotion of equal education and equal economic opportunities for women and girls. "Greater gender equality," the report's authors wrote, is key to "enhancing productivity and improving other development outcomes, including prospects for the next generation and for the quality of societal policies and institutions."

Women are also driving growth for the companies that appreciate the value they bring to the table. Companies with more women in their top ranks perform better. A 2011 analysis by Catalyst, a nonprofit devoted to expanding opportunities for women in business, found that Fortune 500 companies that consistently had three or more female board directors over a five-year period had nearly a 50 percent higher return on equity than companies with no women on their boards. Credit Suisse has found that companies with more than 15 percent of women in top management have a higher return on equity than companies where women comprise less than 10 percent of top management. A 2015 analysis found that the Fortune 1000 companies with women CEOs performed three times better than the benchmark S&P 500 between 2002 and 2014. In the words of the former president of the World Bank, Robert Zoellick, "Gender equality is smart economics."

As a result, corporate executives and government leaders alike are waking up to the fact that women are drivers of both economic growth and social progress. Armed with the data, women and men leading communities, nonprofits, companies, and countries are increasingly making the case for putting women at the center of their strategies. From the village to the boardroom we have seen individuals using the data to shift mindsets, changing how we think about the power and role of half the world's population. In some instances, making the case has meant giving families incentives to keep their daughters in school. In others, it has meant lobbying leading CEOs to take a hard look at the correlation between diversity and profitability.

And as more women ascend to senior positions, they are increasingly using their newfound power for a common purpose: to advance other women, to "lift as they climb." They are reaching across sectors, nations, and socioeconomic strata to form networks propelled by a shared belief that women and girls have the potential to ignite change. These are not the old-boys clubs of yesterday where deals got cut in back rooms. Today's women-led networks, purposeful and inclusive, are turning that paradigm on its head.

These purpose-driven partnerships yield their own double dividends for women. In a world where women and men are increasingly suffering from time constraints, being able to make a positive contribution while connecting with others can create both personal satisfaction and professional success.

A substantial cohort of women has reached the upper echelons of government, business, and civil society. Leaders like Hillary Clinton, Christine Lagarde, and Melinda Gates are using their high visibility to draw attention to the importance of women and girls in today's global economy and development. Women CEOs of DuPont, IBM, Xerox, PepsiCo, Sam's Club, Campbell Soup, and General Motors, to name a few, oversee global companies collectively worth billions of dollars. Women presidents and prime ministers in countries including Germany, Denmark, South Korea, Chile, and Brazil are modeling female leadership and exercising hard power in the global arena. Media stars like Oprah Winfrey, Arianna Huffington, and Tina Brown are shaping the discourse around women and power, using their reach to tell women's stories. High-profile business leaders like Diane von Furstenberg and Sheryl Sandberg have made women a central focus of their leadership, using their positions to empower other women. At the same time, women have also entered middle management in large numbers, where they are leveraging their influence and expertise to make the case for women and girls. At the base of the pyramid, too, women are creating inclusive networks that are yielding enormous transformation.

Obstacles to unleashing the potential of women, however, still stand in our way. They range from discrimination to widespread violence against women to the design flaws in the system that make it difficult for women to reconcile today's economic realities with caregiving and other responsibilities. We must continue to work to eradicate these injustices and secure fundamental human rights for women.

But an undeniable momentum is building, as more women ascend to leadership and an increasing number of women and men recognize women's potential to fast-forward us to a better world. We stand today on the cusp of a global power shift, one that has the potential to redefine the way we work and live. What follows is an explanation of what this unprecedented power shift could mean for each of us, and for our global community.

Through the stories and wisdom of women and men we know and admire, hailing from diverse industries, nations, and socioeconomic strata, we show how women's growing economic power is creating social progress. This book lays out the many ways in which women drive the economy — as managers, employees, entrepreneurs, and consumers — and how this is changing the way we do business, define success, and create social impact. You will see how these women are using their power to drive their purpose, building businesses that give back, leveraging resources to empower other women, and engaging in skills-based volunteerism and philanthropy. This is a reference book for those who want to master and disseminate the data on the business case for women, and a how-to manual for those who want to harness their own power and combine it with purpose. To that end, we have included in the appendices a toolkit with some practical advice as well as selected resources that can help you continue on your personal journey. More advice and resources can be found at www.senecawomen.com.

Our collective experience spans more than fifty years and one hundred countries. We've met thousands of women, from British parliamentarians to Afghan peace activists, from the most glamorous cities in the world to war-torn villages. We have met with American combat veterans and women who serve in UN peacekeeping missions, with Supreme Court justices and survivors of brutal acid attacks. And we have found that while the stories have a thousand faces, in the end it is the same story being told over and over again. It's the story of women and their aspirations for themselves, for their families, and for their communities. It's the story of how, when given the opportunity, women can fast-forward us to the world we all want to see. This is the story we knew we wanted to share.

What we have learned from our research, from our work, and from speaking to these thousands of women, including more than seventy female leaders and some male champions interviewed for this book, is that advancing and investing in women and girls can unlock the potential of countries, companies, and communities. Doing so can also unlock the potential of individual women too, beginning with the recognition of our own power and potential to lift one another up.

In fact, change always starts with individuals — in this case, people who found their purpose in advancing women and girls. And in speaking to these women and men who share our purpose, we have found that despite the diversity of our experiences, one simple approach holds constant. It's an approach that can also ignite your own potential, transforming the way you think about your life and work. It can be described in three simple steps:

- Know your power.
- Find your purpose.
- Connect with others.

Whether you work in the nonprofit world, log hours as a corporate lawyer, educate the next generation as a teacher, run a business, or raise children full-time — whatever your calling — this approach results in success. It brings success the way we're defining it: a success that includes not only personal achievement but also meaning, impact, and fulfillment.

As you will see, change often begins with a shift in perspective in one individual, which then ripples through her own life, organization, community, and beyond. And just as women are coming to embrace their own power to effect change, men are also expanding their perspectives, to understand that women are true partners in global progress.

Since 1848 in Seneca Falls, New York, where more than three hundred participants gathered for the first women's rights convention in the United States, women and men have advocated for women's equal participation. The progress of history, a wealth of new, evidence-based research, and the imperatives of growth have lent stunning velocity to women's advancement in just the past few years. What follows is what that unprecedented power shift could mean for countries, companies, and communities, and what it can mean for you.

2

Know the Power of Women:
Make the Case

IN 1991, ANN MOORE BECAME the publisher of the celebrity magazine *People*. She thought the magazine would be more successful if she could pivot the content toward female readers. Her male colleagues, however, were not so sure. A female readership? That would alienate some of their biggest advertisers — the auto companies in Detroit. Everyone "knew" women didn't care about cars.

Ann, a seasoned media executive who had spent time at *Fortune* and *Money* magazines and was the founding publisher of *Sports Illustrated for Kids*, knew better; she just needed proof. She started with minivans. At the time, most ads for minivans appeared in magazines geared toward men, like *Fortune*. She sent a videographer to Detroit to film cars that pulled into the parking lot next door to an upscale hotel favored by Time Inc. executives.

"Every time a minivan rolled up, we had a microphone, and we said to the driver who got out of the minivan, 'What's your favorite magazine?'" Ann recalls. "Every one of them getting out of a minivan was a woman, and she said, '*People*.' We spliced together the tape and mailed it to the product managers of all of the minivan manufacturers in Detroit. And we got the business." She used the same method for other models of cars and got the same results. Soon, many carmakers were advertising in *People*.

It took the help of a few videographers for Ann, who later became the first female chief executive officer of the Time Inc. publishing empire, to make her point: women are an economic force to be reckoned with.

Eight years later, Kathy Matsui, then a managing director at Goldman Sachs in Tokyo, needed to prove a similar point. Her job was to advise clients on how to invest in Japan, but the country was in a recession. At the same time, she noticed that her highly educated female friends, many of whom had recently had children, were having trouble returning to the workforce after taking a year or two off. Between Japan's stagnant economy and her friends' failed attempts to find work, Kathy identified a potential bright spot.

"On the one hand, the reality of investing in Japan looked so bleak, and on the other hand, there is this untapped hidden resource staring us right in the face," Kathy told us, referring to Japan's highly skilled women who were not in the labor force. "What if you could equalize the gender gap? What would that mean in macroeconomic terms?"

Kathy didn't have to depend on videos. The government and private sector companies had already collected reams of data on Japanese citizens and consumers. In less than two weeks, she fleshed out her insight into women's role in the Japanese economy and released a groundbreaking report in 1999, *Women-omics: Buy the Female Economy.*

The report posited a radical new investment thesis: women are critical to driving Japan's economy. Her research wove together social observations, like the fact that women who maintain a family and a career often face criticism; demographic trends, such as the rise of single-women households and figures on women's spending; and consumer data showing that demand by women was supporting growing industries such as Internet and cellphone services, condominium sales, and luxury goods.

For over a decade, the Japanese economy continued to founder. And Kathy's analysis got little attention.

Fast-forward to today. Sixteen years later, Kathy is vice chair of Goldman Sachs Japan, and her "womenomics" research has captured the attention of a growing number of executives and government leaders — including Japanese prime minister Shinzō Abe — who increasingly understand that women are the key drivers of both economic growth and social progress. In this chapter, we'll see how women and men in government and at major companies are using research and data to make the case for putting women at the center of their strategies. And we'll see how the multiplier effect works in practice — that is, how advancing women and girls yields a double dividend, improving conditions for the women themselves while having a significant impact on countries and companies around the world.

What It Means for Countries

Christine Lagarde, the first female managing director of the International Monetary Fund, has a vision for achieving a more stable and prosperous world economy. She leads the organization that provides policy advice and financing to numerous countries, and has made the "inclusive economy" — an economic strategy based on equitable opportunities — a central tenet of her leadership. Since taking over the IMF in 2011, she has been making the case that women are, in IMF parlance, "macro critical," integral to the institution's core mission.

How critical? Increasing women's workforce participation to equal that of men's could potentially raise GDP by 34 percent in Egypt, 9 percent in Japan, 12 percent in the United Arab Emirates, and 5 percent in the United States, according to one 2012 estimate.

During Lagarde's tenure, the IMF has produced studies and papers demonstrating that women's economic participation can be a powerful driver of growth. A recent report highlighted the importance of removing legal obstacles that inhibit women from working, such as barring them from pursuing certain professions, working without their husband's permission, working at night, or opening a bank account. "It would be beneficial to level the playing field by removing obstacles that prevent women from becoming economically active if they choose to do so," the report suggests.

"From the IMF perspective . . . we can contribute the facts, the figures, the numbers which actually document the very valid cause for the integration of women, the elimination of discrimination, and what I have called 'the fair and level playing field' for all to accomplish their talents," Lagarde told us. "I believe in the cause of women, and I believe in the strength of their contribution to the economy."

Economists from the World Economic Forum and the World Bank

concur. Each organization has, in recent years, added momentum to this growing body of macroeconomic data with new reports and research that are influencing executives and world leaders alike. In 2006, the World Economic Forum issued the *Global Gender Gap Report*. Under the leadership of Saadia Zahidi, the report analyzed the gap between men and women by country, using four metrics: access to health care, education, economic participation, and political empowerment. While no country has yet to close all the gaps completely, those with narrower gaps are far more economically competitive. The *Global Gender Gap Report* has become an influential reference tool on women's progress.

Luis Alberto Moreno, president of the Inter-American Development Bank (IDB), understands the potential economic impact of closing the gender gap. In particular, he has seen how women's increased workforce participation has been critical to the growth of Latin American economies. From 2000 to 2010, the rate of women's participation in the formal labor market grew by 15 percent across the Latin American–Caribbean region; a World Bank study concluded that women's additional earnings helped provide a bulwark during the economic crisis of the late 2000s. Indeed, extreme poverty throughout the region would have been 30 percent higher by 2010 without women's contributions to the labor force in the previous decade. "Women are key to driving growth in Latin America," Luis told us.

He also understands that when women control how they spend their money, their families and communities benefit. In Brazil, for example, children in households where women were the primary breadwinners were up to 14 percent more likely to attend secondary school.

Luis is doing his part to stimulate this multiplier effect by investing in cross-sector collaborations that support female entrepreneurs. "I realized that over time we needed to be much more inclusive, bringing in the private sector, bringing in civil society, and finding partnerships, because at the end of the day, this is what it's all about," he said. Even for an institution as large as the IDB, which loaned $14 billion in 2013, Luis pointed out, "it doesn't make sense" to tackle an issue as large and fundamental as women's economic participation in isolation.

The benefits of women's economic participation have, however, not reached every country equally. In 2009, Melanne had an opportunity to make the case to leaders from the Asia-Pacific region. She was reviewing the agenda for an upcoming summit, to be held in Japan in 2010 during its turn as the Asia-Pacific Economic Cooperation (APEC) host country, when she noticed a conspicuous absence on the agenda of the role of women in the economies of the area, despite the fact that a recent United Nations study had estimated that the region (which includes the United States and China) lost in excess of $42 billion annually in GDP because women's potential was not being tapped. She was told she could request to make a presentation during one of the early planning meetings. She assembled the data on how women could boost the economic output of the region, then flew to Tokyo to address the ambassadors from twenty-one economies.

After she made her case, one of the ambassadors approached her with a pleased look on his face and said, "You talked about economic growth." By the time the October meetings rolled around, Japan had scheduled a Women's Entrepreneurship Summit on the sidelines of its small and medium-sized enterprises' ministerial meeting, which gathered women entrepreneurs and government and business leaders from across the APEC region. There, too, Kathy Matsui presented her "womenomics" thesis.

Melanne had a strong ally in Robert Hormats, then the under secretary of state for economic growth, energy, and the environment, who in his diplomatic role helped make the case for women at APEC and beyond. Recently, Hormats explained to us why he fought to make women's economic participation a key part of the ongoing APEC meetings.

"If a country doesn't use all of its talent, it's like fighting in a ring with one hand behind your back," he said. "It's the laws of arithmetic. You can't afford to just marginalize one group, certainly not half of your economy."

One year later, in San Francisco, the United States hosted the inaugural APEC Women in the Economy Summit. More than seven hundred leaders from the public and private sectors came together to create the San Francisco Declaration, which identified key areas in which countries can support women entrepreneurs, including greater access to financial services, access to markets, capacity and skills building, and enhancing women's leadership. When then secretary of state Hillary

Clinton addressed the summit, she laid out the evidence-based case. "To achieve the economic expansion we all seek, we need to unlock a vital source of growth that can power our economies in the decades to come. And that vital source of growth is women," she declared.

What It Means for Companies

Today, some of the biggest companies in the world are recognizing that partnering with women brings a multitude of benefits, both for society and for the companies themselves. This recognition has enabled them to reach and support new markets and encouraged them to find ways to allow their most talented employees to thrive, adding to their top and bottom lines while contributing to social good.

Although early efforts often focused purely on philanthropy and corporate social responsibility, today more and more companies are partnering with women as part of their core business strategy—with measurable returns. That means taking stock of their business models to understand where women intersect with their goals.

Bob Moritz, the chairman and senior partner of the auditing and consulting firm PwC, knows that women are essential to his firm's success. He's committed to ensuring that PwC become, and be known as, an inclusive, diverse place to work. Why? Because that's what produces results.

"In order for organizations to maximize their potential, they need to have the best thinking," Bob said. "In order to have the best thinking, you need the most diverse people around the table. If you want to have the best performance, you need the best talent."

Joseph Keefe, the CEO of Pax World Funds, a financial firm whose Pax Ellevate Global Women's Index Fund, designed in partnership with Wall Street veteran Sallie Krawcheck, invests in companies with a record of promoting women, said it simply: "The biggest destroyer of wealth creation is patriarchy." It's not just up to women to "lean in," he has said. "Shareholders seeking better returns would do well to lean *on* companies to appoint and promote more women."

Why is this? Women have vital roles to play as strategists, managers, employees, researchers, designers, distributors, suppliers, and customers. They help companies reach new markets and regions, and develop innovative products that resonate with female consumers. At companies ranging from espnW to Ann Taylor to Marriott, the presence of women at the top translates into policies, products, and initiatives targeted at improving the lives of other women while benefiting the bottom line.

In the examples that follow, you'll see how forward-thinking women and men successfully made the case for investing in women in the private sector. It's worth noting that in each of the examples below, companies have joined forces with complementary organizations across sectors — nonprofits, governments, or multilateral institutions. These kinds of public-private ventures leverage the strengths of each sector, ultimately enhancing the capacities of all partners. The initiative or approach these leaders proposed often aligned with their company's core business strategy, as they took the time to understand where their organizations' goals and expertise intersected with opportunities for advancing women and girls. With thoughtful design and the right partners, this approach can result in more sustainable outcomes for all.

Tying It to the Bottom Line

Seventeen years after Ann Moore made her point about minivans at *People,* Laura Gentile found herself in a similar situation at ESPN, the global sports broadcaster. In 2008, as chief of staff to ESPN's then president George Bodenheimer, she analyzed data that showed the network would reach saturation of the 18-to-49-year-old male market in the next few years. To sustain its growth, ESPN would clearly need to reach a new audience. She had a good idea of who that could be. "It dawned on me that we needed to look at new audiences and new opportunities for growth. And when you start asking that question, pretty quickly you get to women," Laura told us.

She got a little bit of funding to put together market research. The numbers bore out her suspicion. "You look at trend lines of what's happened since the passage of Title IX in 1972" — which mandated equal opportunities for girls' participation in school sports — "and there's been a 600 percent increase in girls playing at the college level and literally a 1,000 percent increase of girls playing at the high school level," Laura said. "This is major, major growth, leading to more girls not only understanding sports, but truly caring about sports and really feeling like 'Sports is mine. It's not my dad's thing, it's not my brother's thing — sports is mine.'"

Laura soon hatched the idea of satisfying this demand with a new network: espnW.

A former all-American college field hockey player (she also played varsity basketball and softball in high school), Laura knew from her own experience that for girls the benefits of playing sports are not only physical. Female high school athletes have lower dropout rates. The global consultancy EY (formerly Ernst & Young) and espnW surveyed four hundred women business executives, nearly half of whom held C-suite titles (CEO, CFO, COO, etc.), and found that an astonishing 94 percent had participated in sports; three-fourths of them said that sports can accelerate women's leadership and career potential. For Laura, sports training instilled a drive to succeed and the discipline to set goals and plan on how to achieve them. Step one in getting buy-in for espnW was gathering the data to make the business case to her colleagues.

After a year of pitching the concept around the company, Laura and her team hadn't seen the progress they'd hoped. She rolled out the "W" brand at a retreat in San Diego in September 2010. The espnW blog launched in December and five months later evolved into a premier website devoted to women's sports.

Around that time, Dionne Colvin Lovely, a senior marketing executive at Toyota, and John Lisko, a senior advertising executive at Saatchi & Saatchi, were looking for ways Toyota could better reach its female customers. Dionne, a twenty-six-year veteran of the Japanese carmaker, had seen a shift in women's purchasing power over the past ten years. Women used to only influence purchasing decisions; now, she says, they are increasingly the sole decision maker.

This was just the data Dionne and John needed to bring their companies on board with the women-focused and purpose-driven initiatives they had in mind. They backed empowering conferences, ranging from the espnW: Women + Sports Summit to Tina Brown's Women in the World to Oprah's The Life You Want tour, creating awards and grants for "Everyday Heroes" (women using sports to make a difference in their community) and "Mothers of Invention" (women innovators creating solutions to intractable problems), which they presented on-stage at these live events and featured online. For Dionne and John, us-ing Toyota's considerable advertising dollars to honor women who make change happen was a chance to do well by the company while creating social good — and while helping expand the reach of media initiatives whose purpose is telling inspiring stories of women.

As espnW started to grow, Laura got an unexpected call from the State Department. As part of Secretary Clinton's commitment to wom-en's and girls' empowerment, the department was creating a sports-based initiative, at the impetus of the Center for Sport, Peace, and Soci-ety at the University of Tennessee at Knoxville. Studies have shown that girls who compete in sports are more likely to attend school and par-ticipate in society. The partnership between the State Department and espnW resulted in the Global Sports Mentoring program, which brings emerging overseas leaders in the athletics field to the United States to learn skills from American women working in sports and other indus-tries.

Maqulate Onyango, a graduate of the 2014 program, called it "life-changing." Maqulate joined the program from Kenya, where she grew up in Mathare, a large Nairobi slum with little in the way of basic services like electricity and water. Her parents didn't have the money to send her to school, and for the first years of her life encouraged her to think about one day getting married, which was the last thing she wanted to do. At age thirteen, she joined the Mathare Youth Sports Association (MYSA), first as a football (soccer) player, community volunteer, and youth coun-selor, and later as one of Kenya's few female referees. (She subsequently became the country's first female match commissioner.) MYSA paid her school fees, and within four years she had not only learned to read and write, but graduated from high school. She's now MYSA's sports direc-tor, paying it forward to other girls in the neighborhood so they can ex-perience the benefits that football offered her.

"I think when they look at football, they see hope," Maqulate told us. "We all have challenges from different backgrounds. Maybe you didn't have dinner, maybe you're not going to school, maybe your parents are fighting every day in the house. So I think coming to a place where you feel safe and secure, where you are on a team, you get to share your experiences with your sisters."

The Global Sports Mentoring program matched Maqulate with mentors from Saatchi & Saatchi, led by John Lisko. Through the program, she developed skills in leadership, communications, marketing, and management. She told us that above and beyond the practical lessons (and the chance to visit America, a lifelong dream of hers), the encouragement and support she got from her mentors was crucial in teaching her to aim high. Since returning to Kenya, she's already started two new programs: one for teenage girls to learn photography and document their lives through images, and a girls' education nonprofit in the impoverished rural Turkana area in the northwest of the country.

"I found a push and I got encouragement from my mentor," she said. "You feel you can do anything, because they believe in change and they are going to support you."

Laura told us that the espnW program had just as much impact on the mentors who participated in it, who came from a variety of organizations, including Toyota, Gatorade, and the Women's National Basketball Association. It also helped espnW gain increasing credibility within ESPN. "It changes hearts and minds when ten executives get to go to the State Department and shake hands with Secretary Clinton, and she waxes poetic about the power of sports for women and girls, or about the importance of espnW," Laura recalled.

Four years later, the business case has been borne out. The conference has become one of ESPN's strong business lines and a profitable endeavor for the company. Laura told us that beyond the business case, one of espnW's biggest successes is amplifying women's voices across the larger network.

Understanding the Value Chain

Senior managers at ESPN are not the only ones who recognize the potential value of half the world's population.

Muhtar Kent is a CEO at the forefront of partnering with women for growth. When he became head of the Coca-Cola Company's international operations in 2006, he was keenly aware that 65 to 70 percent of the people buying its products around the world were women. Then, shortly after becoming CEO in 2008, he pledged to make "recruiting, developing, and advancing women and achieving true diversity" one of the centerpieces of the company's — and its bottling partners' — 2020 Vision for growth. Muhtar knew that women were critical to the future of Coca-Cola's business. He started internally, creating the company's Women's Leadership Council in 2008, a group of seventeen executives tasked with figuring out how Coca-Cola could best recruit and promote its female talent.

"Muhtar called us together and asked us to write a multiyear plan on accelerating women into senior operating roles," remembers Bea Perez, now Coca-Cola's chief sustainability officer. "When I presented him with the metrics part of the plan, he said, 'Your numbers aren't aggressive enough. I want to do more.'"

Shortly after the Women's Leadership Council was formed, its members realized that the world's largest beverage company could use its corporate heft to further the UN Millennium Development Goals, eight targets aimed at bettering the lives of the world's poorest people. With those targets in mind, the leadership council created the 5by20 program led by Charlotte Oades, which leverages Coca-Cola's resources and reach to empower 5 million female entrepreneurs along its value chain by 2020, including farmers, small-scale shop owners, and bottle and can recyclers.

The 5by20 program is designed to help women entrepreneurs overcome three hurdles: difficulty obtaining capital, a lack of business training, and inadequate networks of mentors and peers. Since the initiative launched in 2010, 865,000 women have participated across 52 countries. In Kenya and Uganda, for example, Coca-Cola, the Bill and Melinda Gates Foundation, and the international nonprofit TechnoServe recently completed an initiative called Project Nurture, which reached more than 53,000 farmers over four years, 30 percent of whom were women. The farmers received skills training in mango and passionfruit production, basic agricultural practices, farm management, and business skills. TechnoServe trains female farmers and their male peers, helping to increase women's representation in local farming groups and building their technical capacity. TechnoServe also links women farmers to local banks that provide them credit, and to the processors and exporters who turn their fruit into puree or help get them to the international market.

Women farmers who participated in Project Nurture saw their average incomes increase by 140 percent over the four-year program. Through Coca-Cola's ongoing investments in mango production in Kenya, two processors using produce from Project Nurture farmers now supply 100 percent of the mango puree for Minute Maid Mango in Kenya, Uganda, Senegal, South Africa, Zimbabwe, and the Democratic Republic of Congo. More than 36,000 metric tons of fresh fruit from this project have been harvested and sold for use in the mango juice.

In Brazil, Coca-Cola funds an economic empowerment and life skills training program called Coletivo, including programs targeting youth, artisans, women, and others, from low-income urban communities all the way to the Amazon rainforest. Kim saw the power of 5by20 firsthand in 2012, when she visited a favela in the hillsides of Rio de Janeiro that had been overrun by drug lords and isolated from the outside world. During those years, many residents were afraid to walk the streets for fear of being caught in an all-too-frequent shootout. As a result, 90 percent of adults had not completed high school and 57 percent of homes were headed by a single parent.

Tragically, during that particularly violent period, community member Regina Maria Silva Gomes had lost her husband as well as her two sons. She was despondent and depressed, and she now had five grandchildren to care for. Her close friend Dona Ana, a neighborhood leader who saved the favela by bringing municipal services and starting an informal school and community center, asked if Regina would spearhead an initiative to clean up the streets, which were littered with trash. What else could she do? Regina accepted the job, finding dignity in the dirt and income to provide for her grandchildren.

At first she was embarrassed, picking up trash. Neighbors jeered her, calling her "garbage." And she half-believed them, she later told Kim, who met her in Brazil. But Dona Ana encouraged her to sort the garbage for recyclables, and Regina started a recycling center, where favela residents could bring in bottles and other recyclable items and trade them in for credit at the neighborhood grocery store. Through Coletivo Recycling, Regina received business training and developed a computer program to track the credit that residents earned, which could then be used at the local grocery store to buy the food and supplies they needed. It was an incentive the residents needed to participate in the recycling and cleanup effort.

But Regina also knew that there was more to the garbage than what people saw. In fact, there was even beauty in there somewhere. Regina united women artisans to transform the empty bottles into little works of art: she cleaned them and made beautiful bird feeders, decorative items, and toys. Through Coca-Cola's Coletivo Artisans program, Regina received training from a designer to ensure her handiwork was of a consistent quality and business skills to formalize her enterprise. Coca-Cola also helped her sell her crafts to a larger market, through a partnership with ASTA, a local NGO, which has a catalog business and retail shop. Eventually, Regina purchased her first home, and she went from being an outcast in her community to a role model who supports seven hundred families through her business.

What Women Want

Until the mid-1990s, marketing and advertising departments were often male-dominated, reminiscent of the *Mad Men* era. That has begun to change. By 1995, women made up almost 36 percent of Americans working in marketing and advertising, up from almost 24 percent one decade earlier. With that critical mass, women in various industries have pushed to focus more resources on truly understanding the female consumer, with lucrative results.

As Laura Gentile learned, the effort has to be authentic or the product won't resonate. As the mastermind behind the sports site espnW, she worked hard to ensure the website, the related conference, and the conversation they sparked answered women's needs. "It can't feel like a marketing ploy," said Laura. "It can't feel like five guys in a conference room high-fiving each other because they got me [the female viewer]. It's got to be genuine."

ANN INC., a U.S.-based clothing retailer with 1,030 stores and a

20,000-strong workforce that's almost 95 percent female, is an example of a company that understands how to put women at the center of its strategy. In 2005, when Kay Krill took over as CEO, she held a series of brown-bag lunches with her employees at every level of the company to get their ideas on how the company could better connect with customers. Some of her most productive meetings were with her troops on the front lines: ANN INC.'s sales associates, who told her they wanted the company to put a more philanthropic face forward. "They said, 'We want to be a more giving company. We want to connect with our communities and give back. We want to connect with our clients,'" Kay recalled.

The result was ANN Cares, which has raised and donated more than $50 million to support women and children since 2005. As with so many bright ideas, this one was born from women talking to other women. Since then, the company has launched several other corporate social responsibility initiatives, including ANNpower, a national mentoring program for high school girls, under the rubric of ANN Cares, the company's charitable arm.

Catherine Fisher, ANN INC.'s vice president of corporate communications, believes that the company's giving programs more than pay for themselves, because they create tremendous buy-in among employees and generate lasting loyalty among shoppers, who love knowing their purchases count toward supporting important women's causes. "Our store associates are over the moon," said Catherine. "I have walked into a store anonymously and I hear them tell me excitedly about ANN Cares, what we do for breast cancer, what we do for St. Jude's Children's Research Hospital. They will repeat back to me all this information with such passion . . . They get me excited about it! It resonates so well with our clients and employees."

The experience of ANN INC.'s employees dovetails with emerging research that shows that adding meaning to work leads to greater professional satisfaction — especially for women. The Center for Talent Innovation, led by the management expert Sylvia Ann Hewlett, found in a recent study that women, more than men, value the ability to "advance causes important to them" in their work. In the United States, 80 percent of women between the ages of thirty-five and fifty (as well as 75 percent in Great Britain and 78 percent in Germany) said it was very important to them to "reach for meaning and purpose" in their careers.

Of course, it's not only women who want purpose. A 2014 survey of nearly twenty thousand employees by the workplace consultancy The Energy Project and the *Harvard Business Review* found that the 36 percent of respondents who had found meaning in their work were more than twice as likely to report being satisfied in their jobs, and were over 90 percent more engaged at work. For the next generation, purpose at work may not be optional: a 2015 survey by Deloitte found that among the 7,800 millennials surveyed, 60 percent described "a sense of purpose" as "part of the reason they chose to work for their current employers."

As women increasingly rise to positions of power, they're controlling the purse strings within companies too, and becoming responsible for an ever-greater share of business-to-business (B2B) spending. Cathy Benko, vice chairman and managing principal at Deloitte LLP, recognized this after noticing that Deloitte was consistently failing to win business from potential female clients. "How Women Decide," a 2013 article in the *Harvard Business Review* that Cathy coauthored with Bill Pelster, describes how many male employees failed to take women's processes seriously: simply put, their selling techniques didn't align with the decision-making methods of female clients. Women, she said, often seek to establish a rapport with the people they will be working with. During training sessions for Deloitte employees, the company found that "the failure to establish rapport is the most frequent mistake our male professionals make."

> In most cases, the male team members go directly to the purpose of the meeting and work through their content agenda. They may be unaware that the female client sees the meeting as a way to get to know the people she is being asked to trust with her business. Or they may not know how to respond to that objective. So the listening challenge is to discover what she wants to achieve and what she feels is the most comfortable way to do so.

Deloitte's in-house training not only helped the company win more business from female buyers, but also increased employees' commitment to diversity, since it clearly illustrated to them why diversity matters. They could see for themselves that it wasn't diversity for diversity's sake — there were real costs to bringing only one perspective to the table.

Use Your Platform: Drive the Data

In 1981, Beth Brooke-Marciniak was freshly graduated from Purdue University when she arrived in Atlanta for her first job, at an accounting firm. She didn't have a place to stay, but as it turned out, one of her female managers needed a roommate, and Beth was grateful for the shelter — until she noticed one thing: "I move in, and within forty-eight hours it became really apparent that there were things you had to do to get ahead that I was not willing to do."

Her instincts told her that this was not the job for her, so she decided to make a midnight phone call to Indiana. She woke up the man who headed the Indianapolis office of Ernst & Young (now EY), asking him for another shot at a job she'd turned down just a few months earlier. He indicated he'd be willing to hire her, but he had one last question: "Can you be here tomorrow?" She promptly jumped in her car and drove for nine straight hours, showing up at the office by 10 a.m.

Her instincts served her well. Thirty-four years after her midnight getaway, Beth remains with EY today, as its global vice chair of public policy. Like us, she knew what women were capable of, but was searching for a wider audience for her message. In 2008, she stepped out of a meeting of women leaders at Harvard and called Melanne. Both of them were tired of having the same old conversations about women's economic potential, solely among women. The financial crisis had hit, and economies all over the globe were imploding. Yet in all the discussions about how to repair the world's fiscal mess, no one was putting women forward as part of the solution.

"We need to get this message out to others and to men, and get the facts," Beth had said to Melanne. "Can you help me get together all the research that's out there?" EY took the lead, with help from Vital Voices, where Melanne had been diligently compiling much of the data on women's impact on the economy. And as Beth recalled, EY's employees were thrilled to use their skills and positions to execute a project with purpose.

"People said, 'I want to help, I want to do this, what can I do?,'" Beth remembered. "And I would ask, 'Where do you sit? What kinds of influence do you have? Think more broadly about the platform that you have, because probably it's right there.' This whole effort surrounding women, this is not my day job. It never has been. It's what we do with our platform."

The result (besides the happy byproduct of increased employee engagement) was the first EY *Groundbreakers* report, published in 2009. It laid out the growing body of data and research to flesh out its theme: "Using the strength of women to rebuild the world economy."

Beth told us she felt like a translator: having spent time in the women's movement, she wanted to take its human rights–based arguments and put them into language that CEOs and businessmen could understand. The *Groundbreakers* report was one of the first steps in that translation process. Beth knew that making the evidence-backed case was the key.

ExxonMobil also knows the value of data and is bringing one of its areas of expertise — research, monitoring, and evaluation — into the women's space to help add to the growing body of data. Suzanne McCarron, president of the ExxonMobil Foundation, told us how ExxonMobil's chairman and CEO Rex Tillerson was keen to put its resources behind explaining the powerful "multiplier effect" of investing in women and girls.

"This is a company of scientists and engineers. If you present data, people listen," Suzanne said. "But Rex wanted to know more. What accounted for the multiplier effect? What really worked? Why? How could it be replicated and scaled?"

Rex Tillerson's questions led to a deep dive into research, which the company undertook with the United Nations Foundation beginning in 2012. Their collaboration resulted in a comprehensive report that analyzed the most effective ways to close the gender gap in areas such as entrepreneurship, agriculture, wage labor, and work for younger women. With the input of experts and economists from multilateral institutions, universities, and nonprofits, the resulting report provided a "roadmap" to more effectively empower women and girls with proven, evidence-backed solutions. Now, Suzanne said, the data is in.

"Today, we are more focused than ever and ready to look at very specific areas that we know from the research are going to make the biggest difference for women, and begin to take them to scale," Suzanne said.

Creating Opportunities for Impact

In 1982, after Kathleen Matthews had worked for five years as a writer and producer at the ABC news affiliate in Washington, D.C., her bosses decided to make her an on-air reporter. Everyone around her, from her husband, Chris Matthews (himself now a broadcast journalist), to her managers, was rooting for her. But by the time the offer came, she was six months pregnant — not exactly the standard look on television at the time.

Kathleen worried that her pregnancy could hinder her career, thanks to age-old stereotypes that peg mothers as less committed to their careers than their male colleagues are, or their female colleagues without children. But hers was an unusual case. Far from being a career-killer, she made on-air pregnancy part of her "personal brand," she said. Viewers eagerly followed her pregnancy's progress, and asked about her baby in the supermarket.

"I also had the education beat at that point, so I was seen as the working mom who cared about good schools," Kathleen told us. "The viewers, I think, took a real interest in women having careers but also starting families."

Executives at the station noticed how powerfully she connected with viewers. One in particular — Jane Cohen, the programming director of WJLA at the time and one of the few women in senior management — saw even further ahead. She envisioned a show that would build on Kathleen's inroads with female viewers, a potentially lucrative demographic that some perceptive advertisers were beginning to notice.

The show launched in 1991, nine years after her on-air pregnancy, at which point Kathleen had three young children. Called *Working Woman*, it saw Toyota as an early advertiser; other companies followed. Over the next five years, Kathleen interviewed guests like Donna Karan, Hillary Clinton, and Martha Stewart. Less than six months after its launch, seventy television stations across the country had picked up the show. Within several years, it aired internationally. The advertisers' hunger to reach a growing demographic of women enabled Kathleen to produce much-needed reportage about the triumphs and challenges of a new generation of professional women.

In 2006, after nearly three decades in journalism and nine Emmy awards, Kathleen found herself being aggressively recruited by the hotel company Marriott International to head its global corporate communications and public affairs. She wondered how she could make positive social impact in this role, and Bill Marriott talked about the jobs and careers created by global tourism. She had just seen Al Gore's environmental documentary *An Inconvenient Truth,* she told us. "I asked Mr. Marriott, 'What is your green policy?' and he wasn't sure what I was talking about. We joke about that now.

"Bill said, 'My green policy, what do you mean my green policy?' And I said, 'Your sustainability policy.' And he said, 'Sustainability, like our business sustainability?' And I said, 'No, your environmental sustainability.' And he said, 'Well, you know, people volunteer to clean up beaches and parks.' And I said, 'But do you have a strategy on global warming? Do you have a strategy for cutting your greenhouse gas emissions?' And he said, 'No, but if you come, you can make it happen.'"

Kathleen realized that she could be "a purpose-driven hotel executive in the same way [she] was a purpose-driven journalist."

In the nine years since Kathleen joined Marriott as chief global communications and public affairs officer, she's had many opportunities to pursue the goals that gave meaning to her journalistic work. With the support of Bill Marriott and his successor, CEO Arne Sorenson, she developed the company's environmental strategy, which not only reduced its carbon footprint but created efficiencies that accrued to the bottom line. She has also developed what we refer to as a global women's strategy.

Recognizing that female business travelers were emerging as a powerful client base, Kathleen saw opportunities to engage with women both inside and outside Marriott. She has successfully advocated for more women at senior levels and on the board, helping to change the face of the company's leadership. In 2012, she formed a partnership with the Akilah Institute for Women, a three-year professional program in Rwanda and Burundi, to place its graduates in Marriott's training programs in Dubai. She also put Marriott's considerable corporate spending in women's pockets, working with the women's business network WE-Connect International to source products and services from women-owned enterprises.

"I truly believe that if you can tap into a sense of purpose and articulate that and people see that in you, it can go a long way, and that's what people are looking for in their companies — they're looking for people who have a vision for something, a better place, a better outcome," Kathleen explained.

Kathleen's style of leadership is every bit as results-driven as that of her male predecessors. She was still a communications professional with her eye on the bottom line. But she was also looking at the qualitative questions: What have I done for other women lately? Whom have I helped? What can my company do to be a greener, more humane actor in the larger economy?

Today Kathleen is running for a congressional seat in the Eighth District of Maryland. If elected, she intends to bring the same sense of purpose to the job, making environmental stewardship and women's empowerment her primary goals.

The women whose successes we've seen firsthand know the answers intuitively, and they are the core of their leadership. These women are redefining success and leadership, often putting the advancement of other women and girls at the center of their strategy. Wherever they sit, women and men in companies, governments, and multilateral institutions are increasingly making the case.

As we shall see, this kind of leadership can be transformative not just for the organizations, but for the leaders themselves. We've witnessed how women leaders at all levels have leveraged their influence to advance women and girls, from a Masai tribeswoman who started the first girls' school in her region of Kenya, to a Harvard student who used her grandmother's medicinal herb blend to invent a low-cost way to keep food fresh in parts of the world that lack refrigeration, to a senior executive at a Fortune 100 company who's redesigning the workplace to accommodate the new parents on her team. They are using their resources and talents to imbue their work with meaning while advancing women and girls — in other words, combining their power with purpose.

3

Find Your Purpose

IN THE IMMEDIATE AFTERMATH OF the global financial crisis, Pam Seagle, a senior marketing executive at Bank of America, found herself facing a daunting task. Her employer was acquiring the investment bank Merrill Lynch, and she was working on the marketing of the merger. The new role had her on a plane between Charlotte, North Carolina, and New York City nearly every week. It was a difficult time to work for any bank, and working in marketing was particularly challenging. A two-decade veteran of Bank of America, Pam had started as a secretary on a temp stint and worked her way up.

After nearly three months of the draining New York–Charlotte commute, Pam was gripped by a dark premonition. On Sunday night, January 11, 2009, she dreamed she was witnessing a plane crash, watching it disappear into a cloud of smoke as she stood on the bank of a river. She was due to travel the following day to Atlanta for a series of focus groups before heading to New York on Tuesday.

The nightmare felt too real. On Monday morning, as she approached the boarding gate, she turned around, ticket in hand, and went back out to her car. She drove home and spent the rest of the day glued to the news, awaiting word of the crash she was sure was imminent. Nothing happened. The next day, more than slightly embarrassed, she took an uneventful flight to New York, and on Thursday boarded US Airways flight 1549 with nineteen other Bank of America colleagues headed back to Charlotte.

Shortly after taking off, the plane encountered an errant flock of Canada geese at three thousand feet. The bodies of the geese, dead on impact, clobbered the plane's exterior. At least several fell into the plane's engines. The engines went silent.

"It was instant panic," Pam recalled. "I realized the pilot had said the words 'brace for impact.' Everyone assumed we were on a plane with no engines, because there was absolute silence when those engines stopped. We were gliding over New York City. I don't think anyone anticipated that we would survive."

Many people say they relive past moments from their life in the onset of a near-death experience. Pam found herself contemplating memories not yet created, future milestones she was fated to miss, like her son's graduation from high school later that year. But as her mind raced, she happened to notice that the plane was moving over a body of water. From her window seat, she saw the Hudson River. She realized then that survival was an option.

"That was a tipping point for me, where I realized I could take some control back," she said. "Maybe I could survive. And then I became very focused on getting out. The minute I had that control back and was creating a plan to get out, I felt better, because suddenly there were things I could do that were going to change the next couple moments of my life."

Captain Chesley "Sully" Sullenberger rescued her from the icy water, in what became known as the "Miracle on the Hudson," and helped her to safety. Then came the ferry ride to New Jersey, the stranger who offered Pam her phone so she could call her husband, a quick trip to the hospital, the flight back to Charlotte, and finally the reunion with her children. As soon as she saw them, she broke down sobbing.

The winter wore on. Pam resumed her weekly commute, but she was feeling less fulfilled than ever. As she began reevaluating her life, she realized some things needed to change. She started by making her family a priority, then learning how to say "no" at work. She grew closer to her sister, with whom she took a long-delayed beach vacation; the two began communicating more deeply than they ever had before. She resolved to schedule meetings and work trips around family commitments, instead of scheduling family get-togethers around her job obligations. She made it a point to be present for the big events in her family's life, and more of the small ones too. She found her relationships more fulfilling, her work improving, and her mind more at ease.

Pam was on to something. Studies have shown that happiness is closely correlated with spending time with our loved ones. Harvard University researchers have found that we are notoriously bad at predicting how happy something will make us, pinning our hopes on what we think will bring long-lasting happiness only to realize after the fact that the happiness we experienced was fleeting and nowhere near as satisfying as we had imagined.

"We know that the best predictor of human happiness is human relationships and the amount of time that people spend with family and friends," Harvard professor Daniel Gilbert told the *New York Times.* "We know that it's significantly more important than money and somewhat more important than health. That's what the data shows." And that's exactly what Pam Seagle found.

Then she found out how fleeting happiness could be. Less than a week after her son's graduation, Pam's sister passed away from a sudden brain aneurism. A few months later, her mother was diagnosed with pancreatic cancer. Pam took some time off to recalibrate. She realized she needed something deeper than happiness. She needed meaning. Her sister's death and her mother's illness had brought her life and its unpredictability into sharp focus. "I knew that there were things in my life that I wanted to reprioritize. I wanted to live with more purpose," she said.

Finding purpose, of course, isn't always a straightforward proposition. Many of us are overworked and pressed for time. But one way to live with purpose is to try to infuse one's work with meaning.

Pam's first step upon returning to work following her sister's death was to meet with her managers and the human resources department at Bank of America. After affirming her commitment to the company, she asked for a job with more meaning, explaining that she couldn't continue in her present role. Her managers knew they couldn't afford to lose her experience and dedication. Together, they created a new position: executive for corporate social responsibility (CSR) marketing.

From her twenty-plus years at the company, Pam knew intimately its employees, its CSR efforts, and the values it stood for. Now she could show the world the side of the bank she had always known and admired. By making the commitment to tie her work to purpose, she had opened up a new set of options for herself and for her employer, using her skill set, her experience, and her knowledge to advance her company's CSR initiatives.

At the same time, though, Bank of America was evolving. With the acquisition of Merrill Lynch, it became more global. "We became aware of the challenges that women are facing in the countries where we were doing business, and needed to create a platform and a strategy to address those," said Pam.

Lucky for Pam, one of the most senior women at Bank of America and on Wall Street, Anne Finucane, had a vision of how the bank could work for women, and how women at the bank could use their skills to advance one another and themselves. Anne, the bank's global chief strategy and marketing officer, had been and continues to be a strong advocate for women in her own institution and in the financial services industry at large. Working with Rena DeSisto, one of her most senior deputies, she outlined an initiative that leveraged the business experience of the bank's top women. The project would pair the bank's senior-level women with emerging female business leaders from around the world, who, as pioneers in their home countries, often lacked role models and advisers. They brought in Vital Voices as a partner, building on its history of training and empowering emerging women leaders and social entrepreneurs.

Under Anne Finucane and Rena DeSisto's leadership, Pam was tapped to work on what came to be called the Global Ambassadors Program. Over the next few months, as they got it up and running, Rena and Pam immersed themselves in the challenges the mentees faced doing business in sometimes hostile environments, developing a deep appreciation for the courage and resilience they showed. Since the program's launch, Bank of America's women employees have mentored leaders from Haiti, South Africa, and India, among other countries. Meanwhile, Pam noticed that as she dedicated herself to helping these women, her job satisfaction and well-being flourished.

She wasn't alone. As Anne told us, "From the very beginning of Global Ambassadors, our women executives have shown huge enthusiasm for the program and for women leaders from across the globe who are participating as mentees. They feel like they're part of a larger community. It is very motivating and energizing to know they can use their skills for good."

Rena herself has been a mentor to the Brazilian graffiti artist Panmela Castro, who combines her love and talent for graffiti art and her passion for women's rights to help end violence against women. After being honored by Vital Voices in 2010, Panmela founded Rede Nami, an all-female art collective that creates street art and graffiti to empower and transform the roles of women in society. Rena and Panmela have worked together to think about how to scale up Panmela's activities. The results have been satisfying for both. "It's rewarding and humbling to find that what you thought would be a teaching experience is a learning opportunity," Rena said. "It's a two-way street. It's entirely possible that I've learned more from Panmela than she has from me."

Their experience illustrates another powerful psychological insight: one of the most important things we can do to bring meaning into our lives is to give of ourselves. As the happiness researcher Daniel Gilbert has said, "One of the most selfish things you can do is help others. Volunteer at a homeless shelter. You may or may not help the homeless, but you will almost surely help yourself."

Pam has continued on, becoming manager of global women's programs for the CSR group at the bank. In addition to her work with Vital Voices, she also works under Anne and Rena's leadership on other initiatives, including Bank of America's small-business lending partnership with the Tory Burch Foundation and the Cherie Blair Foundation's Mentoring Women in Business Programme, in which bank employees and other successful businesswomen mentor women in developing countries through an online platform. With all the travel Pam has done with the Vital Voices program, she's been able to see firsthand how a bank can put its core competencies to work for good.

"It's hands-on," Pam said. "I have had the opportunity to travel with our Vital Voices partnership from Haiti to Singapore, from South Africa to Brazil, and have met every one of our mentors and mentees in person, and I know we're creating impact."

Like Anne, Rena, and Pam, Melanne also feels that she's one of Vital

Voices' biggest beneficiaries, getting back far more than she has put in. Vital Voices was launched in 1997 at a conference organized in Vienna by then ambassador Swanee Hunt; soon it will be celebrating its twentieth year. In the time since it began, Melanne has come to realize how much inspiration, knowledge, and meaning she has gained from working with emerging women leaders.

In 1993, she had gone to work for First Lady Hillary Clinton as her deputy chief of staff, later becoming her chief of staff for the second Clinton term. In 1995, Hillary made her first solo trip as first lady, visiting five countries in South Asia with her daughter, Chelsea. It turned out to be a pivotal journey. At each stop, Hillary met women and girls who, having overcome incredible obstacles, were starting to find their voices.

Early on in the trip, Hillary was due to give an address at the Rajiv Gandhi Foundation in New Delhi. The night before, she and Melanne were up late crafting her speech. Inspiration struck when Hillary, who was reviewing some of the notes and letters that had been handed to her earlier in the day, came across a powerful poem by Anasuya Sengupta, a student at Lady Shri Ram College for Women in Delhi:

> *Too many women in too many countries*
> *speak the same language of silence.*
> *My grandmother was always silent —*
> *always aggrieved —*
> *only her husband had the cosmic right*
> *(or so it was said) to speak and be heard.*
>
> *They say it is different now*
> *(after all, I am always vocal*
> *and my grandmother thinks I talk too much).*
> *But sometimes, I wonder.*
>
> *When a woman gives her love,*
> *as most women do, generously —*
> *it is accepted.*

*

When a woman shares her thoughts,
as some women do, graciously —
it is allowed.

When a woman fights for power,
as all women would like to,
quietly or loudly,
it is questioned.

And yet, there must be freedom —
if we are to speak.
And yes, there must be power —
if we are to be heard.
And when we have both (freedom and power),
let us not be misunderstood.

We seek only to give words
to those who cannot speak
(too many women in too many countries).
I seek only to forget the sorrows
of my grandmother's
silence.

These words captured feelings shared by women everywhere — that women have a right to be heard in their personal and public lives.

The next morning, when Hillary delivered her speech, she recited the poem by this young Indian woman, evoking tremendous national pride among the Indians in the audience.

Long after the speech was delivered, that call to action remained a guiding principle of Hillary's work: to use her platform to amplify the voices of the unheard, and in particular those of women. Sometimes her influence has meant the difference between life and death. Vera Stremkovskaya, a human rights activist from Belarus, is a case in point. On a visit to the White House, a photo was taken of her with the first lady. She asked for a copy of it immediately, and Melanne told her she would receive it in due course. Vera replied, "You don't understand. That is my bullet-proof vest." Like so many others, she would use this public support from one of the world's most visible women as a shield against those who would seek to intimidate her — or even harm her.

On that same trip, in Ahmedabad, India, Hillary (accompanied by Melanne) visited the Self-Employed Women's Association, or SEWA, founded by the lawyer and activist Ela Bhatt. There, she was met by dozens of its members, dressed in a kaleidoscopic array of colorful saris. Many of them were among the poorest of India's poor, who had worked as ragpickers. Hillary asked the women what membership in SEWA had meant for them. A slender elderly woman, her face lined with wrinkles that testified to a life of hardship, stood up to answer.

"I am no longer afraid," she said, her wrinkles deepening as she smiled with pride. "I'm not afraid of my husband. I'm not afraid of the police. I'm not even afraid of my mother-in-law!" The training, camaraderie, and economic independence she got from being part of the women's cooperative had helped her discover the strength to stand up to the people in her life who once had bullied her.

Hillary knew her platform could help make a difference for emerging women leaders in places where their voices were often stifled. To that end, she led the Vital Voices Democracy Initiative, a leadership-training program then housed at the State Department. The program had the strong support of Secretary of State Madeleine Albright, who went on to forge a lasting partnership with Hillary around their shared commitment to advancing women's progress.

The Vital Voices program took Hillary to Eastern Europe, Northern Ireland, and South America, among other places, where she met with emerging women leaders, encouraging them to speak out on the problems they faced in their respective locales. At the first conference, in Vienna in 1997, for example, Hillary met a group of Ukrainian women who told her a real-life horror story: women from their country, and particularly the rural areas, were disappearing. They were promised good jobs in big cities or overseas. Desperate to find work so they could send money home to their families, these women would move to the cities, only to vanish — sold to traffickers.

When she returned to Washington, Hillary was determined to fight this scourge. The first step was getting to the bottom of the situation.

Was this a larger phenomenon? Where were these women going? Who was trafficking them? Why were government officials so slow to respond? Her efforts helped lead to the U.S. government's first-ever study on human trafficking. The Clinton administration set up an interagency task force on the issue, and in 2000 President Bill Clinton signed the Victims of Trafficking and Violence Protection Act. And Vital Voices joined forces with Oksana Horbunova, a Ukrainian trafficking expert with the International Organization for Migration. Oksana used the Vital Voices network to share her expertise on getting governments and the private sector involved with other women waging the same struggle against traffickers in their own countries, from Hungary to Japan.

American women leaders from an array of companies and organizations were and are a prominent part of the Vital Voices network. They volunteer their time and expertise in areas like business development, politics, communications, and advocacy to help train women overseas. Today, Vital Voices, no longer a government program, is a vibrant global network of leaders from different walks of life, united by the shared purpose of advancing women and enabling them to effectively raise their voices in key arenas.

As the Clinton presidency drew to a close, some Vital Voices alumnae gathered one last time for an event with Hillary in the East Room of the White House. There were human rights defenders from Russia, businesswomen from the Middle East, anti-trafficking advocates from Eastern Europe and India, political activists from Nigeria and Kuwait, and peacemakers from Northern Ireland. At a small reception after her speech, in which Hillary made a commitment to support the continuation of Vital Voices as a nonprofit, many of the guests approached Melanne and told her what Vital Voices had meant to them and how relieved they were to know its work would go on. The support network, the camaraderie, the hands-on skills and business training, all were too important to lose.

It was at that moment that Melanne found the purpose that would propel the next phase of her life and career. When she left the White House, she and a small team of people who had been with Vital Voices since its inception got together to transform the program into an independent nonprofit dedicated to building a pipeline of women leaders in human rights, democracy, and the economy. They found pro bono office space, crystallized their mission, and raised the funds needed to get it off the ground. Hillary Clinton, by then a U.S. senator, became the honorary cochair of the new organization, and in the spirit of bipartisanship she was joined by two Republican senators, first Nancy Kassebaum of Kansas and later Kay Bailey Hutchison of Texas.

As she worked to get Vital Voices up and running, Melanne had nights when anxiety over how she would meet the payroll for her two-person staff (she wasn't drawing a salary herself) kept her from sleeping. But her thoughts inevitably drifted back to the women in the East Room, who were on the front lines of change, often risking their lives, and for whom Vital Voices was a lifeline. She would spend the next eight years building and growing the organization.

Early on, Melanne had a strong supporter in Diane von Furstenberg, the fashion designer and businesswoman whose iconic wrap dresses are sold in six dozen countries. Diane's own life had been something of a miracle. Her mother was a Holocaust survivor who emerged, thin and sickly, from Auschwitz in 1945, almost too frail to bear a child. Diane went on to lead a jet-setter's glamorous life: she married a German prince, then launched her eponymous fashion line in 1970. Underneath the glamour, though, she always retained a profound appreciation for the strength and resilience of the women around her.

"I have never met a woman who is not strong," Diane told us. "All women are strong, but because of a religion, a brother, a husband, or themselves, they may hide their strength. Then comes a tragedy, and all of a sudden, miraculously the strength comes out that the woman had always carried. So why don't you let the strength come out before the tragedy?"

When purpose-driven women in various fields get together, each one's power is amplified. Such was the case one evening at the Manhattan apartment of magazine editor and media executive Tina Brown. There, Diane, Melanne, and the other dinner guests listened as Hillary spoke on the importance of investing in women. Several weeks later, Melanne went to Diane's studio in New York's Meatpacking District to discuss the work of Vital Voices with Diane and her head of philanthropy, Luisella Meloni. It was at that meeting that Diane came up with the Vital Voices slogan: "Invest in women, improve the world." Vital Voices' mission resonated deeply with Diane — its structure allowed women to tap their inner, existing strengths. Shortly after that, Melanne got an email from Diane. She opened an attachment that contained an image of soaring V's against a circular background. The initials represented Vital Voices' many leaders, reaching new heights around the globe. It remains Vital Voices' logo to this day.

One of those soaring leaders is Sunitha Krishnan. Diane and Sunitha first met at the Kennedy Center in Washington in 2011, when Sunitha was being honored for her work fighting human trafficking, and in particular the sexual exploitation of children, through her organization, Prajwala, in the Indian city of Hyderabad.

Sunitha's purpose sprang from tragedy. At the age of fifteen, she was brutally gang-raped by eight men. After her recovery, she found herself ostracized and stigmatized for being a rape victim, a fact she found both absurd and outrageous. In 1996, she moved to Hyderabad. A few days after she arrived, the Hyderabad police moved to disband the city's well-known red-light district. She encountered hundreds of desperate victims of sexual exploitation, who had been turned out on the streets with nowhere to go. Some were being harassed, even tortured, by the authorities. Others, deprived of their sole means of income, committed suicide. All who spoke to Sunitha feared for their children — how could they support them now that their livelihood was being taken away? With her cofounder, Brother Jose Vetticatil, a Catholic missionary, they opened Prajwala, which means "eternal flame."

Prajwala began as a small school for five of these children. Today, in addition to helping thousands of children who have survived commercial sexual exploitation, the organization offers rehabilitation, counseling, and vocational training for women who leave sexual slavery, and works with law enforcement to conduct brothel raids. Some of the children Sunitha has helped were as young as three or four when they were raped, sold into sex trafficking, or abandoned. Yet, she said, they recover and shine. "When I see the same children smiling and embracing life, that is the greatest motivating factor," she has said. "I keep thinking that if this child can smile and forgive humanity, I have no reason to give up or get frustrated."

Unfortunately, the night she met Diane von Furstenberg, her journey with Prajwala was dangerously close to its end. Sunitha, who is barely four foot six, had survived numerous beatings and countless death threats from traffickers enraged by her work. But this challenge was different. Prajwala was on the verge of being shut down after running out of funds for a much-needed expansion. Just before the Kennedy Center event, Sunitha told Diane the story of Prajwala. Diane went "off script" that night. Instead of simply presenting Sunitha with the award as planned, she announced onstage that she would donate $50,000, and urged audience members to join her in raising the additional $150,000 that Sunitha needed to keep Prajwala open. Within twenty-four hours, the money was raised.

Diane calls Sunitha and other Vital Voices leaders "some of the strongest women I know." In her recent autobiography, Diane reflected on how her life has been changed by her encounters with these women: "Though I've dedicated myself to empowering women through my work in fashion, mentoring, and philanthropy, *I* am empowered, mentored, and filled with riches from these women. It is they, and many others like them, who inspire me with their strength and beauty."

Integrating purpose into one's life and work can be transformative. Our experience and the experience of many of those whom we have worked with confirm Daniel Gilbert's research: ultimately, it is we who are the greatest beneficiaries of the purpose-driven work we do. Finding our purpose and letting it guide us have made our careers more fulfilling and our lives richer. While our commitment to advancing women and girls was something that grew at different paces and was catalyzed by different events, for each of us it created pathways and set in motion events and connections we never could have imagined. Sometimes that purpose led us to make what outside observers might see as unorthodox choices — at times veering off traditional career tracks in order to take a chance to make an impact. Most important, following our purpose has put us in the company of people who share our values, and are as committed as we are to translating those values into action.

4

Connect with Others:
Partner for Purpose

SOPHIE WAS BARELY ONE MONTH old when she was attacked with acid. The surprise assault occurred while she was breastfeeding, as she and her mother, Chan,* lay in bed half asleep in their hut in rural Cambodia. Earlier that day, a woman who claimed to be the mistress of Chan's husband had stopped by their home, insisting, as she had on earlier visits, that Chan leave the premises.

As a last resort, Chan gathered up one dollar and gave it to the woman in the hope that she would go away for good and leave the family alone. Life was already difficult for Chan, with three children and limited means to support them. Instead of honoring her side of the bargain, the woman went to the marketplace and used the money to buy battery acid, which was cheap and readily available.

She returned to Chan's home and poured the acid through the window, dousing Chan and Sophie as they slept. The impact was immediate—the acid burned through their flesh down to the bone, splashing Chan's body and baby Sophie's face and eyes. Unaware of what had happened and how to remedy it, and with limited access to clean water, they suffered for several days before finally making their way to the capital, Phnom Penh. By the time they reached the city, the baby had been blinded in one eye, with burns covering a large portion of her face, and Chan had suffered extensive damage to her right ear, face, and a large

---

* Sophie and Chan are pseudonyms.

portion of her body and arms. The baby was so badly injured that a relative was overheard suggesting that Chan "throw her out and make another."

In Phnom Penh, they checked into the acid ward of what is now called the Children's Surgical Center, where mother and child waited to receive treatment alongside half a dozen other women and men who had experienced the same fate. Acid attacks are a frequent form of violence around the world, often used to resolve personal disputes and to punish women who have transgressed gender stereotypes — by seeking financial independence through work, for example, or dating before marriage or, in some countries, simply attending school. The goal of using acid as a weapon is usually not to kill but rather to disfigure a woman — "stealing her beauty" and making it impossible for her to function in society and lead a normal life. The mere existence of an acid ward in Phnom Penh demonstrates the frequency of this type of violence in Cambodia, where it is often committed with relative impunity. In December of 2004, when Chan and Sophie were placed in the ward, it was running at full capacity.

That same month, Dr. Ebby Elahi, a New York–based oculofacial surgeon and friend of Kim's since college, was visiting the Children's Surgical Center acid ward, where he first met Chan and Sophie. That meeting not only would change the course of the lives of Chan, Sophie, Ebby, and Kim, but would also have an unexpected ripple effect for years to come, inspiring the formation of a coalition united by a purpose.

Ebby had gone to Cambodia that month on a medical expedition on behalf of the Virtue Foundation, a nonprofit organization he and several colleagues founded in the aftermath of the September 11 attacks.

Ebby's skills were desperately needed in the ward, as acid violence often causes severe injury to the eyes and face. Though he had been on surgical missions before and had previously encountered harrowing diseases and injuries around the globe, that day he was particularly disheartened to see the suffering of Sophie, the youngest known victim of acid violence to date. After examining her and performing some initial surgery, he knew that in order to address her visual disability and injuries, he would need the comprehensive resources of a major medical center such as Mount Sinai Hospital in New York. He also knew his colleagues could help treat the mother's injuries and aid in her rehabilitation.

"This baby was hard to bear. It was difficult for me," Ebby said, "because she is living in an environment where you need all your faculties to survive."

The necessary surgeries and follow-up treatments would be extensive and costly, but Ebby believed that if he could create a coalition of support in New York, he could change the fate of this child and mother.

At that time, in 2005, Kim was working at Avon, where she recently had been promoted to corporate secretary, a position that came with increased responsibilities. Soon after Ebby's return to New York, the two friends were catching up at his office. At one point, Kim told Ebby about the burden of her demanding workload. He responded by suggesting that she consider something that might change her perspective, perhaps travel to another part of the world where she could experience how others truly lived. She smiled politely, wondering how that would help with her already overbooked schedule.

Soon after, Ebby invited Kim to an event on the topic of extreme poverty and sustainable development at Rockefeller University that he had helped organize, and where he would be speaking alongside senior executives from Refugees International and the International Rescue Committee. Kim walked into the auditorium expecting an engaging event, but what she saw changed her life. Confronted with the image of little Sophie, her left eye seared shut, her face and scalp covered in braids of scar tissue, she was appalled by the injustice. As a lawyer, Kim was angered by the attacker's seemingly total impunity. Despite the prevalence of acid violence in Cambodia, there seemed to be little if any legal recourse for what had happened to Chan and Sophie and so many others.

As she sat in that auditorium, Ebby's suggestion began to make sense. Kim realized how fortunate she was in her life, but also that she was in a position to make a difference: she could use the resources, skills, and power she had worked for toward a positive purpose. Shortly after the event, she called Ebby to ask how to get involved. Their next conversation accelerated a change in the way she thought about her job and her life.

Ebby told Kim how his own perspective had shifted as a result of his work overseas. He recounted how, one day shortly after his return to New York, a piercing winter wind struck his face as he left for work. That stinging sensation, which ordinarily would have caused him to wince in discomfort, instead prompted him to think of Chan, Sophie, and all the others who had passed through the acid ward, whose burns had resulted in significant loss of sensation in their faces. In that moment, he almost felt grateful for the pain; it was a reminder of the fact that he could feel his face, which until then he had taken for granted. Reframing one's perspective through the lens of gratitude, he told Kim, can have a profound impact on the way we experience and perceive the events in our lives.

"We live with blinders on," Ebby explained. "When I came back from working with the acid burn victims in Cambodia, I started to focus on the things I took for granted. When was the last time I thought about the fact that I can feel my face, that my limbs can move, that I can open my eyes and see? There are 285 million people around the world who are visually impaired, of whom nearly 40 million are completely blind." He pointed out that until we are exposed to these facts, we take many aspects of our lives for granted. He went on to explain that this is due to the fact that we naturally tend to calibrate our frame of reference to those in our immediate vicinity or in the media. Their lifestyles form our sense of what's "normal."

Swarthmore psychology professor Barry Schwartz, author of *The Paradox of Choice*, agrees. He refers to this phenomenon as the "curse of social comparison." Schwartz found that when people compare themselves to others who "do better" (what he calls "upward social comparison"), they are more likely to experience "jealousy, hostility, negative mood, frustration, lowered self-esteem, decreased happiness, and symptoms of stress." Schwartz suggests that we challenge our natural tendency to compare ourselves to the narrow slice of those who have a world of wealth and resources at their fingertips.

"It's a shift in perspective," Ebby told Kim, "meaning that your sense of life satisfaction ultimately depends on your personal, chosen frame of reference."

He continued: "Our immediate environment and day-to-day experiences make us prone to the 'normality bias.' If I am surrounded by abundant goods and services, their relevance in my life slowly shifts from being optional to necessary. I can experience unhappiness and even anger if I feel excluded from such privileges. By widening our frame of reference beyond the distortions of the media and our immediate social environment, we can begin to appreciate aspects of our lives we may have taken for granted. This experience of gratitude is often accompanied by a solemn sense of contentment, if not happiness."

For most of us, it takes a conscious act to reframe our perspectives. It means seeking out information and experiences that fall outside our daily lives, and trying to rid ourselves of the notion that we're competing with the celebrities who get so much airtime, the people whom Boston College sociology professor Juliet Schor calls "our media 'friends.'" In her book *The Overspent American,* she compares Americans in the 1950s, who felt a need to keep up with the Joneses, with Americans today, who measure themselves against people whose earnings and net worth are often many multiples of the median.

Barry Schwartz has a name for this too: the "curse of high expectations." He describes how distorted our expectations have become of what life should look like, and how this contributes to a vicious cycle of disappointment as we fail to meet unrealistic expectations. Instead, Schwartz suggests that we cultivate an "attitude of gratitude," by "consciously striving to be grateful more often for what is good about a choice or an experience, and to be disappointed less by what is bad about it."

Ebby has found that one of the most effective ways to reframe one's perspective and cultivate this attitude of gratitude is through volunteerism and service. "To paraphrase my grandfather Ostad Elahi, we should be grateful for the opportunity to do good, in part because we ourselves have the most to gain by doing so," he said. "When you view your life through the lens of a larger purpose, you create a larger arc for your life, where day-to-day events become subservient to your greater goal. The momentary ups and downs become dusty winds on the road of your larger journey."

His experience echoes what a growing body of research tells us — that connecting to a cause larger than ourselves is one of the surest steps toward a meaningful life. And just as important, research also shows that meaning, not happiness, is the key to a successful life.

Martin Seligman, a pioneer in the field of positive psychology, describes three dimensions of happiness one can pursue: the pleasant life, in which our basic needs are met; the good life, in which one finds ways to creatively deploy one's strengths and virtues; and the meaningful life. He defines the meaningful life as one in which you are able to use "your signature strengths and virtues in the service of something much larger than you are." In other words, when you are able to use your power for purpose.

When Kim met Sophie, she gained a new perspective. Seeing that innocent baby and knowing she had suffered for days without medical attention inspired her to want to do more. The Virtue Foundation was built on the notion that everyone has something to contribute. She knew she could put her resources to work.

She was at the right company. Avon had a long history of empowering women — indeed, it was in the business of empowering women entrepreneurs through its direct-selling model. The company had a legacy of women-focused initiatives, including awareness campaigns on issues like breast cancer and domestic violence, and it prided itself on being "the company for women." Its new CEO at the time, Andrea Jung, then the youngest woman ever to lead a Fortune 500 company, had made it a personal priority to ensure that the company lived up to its tag line. From what Kim had seen of Andrea's leadership, she knew that if she presented her with Sophie's story, Andrea would want to use her power to help.

Shortly after her promotion, Kim was headed to a conference in western Canada with Andrea. As they pulled away from their Sixth Avenue headquarters for the airport, Kim sensed it was the ideal moment to bring up the subject. "Have you heard about acid violence?" she asked.

Andrea was shocked by Sophie's story, and by the fact that this horrific crime affected women in many countries. Before they reached the airport, she had made a commitment to do what she could to help combat this scourge; it seemed only logical. And that was only the beginning. During the rest of the trip and for years to come, Kim and Andrea bonded over how they could use their platforms to make an impact. Andrea became an early member of Kim's purpose coalition.

In the months that followed, that coalition grew. Ebby was able to round up dozens of volunteers to care for and perform pro bono surgery on Chan and Sophie, ultimately restoring much of Sophie's sight and repairing many of their injuries and disfigurements. The Virtue Foundation hosted a conversation on acid violence at the United Nations. A volunteer documentary filmmaker who had been traveling with Ebby captured the issue in *Stolen Faces*. As awareness of acid violence grew, so did Kim's responsibilities at work. She became increasingly aware of how her work at the company could help advance women and girls around the world.

Kim quickly became "addicted to purpose." She found herself energized and excited about her work, since it gave her the chance to give back. Her experience was backed by decades of research showing that volunteering is correlated with positive health benefits, including increased energy and lower stress levels. Allan Luks, a social entrepreneur and thought leader, coined the term "helper's high" to describe the "powerful physical feelings people experience when directly helping others."

Inspired by Sophie, Kim continued to seek out new ways to harness her skills and the resources at her disposal. One such opportunity arose in 2008, when she was asked to attend a gathering at the White House for women from the Middle East.

On that occasion, she had a chance encounter with one of then secretary of state Condoleezza Rice's top aides, Ambassador Shirin Tahir-Kelly, who was responsible for women's issues globally. Shirin introduced herself to Kim and asked her whether Avon would partner with the State Department on an economic empowerment project. Thinking of Sophie, Kim had another idea. "How do you feel about women and justice?" she ventured.

Nine months later, Condoleezza Rice, Andrea, Shirin, Kim, and Justice Sandra Day O'Connor convened a daylong conference at the State Department. Judges and legal professionals from seventy-five countries shared best practices and strategized on how to combat violence against women using judicial and legal tools.

As Kim gave the closing remarks, inspired by the women judges before her, she felt she could not let this day end without establishing some way to continue the dialogue. Smiling from the podium, she made a silent promise to the little Cambodian girl and other acid violence victims around the world, and announced the creation of a center for women and justice. Stepping back from the podium, Kim maintained her smile but hoped that she could deliver on this promise. Somehow, though, she trusted that the women and men present that day would be just as committed as she was to bringing such a center to fruition.

Her faith was soon borne out. A few days after the event, Kim decided to take a chance and put in a call to Justice O'Connor. She left a message with the justice's assistant, only half expecting a response. Soon thereafter, her office phone rang. A voice Kim recognized said, "Is this Kim Azzarelli? This is Justice Sandra Day O'Connor." Kim described her vision for an institution that would support women judges around the world in combating violence against women. "I would be happy to support your proposed center for women judges. I think it could be very helpful," Justice O'Connor replied. When she heard those words, Kim knew her vision would become a reality.

Her next stop was the Virtue Foundation, where she raised the idea with Ebby and his colleagues. The foundation quickly offered to fund the first fellow. Then there was the question of where to house the center. Kim approached her alma mater, Cornell Law School. Just a few weeks after the event at the State Department, Kim traveled to Ithaca, New York, to meet the dean of the law school at the time, Stewart Schwab. Until that day she had had little contact with him, and as she walked into his office, she prepared herself for what she expected to be a difficult pitch.

To her surprise, Dean Schwab greeted her with a big smile, a warm handshake, and his utmost assurances that of course Cornell would be a part of this exciting and important initiative. As she wondered why the conversation was going so smoothly, her eyes landed on a photograph on the dean's desk. In it, a much younger Stewart Schwab stood with Justice Sandra Day O'Connor, the two of them smiling at each other. Seeing Kim's face, Dean Schwab turned to look at the picture as well. "Oh, yes," he said. "I was one of her first law clerks."

The last step was marshaling the resources to make the center a reality. Soon after the meeting in Ithaca, Andrea called Kim into a private conference room. As Kim sat down, Andrea said, "I understand you're starting a center for women and justice at Cornell." Her follow-up question blew Kim away: "How can we support you and the women judges?"

Within a year, the center was up and running, thanks in large part to Sital Kalantry, a human rights professor at Cornell Law School, and Sara Lulo, the center's first executive director. The center drew on the expertise and leadership of judges, practicing attorneys, businesspeople, academics, and physicians, demonstrating that everyone had something to bring to the table. Now six years old, Cornell Law School's Avon Global Center for Women and Justice has provided pro bono assistance and training to judges around the world on issues ranging from child marriage to human trafficking to peace building and domestic violence processes. One of its first reports, a three-country study of acid violence, spearheaded by Sital and Jocelyn Getgen Kestenbaum, the center's first fellow, resulted in a model legal code that would hold perpetrators of acid violence accountable — ultimately influencing changes in Cambodian law.

Little Sophie's plight had unleashed a range of far-reaching purpose-driven initiatives, including contributing to the passage of new laws in her own country. Sophie's story had even reached the first woman to serve on the Supreme Court, who not only supported the creation of the center, but each year was eager to learn about its progress and host the women judges at the Supreme Court. In 2011, Kim received another memorable call from Justice O'Connor as she was preparing to receive the international judges.

"Kim, this is Sandra." (It was always "Justice O'Connor" to Kim.) "I have good news and I have bad news. Which do you want first?"

"Definitely the bad news," Kim said.

"Well, the bad news is that I won't be able to host the women judges at the Supreme Court this year, as I have a conflict I can't resolve. The good news is that I've asked the other girls to host. Would that be satisfactory?" By "the other girls," Justice O'Connor was referring to Justices Ruth Bader Ginsburg, Sonia Sotomayor, and Elena Kagan, who all enthusiastically honored her request.

In addition, with the help of Justice O'Connor, the Sandra Day O'Connor College of Law at Arizona State University, in collaboration with the O'Connor House, expanded its advocacy against domestic violence, creating the Diane Halle Center for Family Justice. Years later, the justice was walking with Kim in New York. She stopped, turned to Kim, placed both hands on her shoulders, and said, "Do you know how many women are not being beaten right now because of these efforts? I hope you realize this."

Networking around purpose has put us in the room with women and men who have widely varied skill sets, backgrounds, and accomplishments. But purpose has always been a great democratizer: it brought together Cambodian health care workers, New York doctors, and top corporate executives in order to restore the health of a little girl burned with acid. Purpose gathers judges from many nations who are committed to ending violence against women. It erases rank and values everyone's skills and commitment to the cause.

We have seen purpose uniting women at all levels of society. From the rural women of Bangladesh who join together to form microcredit borrowing circles; to the earthshaking 1995 Fourth World Conference on Women in Beijing; to women executives who are working together to put women at the center of their companies' agendas; to the diplomats, celebrities, and activists who converge on Tina Brown's Women in the World summits — when people come together around purpose, extraordinary things can happen.

5

Leadership and Networks at the Top

IN MARCH 2014, HILLARY CLINTON and Christine Lagarde, the managing director of the International Monetary Fund, shared the stage at Lincoln Center with *New York Times* columnist Thomas Friedman at the Women in the World Summit in New York. Friedman had just made the point that the European Commission was in dire need of new leadership, which, he observed, Lagarde was abundantly qualified to provide. Addressing Lagarde, he asked, "President of the European Commission? Which would be very interesting, if you're the president of Europe and," he added, turning to Clinton, "you're the president of America."

As the two women's hands met in the air for a high-five, the crowd erupted in thundering cheers. It was an image to remember: two powerful leaders, hands meeting in a joyful acknowledgment of the many world-changing possibilities that still lay ahead for each of them and the potential power of a network of women at the top.

For the first time in history, a critical mass of women has reached the summits of business, government, and culture. The glass ceiling — that frustrating barrier that prevents women from getting to the top — is showing cracks, although it is far from shattered. Women today lead nations, multilateral organizations, and Fortune 500 companies. They conduct diplomacy, design U.S. technology policy, and sit on the Supreme Court. They are role models and they are mentors. Often, working together, they use their power for the purpose of advancing other women.

Tina Brown understands the power of networks better than most. Over the course of her journalism career, which took her from the British society magazine *Tatler* to *Vanity Fair* and then to *The New Yorker* (as its first female editor since its founding in 1925), she has reported on some of the most accomplished people in politics, business, entertainment, and the arts. But the stories that have stayed with her, the people who impressed her most, were women on the ground leading change, whom she often met through the Vital Voices network. Their struggle to better their communities, fought with little fanfare and often at great personal risk, were the stories she wanted to tell.

One of those women was Leymah Gbowee. In the early 2000s, Leymah led a movement of Christian and Muslim women to protest the gruesome civil war in Liberia, which had raged on and off since the 1980s. Disgusted with the violence they had experienced for far too long, Leymah and women from her church joined with Muslim women allies to distribute flyers around the capital, Monrovia — at daily markets, after Friday prayers at mosques, and at churches on Sundays. The women's desire for peace dissolved ethnic and religious boundaries, leading them to stage nonviolent prayer vigils protesting the war at a fish market visible from the residence of Liberia's president, Charles Taylor.

In 2003, in an act of extreme bravery, Leymah confronted Taylor, a former guerrilla fighter who was later convicted of crimes against humanity, including sexual slavery and recruiting child soldiers. She stated: "The women of Liberia . . . are tired of war. We are tired of running. We are tired of begging for bulgur wheat. We are tired of our children being raped. We are now taking this stand to secure the future of our children because we believe, as custodians of society, tomorrow our children will ask us, 'Mama, what was your role during the crisis?'"

Her actions and those of the thousands of women protesters pushed forward stalled peace negotiations, which would ultimately contribute to ending the war and later to Taylor's removal from power. For years, these women's role in ending the conflict was little known outside Liberia, until filmmaker Abigail Disney chronicled Leymah's story in the 2008 documentary *Pray the Devil Back to Hell*.

By 2009, Tina Brown had created the digital news website the *Daily Beast*, which would later merge with *Newsweek*. There she began to use her platform to tell the stories of the women who, in her words, "live between the lines of the news." She knew how powerful a live event could be and wanted others to hear the stories of these inspiring women directly from them, unmediated and unscripted. She also knew she could use her media reach to bring attention to these underreported stories.

Now was the time to get her network on board. Tina called on leaders in the media industry and in literary circles, on Wall Street, in Hollywood, and in Washington. Top reporters, television anchors, and well-known Hollywood stars showed up to interview and honor more than a dozen human rights activists and social entrepreneurs at the first Women in the World Summit, held in New York in March of 2010.

The summit opened with a powerful stage performance, *SEVEN*, an innovative documentary theater piece that told the stories of the lives of seven courageous women from the Vital Voices network, from a congresswoman in Guatemala fighting corruption, to an anti-trafficking advocate and parliamentarian in Cambodia, to a courageous advocate for women's rights in Afghanistan, Farida Azizi. The play itself was the product of another women's network. Carol Mack, an award-winning playwright and author, had been struck by the drama of Farida's story when Carol heard her speak at a small Vital Voices gathering. Carol knew that story could impact others as well. She asked Melanne if there were others like Farida in the Vital Voices network. Melanne told her there were hundreds. So Carol reached out to her own network of friends in the theater. She and six of her playwright colleagues worked with Vital Voices to select seven leaders, including Farida, whose stories they would bring to life on the stage. Each playwright was paired with one of the women's rights champions and, through interviews and research, created a monologue based on her story. The result was the documentary drama *SEVEN*.

Meryl Streep portrayed Inez McCormack, the renowned Irish trade-union activist who had played a critical role in the 1998 Good Friday Agreement. As the last of the seven monologues concluded, the audience burst into applause. But the show wasn't over: all but one of the seven featured activists walked onto the stage. Their presence reminded the audience that this wasn't fiction — their harrowing stories were all too real.

In the six years since the summit was first held, many of the courageous women featured onstage have themselves become household names. Leymah Gbowee went on to win the Nobel Peace Prize in 2011 (along with Liberian president Ellen Johnson Sirleaf and Yemeni human rights activist Tawakkol Karman). Malala Yousafzai, who was honored by Angelina Jolie onstage in 2013, won the peace prize in 2014. It is clear that coverage of women in leadership and of so-called women's issues is finally becoming more mainstream.

Every year there are an increasing number of important events that bring together influential women committed to discussing issues affecting them and their professions, as well as ways to improve the lives of women and girls globally. One of the first was the Women's Forum for the Economy and Society, launched in 2005 by Aude de Thuin in the seaside town of Deauville, France. Aude recognized that a large number of women leaders were looking for opportunities to come together in a setting conducive to networking, much like the World Economic Forum in Davos, Switzerland, but featuring a wider range of issues, from the economy to human rights. The Women's Forum, under CEO Jacqueline Franjou, has expanded to conferences in Myanmar, Mexico, and Brazil, in addition to France. In recent years, these kinds of gatherings have expanded and enhanced women's networks, advancing solutions and igniting purpose-driven initiatives around the world. "The goal of the Women's Forum for the Economy and Society at Deauville," explained Clara Gaymard, the president and CEO of GE France and the president of the forum, "is to provide a unique business and social environment where both women and men can collaborate. These meetings are about learning and sharing best practices, anticipating the future, and networking across generations. We focus on making the right choices and investing in what matters, and enabling everyone to have an opportunity to make an impact."

Jacki Zehner is another leader in her field using her network to amplify the power of women's philanthropy. In 2002, after an extraordinarily successful career on Wall Street (she was the youngest woman and the first female trader to be made a partner at Goldman Sachs), she became a founding member of the Circle Financial Group, a private wealth-management firm run by a dozen Wall Street women, each with expertise in a particular asset class. In 2009, with the fruits of her professional success, Jacki made a public pledge of $1 million to the Women's Funding Network.

That million-dollar gift made Jacki a full-fledged member of the group Women Moving Millions, of which she is now chief engagement officer. Women Moving Millions aims to raise the bar of philanthropic giving by American women, which the organization estimates should be as high as $230 billion *annually,* to advance the causes of women and girls. The organization encourages women to publicly pledge their gifts of $1 million or more, but also holds events to educate potential donors about the philanthropic undertaking, potential beneficiaries, and how to maximize impact. Jacki noted that in the eight years since Women Moving Millions was started by philanthropist Helen LaKelly Hunt, more than 220 people in eleven countries have made pledges of $1 million or more, with a total of more than $500 million pledged.

"At the time Women Moving Millions was launched, there were very few big gifts to women-led organizations that focused on women and girls. That's why I love this community — they put a gender lens on philanthropic strategy," Jacki told us. "We know that women love to do things in community, so why not do philanthropy in community? It creates so much leverage and shared expertise."

Melinda Gates is another woman who is seeking to put a gender lens on global philanthropy. She is increasingly putting women and girls at the center of the work of the Bill and Melinda Gates Foundation, concentrating on a range of issues, from maternal and child health to family planning and access to financial services, especially for underserved women. Recently, she has partnered with the Clinton Foundation on No Ceilings: The Full Participation Project, a data-driven analysis of the progress and gaps remaining for women's and girls' equal participation.

"I've thought a lot about empowerment," Melinda told us. "What does that mean? To me, it means three things. For women to be empowered, they need basic health, they need decision-making power, and they need economic opportunities. We can and need to make all sorts of investments to help women and girls be healthy and seize power and opportunity. Girls' education actually impacts all three categories," she said. "Another example is ensuring that women have access to a bank account where they can save the money they earn, because it makes it easier for them to decide how their family will spend its income. In the end, having control over resources is a pathway to greater economic opportunities. The beauty of these types of investments is that, when they result in empowered women, the women themselves become engines of development. An empowered woman is busy making investments in everyone around her, so the ripple effects of investments in empowerment are very significant."

We've seen over and over that as women seize a greater number of leadership positions, they amplify their impact by working together to advance women and girls.

From Sixteen to Thirty

And while we are seeing historic levels of women in leadership positions, unfortunately we're still some distance from equal participation. Indeed, in nearly every sector, women still struggle to reach leadership posts in meaningful numbers. "Women remain hugely underrepresented at positions of power in every single sector across this country," Barnard College president Debora Spar has said. "We have fallen into what I call the 16 percent ghetto, which is that if you look at any sector, be it aerospace engineering, Hollywood films, higher education, or Fortune 500 leading positions, women max out at roughly 16 percent . . . That is a crime, and it is a waste of incredible talent."

The higher up the chain you go, the worse it gets. While women in the United States hold 19 percent of board seats in S&P 500 companies, they make up only 3.1 percent of board chairs and less than 5 percent of CEOs. In both 2012 and 2013, one out of ten companies had no women serving on their boards at all. Worse still, women of color hold a mere 3.1 percent of board seats in Fortune 500 companies. A recent study by EY found that the number of board directors named John, Robert, William, and James at S&P 1500 companies exceeded the total number of female board directors.

Helena Morrissey is one woman who is using her platform and network to change these numbers. Helena is the CEO of the London-based Newton Investment Management and a founder of the 30% Club, which aims to get women into 30 percent of board seats. Why 30 percent? Research dating back to the late 1970s suggests that 30 percent representation of women's voices in a group setting constitutes a "critical mass." At that point, those people can begin to be heard for themselves, not merely as representatives or tokens of an "other" perspective.

Helena began her campaign by leveraging her network, sending personal notes to some of the CEOs of the top 350 companies on the London FTSE stock exchange. She made her case purely on the data, citing research going back nearly a decade, from the likes of Catalyst, McKinsey & Company, and Credit Suisse, that demonstrates that a more diverse board produces higher returns. One 2012 study, for example, found that 30 percent or more female representation on boards at more than 150 listed German firms led to better performance. And another widely cited nineteen-year study has found that the twenty-five Fortune 500 firms with the best record of promoting women to senior positions also notched higher profitability — between 18 percent and 69 percent higher than the median Fortune 500 companies in their respective industries.

What explains the better performance? Diverse leadership, by its very nature, prevents group-think and leads to better decision making. A study from 2009 found that the simple presence of difference led to better performance in heterogeneous groups than in homogeneous groups; increased tension within a group encourages better problem solving. Research also demonstrates that women lead differently. One study even argues that women make better board directors than men, based on findings that they are more effective at accounting for multiple competing interests, solving problems creatively, and building consensus. By contrast, male directors often made decisions based on rules, regulations, and tradition.

Helena's evidence-based approach seems to be working: in the four years since she launched the 30% Club, the percentage of women on boards of British companies has nearly doubled, to 23 percent. In the United States, where women comprise 19 percent of board seats, organizations like 2020 Women on Boards, DirectWomen, and WomenCorporateDirectors are also promoting the inclusion of more women on boards. This bodes well for company performance in the future.

None of these findings comes as a surprise to Joanna Barsh, who has spent the past decade studying the most accomplished women leaders around the world and what makes them tick. Since 2004, Joanna, a longtime consultant at McKinsey & Company, has interviewed more than two hundred leaders, conducting much of McKinsey's research on the impact of women in the economy while creating an important program on women's leadership. In her 2009 book *How Remarkable Women Lead,* Joanna identified the characteristics that tend to make female leaders thrive: they bring meaning and purpose to work, they lead from their strengths, they embrace positive and negative emotions at work and harness that energy to motivate their colleagues, and they build community and trust in their organization so that everyone feels capable of participating.

That may be one reason behind the increasing acceptance of quotas, which specify a certain number or proportion of women in a given group, to ensure better representation on corporate boards and in politics. Over a decade ago, Norway became the first country to pass legislation requiring up to 40 percent of board seats to be filled by women. Germany, after a public debate that lasted years, followed suit in 2015 with a 30 percent mandate. Many countries, in Europe, Asia, and the Middle East, have similar measures, although not all are mandatory.

Quotas are more widespread when it comes to elected political office. A 2014 report found that some 118 countries and territories, or half of the world, had some sort of gender quota in place for its elected offices. Quotas aside, women are also forming networks with the goal of electing more women to government leadership. In the United States, one of the oldest groups is EMILY's List. Founded by activist and philanthropist Ellen Malcolm in 1985, a time when you could count the number of female senators on one hand, EMILY's List began as a group of twenty-five women gathered in Ellen's basement with their Rolodexes. It has since helped get hundreds of pro-choice Democratic women elected to state, local, and national office. Other nonpartisan groups, like the Women's Campaign Fund and Running Start, are working to help women win political office. And Kirsten Gillibrand, a Democratic senator from New York, has raised millions of dollars in donations to help women take their seats at the decision-making table since launching her Off the Sidelines political action committee in 2012.

In 2011, Secretary Clinton cofounded the Women in Public Service Project in partnership with the Seven Sisters colleges, with the goal of creating a worldwide network to increase the number of women in public service — to get to 50 percent representation by 2050 at all levels — through leadership training and mentorship programs. The program is now housed at the Woodrow Wilson Center, which is led by former congresswoman Jane Harman. Both the International Republican Institute and the National Democratic Institute have programs to increase women's political participation around the world. Madeleine Albright, the chair of the National Democratic Institute, has noted, "Every country deserves to have the best possible leader and that means that women have to be given a chance to compete. If they're never allowed to compete in the electoral process then the countries are really robbing themselves of a great deal of talent."

Governing with Purpose

Women often come to the political table with different priorities, using their power in an expansive, inclusive way. Or, as we like to say, they often lead with purpose.

In India, for example, women's political leadership at the village level has led to outcomes that better reflect women's priorities and the needs of the local community. In 1992, the Seventy-third Amendment to the Indian constitution mandated gender quotas, reserving one-third of seats in the country's 265,000 *panchayats,* or local decision-making bodies, for women. One study found that women-led *panchayats* had made more investments in public services that benefited their female constituents, and another found that villagers were less likely to pay bribes in villages led by women. In particular, female village leaders were more likely to give priority to public services that helped women, like access to safe drinking water, and also to encourage girls' education and discourage extravagant dowries. What amounts to a mass movement of more than one million women into local governments has been called India's "silent revolution in democracy."

Women wielding power in government can make a difference in the lives of many. Mary Goudie, for example, is a life peer in the House of Lords and an impassioned advocate against human trafficking. Baroness Goudie has used her influence to push the British government to sign on to international and regional treaties to combat trafficking.

As she spoke to colleagues, both in her own Labour Party and in the opposition Tory Party, Mary realized that few people in government were familiar with the many dimensions of human trafficking, which involves everything from child labor to bonded and forced domestic servitude to forced agricultural and factory work, as well as trafficking for purposes of sexual exploitation. "They did not understand what human trafficking was, or did not want to understand it," she recalls.

Mary worked to educate them. Her efforts paved the way to the passage of a number of amendments to strengthen the United Kingdom's Modern Slavery Act in March 2015, thanks in part to her work alongside anti-trafficking advocacy groups.

Often, women's common interests and experiences can bridge partisan divides. The experience of women in American politics brings the point home. A 2011 study of the U.S. Congress from 1973 to 2008 found that female legislators are about 10 percent more effective than their male colleagues in passing the bills they sponsor. This outperformance is even more marked for women in the minority party, who are about 33 percent more effective than men in the minority party, a fact the authors attribute to women's ability to work constructively across the aisle.

Since women first entered the Senate in meaningful numbers in the 1990s, they have worked together to pass bills "based on their experience as women," according to a recent *Politico* article. The bonds between female senators grew across party lines at regular off-the-record, informal dinners, hosted on a rotating basis by each woman. In October 2013, with the federal government shuttered after protracted partisan bickering, and facing the prospect of a historic default, the women of the Senate crossed party lines to put forward a plan that would eventually reopen the government. "I probably will have retribution in my state,"

Republican senator Lisa Murkowski of Alaska told the *New York Times*. "That's fine. That doesn't bother me at all. If there is backlash, hey, that's what goes on in D.C., but in the meantime there is a government that is shut down. There are people who are really hurting."

Bipartisanship was also instrumental in sustaining a government program that helped the women of Afghanistan, through the U.S.-Afghan Women's Council, a public-private partnership founded in 2002 by then president George W. Bush and then Afghan president Hamid Karzai. When she was first lady, Laura Bush became the honorary cochair and one of the council's most prominent supporters, traveling to Afghanistan to see its work and raising resources and awareness for it around the world. The council supports businesses and individuals who aim to improve the lives of Afghan women and girls by investing in health, education and literacy, entrepreneurship, and political leadership.

The winding down of the Bush administration could have signaled the end of the council's participation with the government, but then Secretary of State Hillary Clinton saw great merit in its work and encouraged the State Department to continue its engagement with the council. Laura Bush welcomed Hillary as honorary cochair. At Hillary's invitation, Laura Bush and the council celebrated its tenth anniversary at the State Department in 2012, and the women who've participated in the program continue to pay it forward.

Anita McBride, who served as chief of staff to Laura Bush from 2005 to 2009, had a front-row seat to the council's work. In March 2014, Anita visited with emerging women leaders from Afghanistan, representing a variety of sectors, from politics to academia to business. She observed their determination to take the leadership lessons they learned and spread them throughout the country. "They are going deep into communities that are rural and harder to reach, and they're using what they learned and they are training others," said Anita.

In Poland, women from across political, professional, and ideological lines have convened each year since 2009 for the annual Congress of Women, a gathering to foster solidarity and push for better economic, social, and political conditions for women. Henryka Bochniarz, vice president of Boeing International and president of Boeing Central and

Eastern Europe, who helped launch the congress, told Melanne that she was joined by many other senior-level women from Polish and multinational companies, who lobbied their firms to support the effort. These women executives had risen to the top ranks of their companies and made a persuasive case to their firms' leadership that this was an important investment. When Melanne attended the first Congress of Women, she was struck by the hundreds of women who came together from across Poland, rural and urban, of all ages, who have since become an effective lobbying force and are leading the way for women's progress in Eastern Europe.

In its first two years, the Congress of Women was able to pressure the Polish government to adopt a quota mandating that 35 percent of candidates on electoral lists be women. The government also made a commitment to open day care centers for children under three, a measure the congress advocated for, in order to boost labor force participation by women, which, according to the International Labor Organization, hovers around 50 percent. The congress's successes go beyond tangible wins. In the six years it has been running, it has galvanized the national women's movement and inspired a similar congress in Hungary.

Leadership in the Law

Senior-level women in the legal profession are creating their own networks and initiatives to help advance other women in the law, at a time when women's progress in some areas of the legal industry has stalled. More than 40 percent of the student body at American law schools has been female since the mid-1980s, yet as of 2014, only about 17 percent of equity partners at the country's largest two hundred law firms were women.

One recent encouraging trend in the legal field, however, is the increasing number of women serving as general counsels in major corporations. Women hold 21 percent of general counsel positions in Fortune 500 companies. With more women running legal departments, we can also hope to see a demand for more diversity on the supply side of legal services, and therefore better representation of women in the senior management of law firms. This evolution is already under way: in recent years, we've seen more companies demanding a diverse slate of professionals on their outside-counsel teams.

Despite the disappointing number of women at the top of law firms, the bench appears to be a more welcoming place for women, who make up one-third of the justices on the U.S. Supreme Court and 25 percent of judges on U.S. district courts and courts of appeal. The first woman on the Supreme Court, Sandra Day O'Connor, was appointed at a time when women still faced explicit discrimination in the legal profession. But that was hardly going to slow her down. The eldest girl in her family, Justice O'Connor, a born-and-raised cowgirl, grew up herding cattle on an Arizona ranch that had no electricity or running water during her youth. Her enthusiasm for the semiannual cattle roundup meant a break in tradition with what had previously been an all-male ritual.

"Changing it to accommodate a female was probably my first initiation into joining an all-men's club, something I did more than once in my life," she wrote in *Lazy B: Growing Up on a Cattle Ranch in the American Southwest*, her 2002 memoir coauthored with her brother H. Alan Day. "After the cowboys understood that a girl could hold up her end, it was much easier for my sister, my niece, and the other girls and young women who followed to be accepted in that rough-and-tumble world."

Despite graduating near the top of her Stanford Law School class of 1952, she was rejected from every private law firm to which she applied. "We don't hire women" was the only reason they offered. She finally landed an unpaid job with the county attorney's office in San Mateo, where she sat at a desk next to the secretary. By 1981, when President Reagan nominated her to the Supreme Court, she had served as the assistant attorney general in Arizona, in the Arizona Senate, and on two state courts. On September 21, 1981, the U.S. Senate confirmed Sandra Day O'Connor to be the first woman justice, by a vote of 99–0.

Why does having women on the bench matter? Having more women leads to a judiciary that better reflects the society it seeks to serve, and in turn instills more trust in the judicial system. Women also bring valuable perspectives that can result in a more fair and impartial implementation of the law. As Kim recalls, Justice O'Connor described women's fundamental role perfectly at a Cornell Center gathering of international women judges that she hosted with Kim at the Supreme Court: "The key to peace is the rule of law," O'Connor said. "The key to rule of law is an impartial judiciary. And the key to an impartial judiciary is the participation of women."

Another pioneering woman, Justice Ruth Bader Ginsburg, the senior ranking woman on the high court, has been a lifelong champion of women's rights and is sometimes referred to as "the Thurgood Marshall of the women's movement." Like her colleague Justice O'Connor, Justice Ginsburg, who tied for first place in her graduating class at Columbia Law School, similarly struggled to find work because of her gender. She became a fearless litigator at the American Civil Liberties Union, where she led its Women's Rights Project, arguing six and winning five sex-discrimination cases before the Supreme Court. In 1971, her brief to the Court in *Reed v. Reed* compared women's legal and social second-class status to that of African Americans, opening the door for the Court to more closely scrutinize laws that discriminated on the basis of gender.

On the Supreme Court, Justice Ginsburg has continued to be a voice for justice and women's equality under the law — from her early decisions, like opening the all-male Virginia Military Institute to women in 1996, to the landmark employment discrimination case *Ledbetter v. Goodyear Tire & Rubber Co.* in 2007, in which she issued a memorable dissent. "Dissents speak to a future age," Justice Ginsburg told NPR's Nina Totenberg in 2002. "The greatest dissents do become court opinions and gradually over time their views become the dominant view. So that's the dissenter's hope: that they are writing not for today but for tomorrow." Indeed, the first bill signed into law by President Barack Obama was the 2009 Lilly Ledbetter Fair Pay Act.

Today, Justice Ginsburg is joined by Justices Sonia Sotomayor, the Court's first Latina, who graduated summa cum laude from Princeton and was an editor at the *Yale Law Journal,* and Elena Kagan, a former dean of Harvard Law School and the first female solicitor general of the United States.

In April 2015, Justices Ginsburg, Sotomayor, and Kagan joined us in paying tribute to Justice O'Connor's work and life, a rare appearance by the four women justices. Justice Ginsburg provided moving remarks that included a quote by Justice O'Connor: "In Justice O'Connor's own words, for men and women, the first step in getting power is to become visible to others, and then to put on an impressive show. As women achieve power, the barriers will fall. As society sees what women can do, as women see what women can do, there will be more women out there doing things and we'll all be better off for it."

In recent decades, women in the United States have also held highly visible roles in the regulatory sphere, where they have frequently shown insightful and sometimes prescient understanding of the risks in the industries they were overseeing. Sheila Bair served as the nineteenth chairman of the Federal Deposit Insurance Corporation; Brooksley Born warned of the dangers that complex derivatives contracts could pose to the global financial system as chair of the Commodity Futures Trading Commission (CFTC) in the late 1990s; before she became a U.S. senator, Elizabeth Warren was instrumental in creating the Consumer Finance Protection Bureau. Sharon Bowen is the first African-American woman commissioner at the CFTC and has been a powerful mentor to Kim and other female lawyers. Mary Jo White has taken the helm of the Securities and Exchange Commission; Gina McCarthy is administrator at the Environmental Protection Agency; and Janet Yellen, a respected academic, is the first female chair of the Federal Reserve.

Yet despite these great strides, as previously discussed, we still find significant gender gaps in leadership. Before we discuss some potential solutions, it's worth examining the commonly cited excuses we've heard for why women aren't making it to the top.

"Women aren't natural leaders."

For better or worse, leadership is still by and large associated with "male" attributes such as decisiveness and risk taking. When women listen before speaking or lead by building consensus, they're often seen as less effective. Alternatively, women who adopt a "male" leadership style are often labeled too aggressive — or worse.

"Women have a harder time balancing their family lives with work obligations."

While women have historically been designated as caregivers, surely they aren't the only people who want to spend time with their families. The most progressive countries and companies are increasingly recognizing that women and men have responsibilities and commitments outside of work. Legitimizing those obligations and desires, and respecting them, creates more fulfilled and ultimately more productive teams.

"There aren't enough qualified women."

One reason often cited for the failure to diversify corporate boards and senior leadership is the supposed lack of qualified women "in the pipeline." If there's a leak in the pipeline, it is incumbent on the company to fix it, ensuring its talented female employees don't drop out before they reach the top.

"We already have a woman on our board."

One woman? That's not good enough. We've seen how the presence of just one or two female faces in a group can create the illusion of inclusion, leading to complacency.

The firms that have successfully promoted women started by recognizing what's at stake: a tremendous pool of human capital that they can't afford to waste. Bob Moritz, the chairman and senior partner of the auditing and consulting firm PwC, said his company is changing how it operates to better compete for and retain female talent. "If you're not focused on people, you're going to lose sight and not get the best and brightest talent," he told us. "You've really got to spend time thinking about — what is in their best interest?"

Nonetheless, progress at the top may sometimes seem glacial. How can we get to 50 percent?

The "Pipeline Problem"

We often hear complaints about the so-called pipeline problem — that there aren't enough talented women moving through the ranks to promote to senior leadership. We're with Madeleine Albright on this. When she was asked by Charlie Rose, at the 2012 Women in the World Summit, why there are so few women in power, she said: "Men." The typically gracious diplomat continued, "People say, 'There aren't enough qualified women.' That's one of the biggest BS things I've ever heard."

There's clearly a pipeline of talented women, but many institutions, workplaces chief among them, have not yet adjusted to the reality of working women's lives. Flexibility, the Harvard economist Claudia Goldin points out, is the key to creating a work environment that not only retains women, who still do the bulk of society's caring work, but also men, who are increasingly participating in caregiving.

Susan Sobbott was running the small-business division at American Express when she noticed she was losing too many of her female employees to new motherhood. She knew these women didn't want to leave the workforce, but she also understood the challenges of maintaining a full-time job with a newborn at home. She created an internal consulting group to enable new parents to work part-time on discrete projects across the company, rather than maintain a single full-time position. That "allowed them to integrate their life at home and their career," said Susan, now president of global corporate payments at American Express.

The upside, she continued, went even further. "It was so much more dramatic than I thought. I was suddenly building a much more experienced group of employees, because now they were able to rotate into different areas, and they were so much more well-rounded and even more valuable."

Susan created a more inclusive environment for all employees, women and men alike. It's one that acknowledges the full scope of their lives, commitments, and what makes them tick. That attitude, in turn, brought its own benefits to the company.

"What I found," Susan told us, "was that whenever you offer someone flexibility to manage what's important in their lives, you're avoiding them having to make a choice between what's important to them in life, and work will lose every time. The benefit of giving them a third option is that you get loyalty you can't get in any other way, no matter how much money you pay them."

Pipeline problems, of course, also occur when employees are promoted and recruited. Some companies are using the data to encourage an environment where women will be promoted from within. In 2010, executives at Google noticed that its male engineers were sticking their hands up for promotions far more often than their equally qualified female peers. Laszlo Bock, senior vice president of Google's People Operations, designed an experiment to help women feel more confident putting themselves forward.

He had one of his head engineers send out descriptions of two academic studies along with all job announcements. One study found that girls are less likely than boys to raise their hands in class to answer math problems, even though girls' answers were more likely to be correct. Similarly, even though women's contributions to business meetings were judged more favorably by outside observers, they were less likely to volunteer their ideas than their male colleagues.

These studies provided the encouragement that the female engineers needed. Their application rates quickly climbed, and their promotion rates soon outpaced those of their male counterparts.

The benefits of promoting women apply to companies large and small. In 2010, Kah Walla became the first woman to run for president of Cameroon and faced intimidation simply because she was a woman. In a race where she was kidnapped and assaulted by water hoses, she credits a strong network of women for not only helping her stay safe but also helping her get through. Before that, she founded the leadership and management firm STRATEGIES!, in Douala, the economic capital. STRATEGIES! advises clients ranging from large global companies like ExxonMobil and Standard Chartered Bank to hundreds of Cameroon's market women who sell their goods informally.

Kah had started her consultancy with the goal of creating job opportunities for young people across Africa, and in particular young women. After participating in a workshop on gender issues, she realized she needed to formalize her recruitment policies if she wanted to ensure that her hiring procedures were fair. Now, Kah says, it's a simple numbers game: start with an equal number of female and male candidates.

"Any time you have at least 50 percent women at the beginning of the recruitment process, our experience is that you have 60 to 70 percent women in the final top five candidates," she says.

Paying It Forward

Then there's the question of what leadership looks like. As Madeleine Albright famously said, "I never dreamed of one day becoming secretary of state. It's not that I was modest; it's just that I had never seen a secretary of state wearing a skirt."

For most of American history, leadership has had a white male face. By the 1990s, Pattie Sellers, an experienced business reporter, began to notice that the face of corporate America was changing. Women, formerly notable only for their absence in the upper echelons of Fortune 500 companies, were starting to claim positions of power. In 1998, *Fortune* magazine, where Pattie was a writer, ran a cover story naming fifty women to its first-ever Most Powerful Women in Business list. The list and the related coverage recognized the growing prominence of women in corporate and political leadership, and featured women such as Oprah Winfrey and Martha Stewart and senior executives from companies like Cisco, Colgate-Palmolive, Kraft, Microsoft, and Revlon. Since then, the list has spawned an annual, invitation-only conference, the *Fortune* Most Powerful Women Summit, with iterations in Washington, D.C., London, and Hong Kong.

Pattie, who is now an assistant managing editor at *Fortune,* recognized that all this power could be used to serve a purpose. In 2005, she met with Dina Powell, then the assistant secretary for education and cultural programs at the State Department, and the following year they created an international mentoring program to bring emerging business leaders from overseas. These women leaders would be selected by U.S. embassies to receive mentoring and training from senior-level American businesswomen. Dina asked Melanne if Vital Voices would join the partnership, to provide an orientation and an ongoing network for the mentees. Since its inception, the *Fortune* mentoring program has resulted in more than 250 women from 55 countries receiving invaluable lessons from CEOs like Yahoo's Marissa Mayer and Xerox's Ursula Burns.

"The *Fortune*–U.S. State Department Global Women's Mentoring Program is, quite simply, the most meaningful thing I've been involved in," Pattie enthused. "It captures the essence of *Fortune*'s Most Powerful Women — that real power is what you do beyond your job description."

When women rise to the top, they can lift each other up. New research tracking four thousand companies in Norway found that the presence of women at higher ranks of a firm had a positive effect on the advancement of other women in the same firm. Their impact trickles in all directions: horizontally, as they mentor other leaders, and vertically, as they reach into the ranks of an organization. Sometimes their presence can lead to a simple fix: when Sheryl Sandberg was a very pregnant senior executive at Google, she persuaded her male bosses to reserve parking spaces for pregnant employees. Or it can be transformational, as when Sheryl wrote *Lean In: Women, Work, and the Will to Lead*, a groundbreaking book that has resulted in a vibrant community, impacting the way a whole generation of women think about career advancement and their own leadership.

Women's leadership can also help empower women at the lowest rungs of an organization, as with Kathleen Matthews's initiative, developed with Maria Shriver, to boost the visibility and earnings of some of Marriott's least visible employees. Under the new program, called The Envelope Please, envelopes are placed in each hotel room to remind guests to show recognition by leaving a gratuity for the largely female army of housekeepers, who play such an important role in Marriott's operations. While no substitute for good wages, the program recognizes the hard work of women who are not routinely tipped in their daily jobs.

Shriver herself has long been a champion for women. As California's First Lady, the award-winning journalist and author hosted her popular Women's Conferences. Since 2009, her Shriver Report has produced cutting-edge studies that address the conditions facing American women, including the alarming rates of economic insecurity, and offer blueprints for action. In print, TV, and digital media, Shriver creates positive impact in the world.

These are just a few examples of how women at the top are creating change in the organizations they lead, in their communities, and in concert with other women leaders. But we believe that change just as often comes from the middle. In the next chapter, we explore why this often-overlooked segment is also critical if we are to fast-forward to a better world.

6

Why the Middle Matters

WHEN AMANDA ELLIS JOINED THE World Bank in 2003 as a senior private-sector development specialist, she found that the bank rarely recognized that women had a role to play in accomplishing its mission: ending extreme poverty and boosting prosperity. At that time, talk among the Bank's officers centered around sustainable development, urbanization, and renewable resources. "Gender and growth were considered strange bedfellows when I first proposed the linkages," Amanda recalls.

Luckily, she knew better.

Early in her career, Amanda had overseen development programs for the New Zealand government in Vietnam, Laos, and Cambodia. In Southeast Asia she had witnessed how small loans, combined with business training, had been "transformative, not only for the woman recipient but also for families, given the multiplier effect through higher spending on family nutrition, health, and girls' education."

Early on, Amanda had an experience that left her keenly aware of gender inequality and exclusion. What she faced wasn't just a metaphorical "old boys' club"; it was the real thing: an all-male private club that women were not permitted to visit, let alone join. In New Zealand, one of the most prestigious and oldest of these clubs was the Wellington Club, founded in 1841.

That's where Amanda, then a first-year diplomatic trainee at the Ministry of Foreign Affairs, found herself barred from attending a meeting on economic cooperation with an American delegation. The Americans had booked the venue, she later learned, under the assumption that "A. Ellis" was a man.

There were few female colleagues to whom Amanda could turn for support, but she managed to find one in the secretary for the head of the foreign ministry, who got her an appointment with Merwyn Norrish, then the secretary of foreign affairs. Terribly intimidated, she went into his office at the appointed time and relayed the situation. To drive the point home, she asked Norrish whether she would have been excluded if, for example, she had been Maori, the indigenous people of New Zealand.

He thought long and hard. Finally, he looked her in the eye and promised to write a letter to the Wellington Club in which he would explain that women were entering the workforce in ever greater numbers. Perhaps, he would suggest, it was time to reconsider the club's policies, if only to benefit its bottom line.

"Would that be satisfactory?" Norrish asked Amanda.

She remembers thinking, "That doesn't seem satisfactory at all." It was 1988 — what about equal rights? The fundamental unfairness of being discriminated against on the basis of gender? Far too nervous to say that, instead she thanked him and left.

Whatever Secretary Norrish said in his letter, it worked. A few months later, Amanda enjoyed her first lunch at the Wellington Club, which had changed its rules.

That experience led her to found the women's network within the foreign ministry, with the intention of providing support and professional opportunities for the few other women at the ministry. Shortly thereafter, she joined Westpac, one of Australia's largest banks, as the national manager for women and business. Once again, she knew she could deploy her position to help women succeed.

She had seen surveys showing 40 percent of Australian women felt that banks discriminated against them on the basis of gender. Working with national networks of businesswomen, Amanda grew the women-focused division from zero to more than $500 million in annual lending within three years, helping hundreds of women gain access to capital for the first time and many more to expand their existing businesses. Even her most skeptical colleagues came around.

"The attitudes of my colleagues changed from markedly dismissive to 'let's nominate my best women clients for a Women in Business award,'" she recalls. "It was clear the women's market had huge potential, and cultural attitudes were changing, with visible success."

By the time Amanda arrived at the World Bank, she was a firm believer in the power of women's networks to create change, whether those networks were made up of Cambodian villagers in a lending circle or Australian businesswomen who banked with Westpac. Maybe, she thought, the World Bank needed a women's division.

"It seemed odd to me that the World Bank Group hadn't yet looked into the potential women in private-sector development could have as agents of change at the micro level and as contributors to higher economic growth at the macro level," she remembers. "The initial response wasn't encouraging. 'What do women have to do with private-sector development?' was the common refrain."

Amanda kept looking for openings, and finally found one in her manager, Michael Klein, then the vice president of private-sector development. He considered her track record as a development economist and a commercial banker and agreed to give her a shot. "He told me if I could make a good enough research case, he would ensure he found budget and staff to get a program off the ground," Amanda told us. "He was true to his word."

In 2006, the World Bank published one of its first reports analyzing women's role in economic growth. *Gender and Economic Growth in Uganda* — Amanda was its lead author — demonstrated that Australia was forgoing up to 2 percent in annual growth as a result of gender inequality. "The data on impediments to women being economically active in many countries was compelling — their status as legal minors, inability to own land and hence lack of collateral for loans, differential mobility rules — but it hadn't been categorically assessed," she said.

That has changed dramatically. Since Amanda's report, the World Bank has become a vigorous champion of women as a key to economic growth. In 2012 the bank's flagship *World Development Report* focused on gender for the first time, and the Bank now publishes numerous other thematic and country-specific studies, including the annual *Women, Business, and the Law* report on the legal barriers to women's workforce participation.

Kim, a participant in the World Bank's Private Sector Leaders Forum, helped Amanda to extend the focus of the research to recognize that implementation of law was a critical indicator that needed to be measured too. The result was the Economist Intelligence Unit Women's Economic Opportunity Index, measuring 29 indicators in over 128 countries.

Her line of research was supported by her boss, Robert Zoellick, who served as president of the World Bank from 2007 to 2012. Under his watch, the World Bank produced its first gender-themed *World Development Report* in 2012, a 458-page opus that brought together reams of data to conclude that economic development required specific corrective measures to close gender gaps. Melanne remembers going to the World Bank headquarters, on I Street in Washington, for its annual meeting and being stunned when she pulled up. The squat, modern building had been decorated with banners bearing quotes and statistics from the gender report, which was a major topic of discussion at the proceedings. Zoellick's successor, Dr. Jim Yong Kim, has continued to make the gender gap a priority at the World Bank.

Amanda was only a middle manager in the Bank's private-sector development division when she made her case for the power of women to fast-forward economic growth. But her experience is a clear illustration of one of our core beliefs: there's an abundance of power in the middle, in the vast cadre of women who may not be at the very top, but whose talents and resources make them an essential part of their organizations. While men still dominate the C-suites, women make up a healthy proportion — 36 percent — of manager-level positions in the United States. And as women continue to earn college and advanced degrees at a higher rate than men, that percentage is set to increase.

Women in the middle hold the key to promoting female-focused strategies, as well as creating supportive, flexible work environments and lifting up other women from the lower rungs of their organizations.

Bea Perez, the chief sustainability officer at Coca-Cola, agrees. In her experience, her company's game-changing decisions came from all levels of leadership, not just the highest. Many of their crucial ideas came from the innovative middle.

"It's their leadership that is very powerful," Perez told us. "They're looking at the scenarios, making the tradeoffs, and then making the recommendations, because they're closer to the work on a day-to-day basis."

Managers in the middle have lines to the top, but they also interact on a daily basis with the rank and file of an organization. Ideally, these managers keep in touch with their employees' needs, and are willing to advocate for them with their superiors to ensure those needs are met. We believe that women in the middle are poised to leverage their positions for real change.

Purpose in the Middle

Zainab Salbi saw this potential in the middle when she created Women for Women in Bosnia, now called Women for Women International. In 1993, she came across an article in *Time* magazine describing "rape camps" in Bosnia-Herzegovina and Croatia, usually located in abandoned apartment buildings or schools, where groups of women were held captive as sex slaves for Serbian soldiers. Zainab herself had survived marital rape at the hands of her ex-husband, and the account she read made her weep. She knew she had to do something to help.

But what? After researching the region and various women's groups, she couldn't find a single organization that was helping the women she'd read about. Zainab decided to start her own, calling on women everywhere to support the women of Bosnia through the same one-to-one sponsorship model that was often used to send a child to school or to help a farmer buy livestock. This sponsorship, which would include sending small monthly donations and warm letters of support, could help women in Bosnia get back on their feet and let them know that women elsewhere understood their plight and cared about them. She and her then husband, Amjad, took the money they were saving for a honeymoon in Spain to fly to Croatia to get Women for Women off the ground.

They spent a week touring the country and listening to stories too gruesome to comprehend. She returned three months later with the first sums of sponsorship money they had raised. In her memoir, *Between Two Worlds,* she recalls how the organization grew: "American women, Canadian women — even Bangladeshi women — began signing up as sponsors who sent a monthly check along with a letter to a victim of war. I felt very strongly that this cash should go directly to the women, because it represented freedom to make a choice again in their lives, even if it was a small one. They could buy medicine for their children or fruit or cosmetics if they chose. It was their choice, not ours."

The effect went far beyond the donations, Zainab told us. With the help of a group of volunteers, Zainab sorted and mailed the letters exchanged between each pair of women. She was moved by the unburdening and healing she saw:

I had originally envisioned these letters as helping war victims feel they weren't alone. But as the letters came back from women in Bosnia and Croatia, I realized the survivors of war were using these private letters to tell strangers about the pain they felt they could share with no one else. Through them, they could retain their own identity and yet remain anonymous. The letters were testaments, and the letters the women's sponsors wrote back bore witness to their suffering.

"I got your letters," one Bosnian woman from Sarajevo wrote to her sponsor. "I experienced them like rays of sunlight that reached to the bottom of a dark cave. I lived through the shelling and all the other suffering, but they killed the 'I' in me."

As with Vital Voices and *Fortune*'s mentoring programs, the impact of Women for Women International doesn't flow in just one direction. The organization describes its mission as the "financial, educational and *interpersonal support*" (our emphasis) of women survivors of conflict — and as we learned in chapters 3 and 4, interpersonal relations are what imbue life with meaning. The women who sponsored a "sister," as the organization calls the survivors, felt their own perspectives shift, their worlds open wider, as they saw how even a small action, like writing a letter, could make a difference.

Stronger Together

We've also seen how women who combine their skills and talents at critical moments can create strong networks of support for each other and catalytic change in their communities.

Dana Lerner, a mother living on the Upper West Side of New York, was used to having a quiet impact: she helped people in need of counseling through her work as a psychotherapist. In January of 2014, her nine-year-old son, Cooper, was walking hand in hand with his father, crossing the street near their West End Avenue apartment, when a taxi swerved into the crosswalk and hit Cooper, taking his life; his father survived. The loss of her son devastated Dana. Paralyzed by grief, she all but stopped functioning.

That's when her friends, colleagues, and acquaintances came together to form a powerful network that provided Dana with not only emotional support in the moment, but also the impetus for lasting change in their community. One woman took the lead in setting up a Google Calendar (which she titled "We Love Dana") to coordinate the schedules of twenty of Dana's friends. Another arranged food deliveries. Jackie Kern, an entrepreneur and businesswoman, came up with the idea of memorializing Cooper and his love of basketball through a foundation, Coop's Hoops, that would send young people to basketball camp on a scholarship.

"Dana's biggest fear was that no one is going to remember Cooper, because he's a nine-year-old kid. She couldn't sleep because of that," Jackie remembers. "I woke up one morning and said, 'Let's start a foundation.'"

One of Dana's neighbors, Julie Dermer, worked with Jackie to organize a charity spin class in May 2014, a few months after Cooper's death. Jackie expected to raise between $5,000 and $10,000; the one-hour event pulled in nearly $25,000, enabling more than forty children to attend basketball camp that summer. She aims to send one hundred more this year.

"The support of the entire Upper West Side was behind it," Jackie said, explaining how the fundraiser took in more than twice the anticipated amount. "Complete strangers, because it could have been any of our kids. He was holding his father's hand."

Dana's network expanded further, to include other families who had experienced similar tragedies. Dana became a founding member of Families for Safe Streets and Cab Riders United. Together, they lobbied city hall and the district attorney's office; she testified a number of times before the New York City Council. Less than six months after Cooper's passing, the city council enacted "Cooper's Law," which allows the city's Taxi and Limousine Commission to suspend the license of a driver involved in a serious crash. While motor vehicle–related injuries continue to be the leading cause of injury-related death in New York City for children under twelve, Cooper's Law is one important step toward holding drivers accountable. Dana emphasizes that implementation and enforcement of the law continues to be a significant issue.

"I am fighting for my life, and my family, and my son," Dana says of her newfound role as a public advocate. "I can't do anything else."

She continues to practice as a psychotherapist, and she continues her advocacy every day, in ways great and small, by campaigning and by educating everyone she meets about the importance of driving slowly, wearing a seat belt, and obeying traffic and pedestrian laws. Although she'll always struggle to make sense of the loss of her son, Dana, with the support of her network, has turned a personal tragedy into an opportunity to make positive change.

Taking a Stand

Paul Charron was a man at the top who learned an important lesson from the middle. He became the CEO of the fashion company Liz Claiborne in 1995, charged by the board of directors with reinstituting growth. As part of a total review of the business, it was apparent that costs needed to be cut and assets redeployed. One of the areas targeted for reduction was philanthropic spending. But before he made any decisions, Charron was contacted by a young employee, Jane Randel, who requested an appointment with him. She told him that cutting Liz Claiborne's signature domestic violence awareness program would be a terrible mistake.

"She built a compelling case," Paul said. "As the father of a daughter, recognizing that I was leading a company serving women and populated by women, I found Jane's logic persuasive and changed my mind."

Jane was put in charge of the domestic violence program and eventually became a senior vice president for communications for the company. Paul credits her with having the conviction and the courage to make her case directly to him, educating him about the problem. "I did not know all this," he admitted, referring to the prevalence of domestic violence. "As soon as I became educated, it all started to flow, because I knew it was the right thing to do. It became a question of empowering and encouraging people, providing the budgets, providing support."

Liz Claiborne went on to fund influential research, including studies that demonstrated the impact of domestic violence on workers' productivity and the extent of dating abuse among teenagers. The company also sponsored awareness and advocacy campaigns, such as Love Is Respect and Love Is Not Abuse. Indeed, Liz Claiborne's historic leadership on violence against women, as well as wider support from the business community, was vital in getting the Violence Against Women Act passed in 1994. Paul, for his part, knew that by doing good, he was also doing well by his company. Jane went on to cofound NO MORE, a nationwide awareness campaign dedicated to helping reduce sexual assault and domestic violence, and she is one of a handful of experts retained by the National Football League to help define the league's policies around these issues.

"We knew our engagement would be of benefit to the company, but we were really doing it because it was the right thing to do, because domestic violence adversely impacted our customers and our colleagues," Paul said. "We had people who had seen the damage done by violence against women in ways that I had never observed. It was a deeply personal issue for them. By taking a stand, both customers and colleagues were very proud of our company."

While CEOs like Paul Charron may have the final say, they rely on their middle managers for ideas, since it is they who often have a firmer grasp on operational details. One of the best ways to influence senior management is to be well prepared — to understand the goals of the organization and, if possible, to make the evidence-based case.

At Westpac, Amanda Ellis knew she needed data on her side when she first proposed to expand the bank's outreach to women. "At Westpac there had initially been a lot of skepticism of the need to focus on women clients," she told us, "but two independent surveys suggested around 40 percent of Australian women felt discriminated against by banks purely on the basis of gender. Male colleagues for the most part scoffed at these results, saying that the women's perceptions were 'just wrong.' But perception is reality for the customer, so we substantiated this with original research at fifty bank branches across Australia, and the results were corroborated."

By doing her homework, Amanda brought hard data to the table and was able to make a convincing case for scaling up women's lending. Half a billion dollars in loans later, her case was made. The power of women at all levels — from the top to the middle to the grassroots — should not go untapped or underestimated.

7

Power at the Base

ON ANY GIVEN DAY, THE Kate Spade store on Broome Street, in New York's fashionable SoHo, is packed with shoppers browsing the airy, high-ceilinged clothing boutique. Kate Spade started as a handbag line: chic tote bags that Spade herself designed and launched in 1993. After establishing itself as a full-fledged lifestyle brand, the company decided in 2005 to add a new dimension: purpose.

On Purpose, Kate Spade's initiative to give back, began as a partnership between Kate Spade and Women for Women International, the organization founded by Zainab Salbi that connected American women with women in the Balkans in the aftermath of its brutal war in the 1990s. Kate Spade and Women for Women set up yearlong trade and training programs in several postconflict settings, including Bosnia, Afghanistan, and Rwanda, with the fashion brand providing the materials and handicrafts training, then buying back the finished products (including items such as dog sweaters, which were slightly incomprehensible and more than a little amusing to the Bosnian women knitting them) and selling them to its ready client base.

Many of the styles sold out immediately, generating income that was higher than the local average for the participants for the twelve-month period of the partnership. But as Sydney Price, senior vice president of corporate social responsibility at Kate Spade, explained to us, the company saw ways to improve. She realized that the materials, which Kate Spade obtained at low cost by buying in volume, and the know-how were coming directly from the company. In this instance, working through a nonprofit added an unnecessary layer of complexity. So Kate Spade tried another approach.

In the hills about twelve miles north of Kigali sits Masoro, a village of around twenty thousand people, which, despite its proximity to the Rwandan capital, suffered higher unemployment and lower earnings than the national average. But Masoro did have a basic infrastructure, which Kate Spade knew was essential to investing for the long term. The village also had, as Sydney discovered, a tradition of producing exquisite embroidery.

"I had been a merchant with the Neiman Marcus group for eighteen years and traveled all over the world, and I was blown away by the attention to detail," Sydney told us. "So even though they had no market and they were making these products, I knew they were going to have the capacity to learn a lot more." The company recruited 150 of the village's most talented and committed female artisans and helped them set up their own worker-owned, for-profit business.

Today, when fashion-forward shoppers visit a Kate Spade store or its website, they can choose from a range of embroidered and beaded handbags and pouches, scarves, and jewelry produced by the co-op. As an editor at *Harper's Bazaar*, who fell in love with a beaded linen caftan, put it, "When I found out the story behind the piece, shopping became a lot more purposeful indeed."

Economic opportunity is essential in postconflict environments — the very circumstances under which it's most difficult to achieve. Continued violence and instability, the erosion of civil society, and damaged or destroyed infrastructure present obstacles to entrepreneurship just as much as they characterize a nation rebuilding after war. Women have an especially important economic and political role to play: moving from conflict to peace and prosperity won't happen unless all people can envision a better future and take part in the rebuilding and negotiations after a conflict ends.

Ofra Strauss, the president of Jasmine, the Jewish-Arab Businesswomen's Association, can testify to how women's shared aims can create common ground. With Jasmine, a joint effort is unfolding amid one of the world's intractable political conflicts. Strauss was born into Israeli business royalty: the Strauss Group, a dairy company founded by her grandparents, is Israel's second-largest food company, with more than ten thousand employees. Through Jasmine, which offers training and designs business plans for Israeli entrepreneurs, Palestinian and Jewish, Ofra is ensuring that businesswomen from both communities have the resources and opportunities that enable them to grow and succeed. Recently, she brought WEConnect International, an organization that certifies women-owned businesses and links them to major corporations' supply chains, to Israel, so that local women entrepreneurs can seek opportunities beyond its borders.

"Jasmine is an island. We are Jewish and Arab women sitting together," Ofra told an audience at Georgetown University. "It's about our business, empowerment, making money, and feeding our families. But it's also really about understanding: what does it mean when we share the same goals? The thing about peace is you need an optimistic voice. It can be done, because I can see it in Jasmine."

Sydney Price sees the same potential for the women of Rwanda. She is keen to stress that On Purpose is no charity project. First and foremost, it is a business partnership. "It's sustainable for them as the suppliers, it's profitable to us as the retailer, and we are able to replicate it," she said. "But the most significant thing is that it is business as usual — and creates an incredible positive social impact at the same time."

Price points out that in addition to bringing these artisans into their supply chain, Kate Spade's model includes an explicit commitment to the transfer of knowledge: helping villagers to learn the business skills they need to be independently profitable, so they can take on other clients — even rival fashion houses.

Kate Spade, which in 2014 had sales of more than $1.1 billion, is one of many companies that have recognized the power at the bottom of the economic pyramid. Women represent the vast majority — 70 percent — of the world's 1.3 billion poor. In developed countries they earn between 4 and 36 percent less than what their male counterparts earn, and globally are half as likely as men to have full-time jobs.

Yet women also represent the majority of the world's untapped power, both economic and social. This stance is backed by research from organizations ranging from the International Monetary Fund to the

World Bank. One 2012 analysis by Strategy& (formerly Booz & Company) noted that countries which had taken steps to encourage women's economic empowerment had not only seen their participation in the labor market rise, but also witnessed "broader gains for all citizens in such areas as economic prosperity, health, early childhood development, security, and freedom."

How can we unlock this potential at the base?

One now-widespread strategy is to provide microcredit, small-scale loans to low-income people who have typically been "unbanked." Microlending is often coupled with business training, to help borrowers launch small enterprises and become economically self-sufficient.

The Macro Effect of Microcredit

Although microcredit today is largely associated with the Bangladeshi economist Muhammad Yunus and Grameen Bank, one early advocate for microcredit, Ann Dunham, played a key role in highlighting the impact of this solution at the Fourth World Conference on Women in Beijing. Ann, from her time at Women's World Banking and her years spent in Indonesia, understood the potential power of women's economic advancement. She knew that if women in poverty were treated not as victims but as solid borrowers, they could lift themselves up along with their families and communities. She also knew that if she could bring Hillary Clinton, a champion of microcredit, to the stage at the 1995 Beijing forum to speak on the topic, it could help catapult this effective solution into broader acceptance.

So Ann set out to organize a public conversation at the now-historic Fourth World Conference on Women, with the goal of bringing together Hillary Clinton with Muhammad Yunus and Ela Bhatt of India, the founder of the Self Employed Women's Association (SEWA). There, Hillary would ultimately declare what Ann had known for years: "It's called micro, but its impact on people is gigantic," Hillary said. "When we help these women to sow, we all reap."

What Ann could not have foreseen, however, was that fourteen years after that panel in Beijing, her son, Barack Obama, as president of the United States, would appoint Hillary secretary of state, an office she would use to bring women's rights into the core of American foreign policy. Yunus would go on to win a Nobel Peace Prize for the work he did on microcredit with Grameen Bank.

Sadly, Ann never made it to China in 1995. She died, far too early, of cancer that same year, before she knew that her vision of having Hillary expound the benefits of microfinance on the stage would be realized. Nonetheless, Ann's work on women's economic empowerment, along with that of other early microfinance advocates, and her efforts to get Hillary on the microcredit panel in Beijing have had reverberations that we are continuing to see.

Microcredit programs help overcome one of the biggest challenges women face in becoming microentrepreneurs: lack of access to capital. In 1976, Yunus was a young economics professor researching how to provide credit to the rural poor, who were largely dependent on loan sharks. Yunus was among the first to observe how small loans could lift people out of poverty. He began filling the gap himself, with tiny sums of his own money. The first loan was the equivalent of $27, drawn spontaneously from his pocket in a village called Jobra, in Bangladesh. From that small loan, he started what would become Grameen Bank, which was officially recognized by the Bangladeshi government seven years later.

He was struck by the deep mistrust that characterized women's relationships with money. It worked in both directions: loan sharks often rejected creditworthy female borrowers because of gender bias or a lack of collateral; and, Yunus observed, rural women were often unaccustomed to handling money, and so approached it with trepidation. When he sought to implement a 50 percent quota for women borrowers, some told him they were afraid even to touch the cash.

"They said, 'No, I don't think I should take the money. I don't know what to do with it,'" he recalls.

He realized that the fear stemmed from a historical lack of access to capital. He and his students at the University of Chittagong worked to instill confidence in these women through the use of peer mentorship and support. Once they'd overcome their initial discomfort, the women repaid the loans at astoundingly high rates, particularly when they participated as part of a wider network of peers. Not only that, these newly minted entrepreneurs were lifting their families and villages with them, investing in their children's health and education while providing valuable services, like cellphone charging, to their neighbors. The social benefits were so noticeable that Yunus and his students decided to focus exclusively on women. It turned out to be a wise decision.

"Even during the financial crisis of 2008, Grameen was flourishing when the big banks were collapsing," he said. "It's always a very high repayment rate — no collateral, nothing, still the money gets paid back. But the amazing thing is that still the banking system has not recognized it."

Muhammad Yunus was not the first person to harness the power of women's networks. Avon had pioneered the direct-sales model nearly a hundred years earlier. This way of doing business bypassed retail stores, transforming women with often no business experience into sales representatives and entrepreneurs who sold affordable cosmetic products to women in their community, often from their own homes. The company provided training through a standard curriculum, teaching women sales, accounting, and inventory management skills.

The Avon Lady Goes Global

From the beginning, Avon was never just about selling. In 1886, thirty-four years before women could vote in the United States and just over a century before Yunus launched Grameen Bank, David Hall McConnell recognized that women could, and should be able to, play a role in the economy. As a door-to-door book salesman for the Union Publishing House, McConnell met many housewives on his trips up and down New York State. A nephew of McConnell's wrote that his uncle, when canvassing the cities and towns selling books, "was moved by the way women were struggling 'to make ends meet.'"

The son of Irish immigrant farmers and one of seven children, McConnell knew hardship all too intimately. Fortunately, he proved to be a gifted businessman and quickly ascended through the sales ranks and into management. After spending a decade in the publishing business, though, he was ready for another opportunity. He had begun handing out perfume samples to housewives, to entice them to look at the books for sale. It had not escaped him that they frequently were more delighted with the perfume than with the books, nor was he blind to their economic challenges. Through a great deal of trial and error, McConnell came up with several fragrances, concocted in a homemade lab. His California Perfume Company opened for business in 1886.

McConnell's first employee was Persis Albee, one of his top saleswomen from the book business. She could sell perfume just as well as books, and soon became his "depot manager," in charge of recruiting, training, and managing other saleswomen. The company started out with a staff of four: Albee, McConnell, McConnell's wife Lucy, and a stenographer. Albee was put in charge of recruiting more saleswomen, and revenues increased.

Why only saleswomen? McConnell's early insights were twofold: first, he realized the untapped human capital that was going to waste because of social disapproval of working women; second, he believed that women were better poised to sell to other women.

Although separated by one century and two continents, the experiences of David McConnell and Muhammad Yunus share many similarities. Both men recognized the struggles women faced because of the limits that society needlessly placed on them. Both also saw what women could accomplish if given the chance. In the face of cultural resistance, these visionaries developed cohorts of female entrepreneurs, who tapped into the inherent power of women's social networks, with considerable results: Grameen Bank today lends about $150 million a month, primarily to women. Over a century later, led by CEO Sheri McCoy, Avon's six million sales representatives sell four lipsticks a second, bringing in annual revenue of $8.8 billion. Both models, microcredit and direct selling, have been replicated and expanded around the world.

That confidence in women's economic capabilities was written into "the very DNA of the business model," according to former Avon CEO Andrea Jung. It tapped into what we call "the original social network." As Andrea described it, Avon was built on "women in each other's homes, women in church, women in schools, mothers talking to each other." It's the dynamic we've seen over and over in our careers—women doing their best to help each other and give each other a leg up. By recognizing this, and putting its power to work, David McConnell grew Avon into one of the world's most recognized and trusted brands, with a presence in more than one hundred countries, powered by the energies of a 99 percent–female sales force.

As Andrea notes, leveraging the woman-to-woman distribution model provides benefits beyond the bottom line. Even as the company grew to a multibillion-dollar business, it ensured that its "army of women," as she calls them, were delivering important social messages alongside the newest mascara. Beginning in the 1990s, "Avon ladies," as they became known, were trained to pass on information that might be difficult to obtain or share otherwise. Women trust women, and the intimacy of the sales model allowed for discussion of personal matters. In rural Brazil, for example, Avon saleswomen have been known to travel to remote settlements up and down the Amazon River, advising women on how to do breast self-examinations.

Similarly, Avon representatives fanned throughout Russia to spread vital messages about health and violence against women that their customers were unlikely to hear elsewhere. In the privacy of women's homes, the reps were "able to give you a pamphlet at the same time they were giving you your products, and that you could just read, which said, 'If you become a victim of any kind of abuse, this is what you can do,'" Andrea said. This strategy goes where traditional social services cannot — behind closed doors. A domestic violence victim might face retribution for seeking help from a social worker or a women's advocate. But she can meet her Avon rep without raising suspicion. The Avon lady becomes a link between social services and the women who need them. Avon's latest initiative, Beauty for a Purpose, reflects this history of empowering women through beauty and financial independence.

Rick Goings, a former executive at Avon who is now the chairman and CEO of Tupperware Brands, believes that the "personal development aspect" of direct selling is the key to his company's success. Tupperware's training places strong emphasis on building self-esteem and self-confidence through its signature curricula and formal mentoring between employees of different ranks. Women not only learn how to market Tupperware's food containers, but also build their business acumen and find solidarity by learning from and then training their colleagues.

"Forget the business aspect of it," Rick told us. "You start out with something new and you're timid about it. You don't have confidence. I provide you training, guidance, and you get a taste of confidence, of success. Then you feel confident, and when you have confidence, you have influence. And then you pass it on to others."

Elinor Steele, Tupperware's vice president for global communications and women's initiatives, noted that the mentorship goes from the management ranks down to the sales representative level: new recruits learn from their more experienced peers, joining what is known within the company as "the Tupperware family." Networks of saleswomen also find ways to give back to their communities, either with donations or through time spent volunteering, Elinor said. All of these factors merge to create tremendous meaning for employees, in turn building loyalty to the company.

The impact is particularly dramatic in countries where women are not always expected or encouraged to work. In Indonesia, the world's most populous Muslim country, female labor force participation is around 51 percent. Tupperware has a sales force there of about 250,000, most of them women, nearly all of whom are married and over 80 percent of whom have two or more children.

A recent survey by the company showed that in Indonesia, most of these women came from lower- and middle-class families, where they were largely kept in the domestic sphere. At the time they joined Tupperware, the women reported being shy and insecure. Thanks to regular training sessions on topics like time management and self-motivation, feedback from team and supervisor meetings, and informal sharing of tips and techniques among colleagues, they gained self-confidence and ambition. In a market like Indonesia's, saleswomen typically progress from the entry-level position of consultant to manager, the next higher rung, in as little as six months.

One manager said her experience selling Tupperware had transformed her into "a totally different person" who is confident and has dreams to pursue.

That ambition translates directly to Tupperware's bottom line, helping consultants grow their sales and encouraging them to recruit friends and peers to join. In 2013, Tupperware Indonesia generated more than $200 million in sales. Indonesia is one of its fastest-growing markets, with annual growth of over 30 percent in the past five years.

Empowering Women Workers

The movement of women into factory jobs has also been a big component of the economic growth story of the past few decades. In China, for example, tens of millions of women have migrated from rural towns and villages to the factory towns that power the country's development. In apparel manufacturing, women make up about 80 percent of workers, according to the nonprofit consultancy Business for Social Responsibility. Many of them are uneducated, even illiterate, with little access to elementary information about health and hygiene. For many women, it is their first entry into the formal workforce and their first steady wage.

Unfortunately, not all factory owners have respected workers' rights nor ensured safe working conditions. The tragedies in Bangladesh were examples of a callous disregard for the wellbeing of workers. In 2013, a group of global retailers in apparel formed two organizations — the Alliance for Bangladesh Worker Safety and the Accord on Fire and Building Safety in Bangladesh — to ensure that factory owners, the Bangladesh government, and other stakeholders come together to address unsafe factory conditions, worker safety training, and other problems. As the alliance members have noted, "No garment worker should have to choose between safe working conditions and earning a living." In 2007, Gap Inc. introduced educational learning courses on basic life skills, delivered to women on the factory floor. The courses address topics such as time and stress management, problem solving, effective communication, and health education.

The P.A.C.E. (Personal Advancement and Career Enhancement) program was designed and developed by Gap in partnership with the Swasti–Health Resource Center and the International Center for Research on Women. The program was implemented in partnership with Gap vendors and CARE, a humanitarian and development organization. P.A.C.E. was built on the notion that female garment workers have traditionally experienced little if any social mobility, despite earning a regular paycheck, sometimes for the first time in their lives. Its educational learning course was geared toward helping women grow more confident in expressing themselves and making decisions concerning their lives and careers. Many of the workers reported improved relations with their husbands and in-laws; others described how the training enabled them to better discuss problems with their supervisors and to take responsibility when things went wrong, knowing they could find solutions alongside their colleagues.

The business impact has been striking. Out of a sample of almost one thousand women, the proportion who gave themselves high marks for work efficacy more than doubled, based on criteria such as "meeting production targets on time" and "assuming greater responsibilities at work." In Cambodia, P.A.C.E. program attendees were promoted more than three times faster than other workers. Today, P.A.C.E. operates in more than sixty factories and has reached thirty thousand women.

Dotti Hatcher, executive director of the P.A.C.E. program, has seen great progress over her three decades of working in the garment industry. She told us that the industry is finally acknowledging the link between the executives in the United States and the women in its factories—and why it's so essential to lift them up. "I've seen this go from when nobody was really focusing on anything but making a buck, to really looking at these women," she said. "I realize that whether they're sitting in Guatemala, in India, in Indonesia, if it weren't for these women who were leaving their families every day, going into these factories, working hard, producing these garments, I wouldn't have a job, and our company wouldn't be the company it is. These women have the same capacity to grow, to learn, to advance as any of us has. They just haven't been given the opportunity that many of us have been given."

Dotti and her colleagues understood that Gap is a global company whose community extends far beyond the doors of its nearly 3,700 stores, and that her own well-being is intertwined with those far overseas. Gap has seen how working with female garment workers creates shared value for the company and for their communities.

Partnerships at the Base

When Hillary Clinton visited SEWA in 1995, the Indian trade union of self-employed women had already started its own bank. It was hardly one of the gleaming, glass-and-steel structures then mushrooming around New Delhi and Mumbai, but to those women it was monumental. SEWA's bank was where they could get small sums of credit and where they proudly returned to pay back their loans; where, at the time, their transactions were recorded in massive ledgers that resembled over-sized city phone books.

Reema Nanavaty, SEWA's current director, realized that her constituents were ready for more. SEWA had begun the process of lifting women and communities out of poverty through its organizing, collective bargaining, and microcredit work, but the next step required an expanded network. She reached out to partner with local educational institutions, as well as nonprofits and major corporations. "Very soon I understood that to make small enterprises viable over the long term, to provide economic sustainability to each household, those enterprises had to be mainstream," Reema recalled. "And if you want to be in the mainstream, you have to work at a certain speed. You need to have systems and processes in place. You have to have your value chain in place. Only then will you be confident to go into the market. But we were poor — we'd never run businesses before.

"Therefore, the best way is to have partners," she went on. "We partnered with the Indian Institute of Management and Enterprise, and designed our own management courses and then set up our own SEWA management school. So we have a network for our members who run their enterprises, and a whole range of courses to help them run their enterprises. The second thing was how do you partner with the players in the industry? We partner in such a way that it's a win-win. The enterprises can scale and enter the mainstream market." Reema's efforts have resulted in collaborations with some of the largest corporations in the world, including Vodafone, Staples, and Walmart.

That same year, the Cherie Blair Foundation for Women partnered with SEWA and Vodafone in India to provide mobile phone service to women working in agriculture. A grant from Vodafone led to the development of a simple app, RUDI Sandesha Vyavhar, that allows women to communicate with management in real time, check supply levels, and send orders instantly via text, reducing time and travel costs and increasing efficiency — and their resulting income. The app can be loaded onto any phone, putting mobile technology in the hands of rural women, expanding their business networks and access to information.

"Rural women face a lot of barriers to be financially independent. Given its wide reach, mobile telephony is an effective medium to empower them," Vodafone India CEO Marten Pieters has said. Over the past three years, 1,500 SEWA members have gained access to mobile technology that supports entrepreneurship, enabling them, for example, to sell seeds to farmers and find price and weather information relevant to agricultural sales.

One woman farmer explained that before owning a phone, she would travel long distances to take her produce to a central market, but with no means of communication, she would sometimes arrive to find that the market was being held on another day or in a different location. For a farmer whose goods are perishable, such circumstances could mean the difference between eating and starving. The Cherie Blair Foundation partnership with SEWA and Vodafone is a win-win. Since SEWA's members run their businesses more efficiently, they are better able to invest in their children's education and the well-being of their families and communities. And a growing middle class creates more consumers for Vodafone, and for all companies doing business in the developing world.

Indeed, more and more companies are coming to appreciate the social impact they can have when they make the commitment to connect to women at the base of the pyramid. While past efforts to support women at the base have often been philanthropic in nature, increasingly companies are looking for ways they can complement philanthropy with shared-value initiatives. As we will see in chapter 8, companies can leverage their supply chains to have an enormous impact on women's lives.

One such company is Abbott Labs, a global health care company that is working with women dairy farmers in India in a partnership that seeks to connect women not only to education and skills training, but also to economic opportunity through its suppliers.

"We know that we need to have high-quality milk from our suppliers," said Elaine Leavenworth, senior vice president and chief marketing and external affairs officer at Abbott. "We found that women conduct a lot of the dairy farming, but they have not had access to the training or business literacy they need, or perhaps not as much as their male counterparts have had." With its partner, Technoserve, the Abbott program provides women dairy farmers with skills training as well as instruction on how to manage the health of cows through better nutrition, water quality, and veterinary care. It also provides the infrastructure necessary to maintain a "cold chain," so that the milk stays fresh until it is delivered. "We are putting together programs to empower women dairy farmers so they can address this gap by gaining animal care expertise, which will help them make more money, be more competitive, and be stronger in society," Elaine said.

We hear this time and time again from companies that are successfully engaging with women through business-driven initiatives. Companies that integrate a "women strategy" — that is, figure out how to achieve their business goals while partnering with women — believe these programs will be more sustainable. This is akin to companies that have a "green strategy."

"What is exciting is that we are finding that these types of shared-value initiatives can have a far greater reach and social impact than we could have imagined," said Katherine Pickus, Abbott's divisional vice president of global citizenship and policy. "And they are sustainable."

Bringing Microcredit Back Home

Avon, Tupperware, Vodafone, and Grameen Bank have developed business models that foster the potential of women in developing countries while promoting sustainable growth. These same models can work under very different economic conditions. In 2014, Andrea Jung became the CEO of Grameen America, which operates according to the same principles, this time in underserved communities throughout the United States. As she explained to us: "It's the very same thought as a distributed network of women, who are having an opportunity to access capital, to build a business, to get financial literacy, understand the disciplines of saving, and understand how to get a credit score and achieve creditworthiness, so that it can spur further entrepreneurship for themselves, as well as understanding that they can help others."

Peer mentorship is a critical part of the organization's microfinance model. "The Grameen model is a group lending model where you are one of a group of five women, and in a weekly meeting you have that collegiality and that peer mentorship reinforcement, because entrepreneurship can be lonely," Andrea explained.

At Grameen America, women borrowers are encouraged to save a minimum of $2 a week — a sum too small for most commercial banks to notice. Crucially, Grameen America will open a free savings account to facilitate weekly deposits, which do, of course, grow over time. The savings can be used to invest in a growing enterprise. Muhammad Yunus has noted that Grameen Bank in Bangladesh, once itself a microenterprise, has disbursed more than $16 billion since its inception and currently holds deposits of almost $2.2 billion.

Since Grameen America started operating in 2008, it has seen comparably high repayment rates, illustrating the potential to build up the model to a global level, even in markedly different economic contexts. In its first seven years, the organization has reached more than 45,000 women with nearly 120,000 microloans totaling more than $245 million, and counts 50,000 jobs created as a result of its work. Grameen America is dedicated to helping women entrepreneurs whose businesses range from food services and hair salons to cleaning and pet-grooming companies.

Business leaders, nonprofit organizations, and governments are catching on to the power of women's networks at the base of the socioeconomic pyramid. Brands like Mary Kay and Tupperware followed in Avon's footsteps, building global companies as their products spread through the distribution channels provided by women's relationships. Nonprofits and social enterprises have also adopted the direct-sales model, capitalizing on women's networks to put life-changing goods like malaria nets, solar-powered lamps, clean cookstoves, and birthing kits into the hands of people who need them. The model also provides entrepreneurs with the opportunity to pass on information and give product demonstrations for maximum impact.

Each of these organizations has witnessed how giving women practical skills training helps them become more effective entrepreneurs and employees, and more empowered in their own lives — partners in shared value, in other words. They, like us, understand how much power lies at the base, and how essential it is to invest in these billions of women if we are to fast-forward.

8

Entrepreneurs and Innovators

IF NECESSITY IS THE MOTHER of invention, motherhood surely necessitates its own inventions. Such was the case for Sheila Lirio Marcelo.

Well before her career ever began, Sheila recognized that women were too often pulled off the career track by the demands of family care. An immigrant from the Philippines who had worked at her parents' restaurant in Houston, she was a sophomore economics major at Mount Holyoke College in Massachusetts when she became pregnant with her first son. Her second son arrived just after her graduation from Harvard Business School; soon thereafter her father suffered a heart attack. Three family members now needed her care and attention, while she put in long days at a Boston-based startup firm. "As immigrants without family nearby, my husband and I struggled to find care for our infant son, Ryan," Marcelo has said.

Six years later, Sheila turned that experience into Care.com, the world's largest website connecting pre-screened care providers, like nannies, elderly companions, and tutors, with people in need of their services. The network she built has created jobs for care professionals while providing working families — especially women, who still perform the bulk of care work in the United States — with transparency and convenience, through reviews and an easy payment system.

Marcelo's story illustrates how women entrepreneurs are starting businesses that address women's needs, not to mention growing the economy and creating jobs. As we mentioned earlier, in the United

States women are launching businesses at an incredible pace: the number of female-owned firms has increased by 68 percent between 1997 and 2014, one and a half times the national average of 47 percent. As of 2014, such firms have been an increasingly vital part of the U.S. economy, employing nearly 7.9 million people and generating over $1.4 trillion in revenues. A 2009 study found that if women-owned businesses in America were considered a country, its GDP would rank fifth globally, close to that of the economic powerhouse Germany.

As we saw in the previous chapter, female entrepreneurs are also powerful growth engines in emerging economies. Particularly in countries where women's participation in the workforce may be limited by infrastructure, geography, culture, or educational opportunities, entrepreneurship and home-based work provides a path to financial independence. In emerging markets alone, the 8 to 10 million small and medium-sized enterprises (SMEs) with full or partial female ownership represent over 30 percent of all SMEs.

While women often face a host of barriers that keep them from growing their businesses, including lack of access to capital, formal business training, and networks, they continue to start businesses at a rapid pace across the globe. That may be in part because starting one's own company offers women the chance to be "self-authoring," as one expert put it, and gives them the flexibility to create a workplace culture that fits them and their lifestyles. In fact, a recent survey of entrepreneurs in twenty-five developed countries found that established women business owners in the United States rated their well-being more than twice as high as women non–business owners, and almost as high as men with established businesses. The same study reported that women are increasingly starting new ventures less out of financial necessity than because they see opportunities in the market. This is especially true of women in the early and middle stages of their careers, the period in which women typically begin planning families. It suggests that flexibility and the chance to dictate one's own terms of work are two more reasons entrepreneurship appeals to women.

Women are not only building businesses and investing in their families; they often combine a social mission with their business strategy, putting them at the forefront of the next generation of entrepreneurship.

Building Enterprises with Purpose

Elizabeth Vazquez is one example. A single question drove her to co-found WEConnect International, the nonprofit that links huge corporations like IBM and Boeing to women-owned businesses: what if women building businesses had more money?

For Elizabeth, this question was hardly rhetorical. In fact, it was formed in a dark time in her life. When she was just three years old, she told us, her mother sold the family's belongings, in what she described as "probably Mexico's first yard sale," in her desperation to leave an abusive marriage. Her struggle to bring her two daughters to America and raise them single-handedly inspired Elizabeth to dedicate her entire career to women's economic independence.

In her work with WEConnect International, Elizabeth has met women entrepreneurs from every industry and every region of the world. And she has concluded that she's not alone in seeking to put purpose at the center of her enterprise. All around her, she said, women are redefining success, with purpose at its core. This means seeking to perform better on environmental, social, and governance metrics, making inclusive growth a priority, and finding ways to advance women by doing more business with one another.

"Women tend to build businesses that are good for people and the environment," Elizabeth said. "The women we work with are passionate, innovative, anticipatory multitaskers who are driven by a deep desire to be connected and to make the world a better place. Their success is everyone's success, and it is a privilege to learn from them every day."

"Women have not only intelligence, but EQ — emotional intelligence," said Sung-Joo Kim, a rare female South Korean entrepreneur who specializes in high-end retail, distributing brands like Yves Saint Laurent and Gucci in her country. "EQ plus IQ equals WQ, that's my equation." One of the luxury fashion companies she owns, MCM, gives away 10 percent of its millions of dollars in net income to NGOs working on global health problems, a charitable instinct she says was inspired by her mother.

Elizabeth Schaeffer Brown, a founder of the digital branding company Uncommon Union and the online retailer Maiden Nation, suggests that women's propensity for mission-driven enterprises stems from their historic overrepresentation in caregiving professions like nursing and teaching, as well as their leading roles in charitable and community organizations.

"While philanthropy has always been the domain of wealthy men, the new field of social entrepreneurship is ideally suited to women, who have always had to meet complex demands that pit community against individualism," Elizabeth wrote in *Forbes*. "In short, we understand the necessity of seeing the economy and the world as an interconnected and interdependent system." But, she warns, this comes with the "very real danger in characterizing social entrepreneurship as a kind of lesser, women's work — not quite a business and not quite philanthropy either."

No one could accuse the fashion mogul Tory Burch of running "not quite a business." She attributes the meteoric success of her company to the sense of purpose woven into its mission. Tory built a social mission into her business plan from the get-go. She launched her lifestyle brand intending for it to sustain a foundation (she had at first considered funding humanitarian aid), a notion that confounded many potential investors. Tory put it this way: "When I started the company, one of the key components was fundraising. I met with many investors and I was told by several never to say the words 'social responsibility' and 'business' in the same sentence. They were put off by the idea that starting a foundation was an integral part of our business plan, though the company had to be successful first. I think it actually made me even more determined to make it work.

"Our foundation was incredibly meaningful to us, but we never expected the positive impact it would have on the bottom line of our business. It's important to our employees — it has attracted people to want to work here — and our customers love our mission and like the idea of supporting something they believe in. It has become part of the DNA of our brand. When we talk to entrepreneurs now, we encourage them to incorporate social responsibility from the beginning, even if it is for the long term."

Since 2009, the Tory Burch Foundation has supported women's economic empowerment through access to affordable loans, mentoring and networking programs, and entrepreneurial education. In 2014, the foundation partnered with Bank of America to launch a small-business lending program. With an initial investment from Bank of America, the initiative is making loans to help women entrepreneurs grow and scale up their businesses. Together, they're addressing one of the biggest obstacles women face as they start their own enterprises: lack of access to capital.

The Global Brake

The experience of one Colorado woman illustrates how the obstacles to accessing capital can put the brakes on the accelerating force of women's entrepreneurship. When Hillary Clinton was first lady, she met with a group of small-business owners in Denver. One of the women told her how challenging it had been to get a loan to start her technology company, describing in detail how many times she had been turned down. She eventually secured enough funding to start a successful tech business, but it was a close call. "You know, Mrs. Clinton, the best ideas die in bank parking lots," she said.

Just as women are increasingly understood to be a global accelerator of growth, their difficulty in obtaining capital could be seen as a brake. A 2010 study by the World Bank's International Finance Corporation found that women-owned formal businesses have an unmet need of $260 billion to $320 billion. In the United States, 72 percent of women responding to a survey of 350 tech firms reported that accessing financial capital was a challenge when launching their firms; 80 percent of them had to rely on personal savings. Imagine what these determined women might achieve if that obstacle was removed from their path.

Even in the United States, where widespread credit card use, student loans, and other formal transactions mean that women entrepreneurs often do have a credit history, they still can't always get their hands on the capital they need to jump-start their businesses. Lender discrimination goes back as far as women have been opening businesses. Until 1988, when Congress passed the Women's Business Ownership Act, some states required women to get their husband's or another man's signature in order to obtain a loan. Today, the barriers are less explicit, but still there. American businesswomen often cite factors such as bias from lenders, a lack of sufficient collateral, and limited access to business networks. One study found that women received only 4.4 percent of the dollar amount of conventional small-business loans made in the early 2000s — or around $1 in loans for every $23 loaned to men.

Closing the Financing Gap

Fortunately, programs that integrate loans with business development, training, and mentorship — what are sometimes called wraparound services — go a long way toward solving these problems. The small-business lending partnership between the Tory Burch Foundation and Bank of America works with an existing network of community development financial institutions in underserved communities to provide women entrepreneurs with low-cost capital. The Tory Burch Foundation and Bank of America then host networking and mentoring events for participants, at which they can build up their networks and get advice from experienced businesswomen.

All over the United States, networks of women are taking it into their own hands to get women the capital they need. Golden Seeds is a network of 275 female angel investors who are committed to funding women-led startups; it also runs a Knowledge Institute to train and share best practices among themselves and the public. Belle Capital is a women-led venture capital fund that serves underfunded markets, investing in early-stage companies that have at least one C-level woman or a commitment to recruiting senior female talent.

Natalia Oberti Noguera took another approach to closing the financing gap. In 2010, the year she was developing the Pipeline Fellowship, only 13 percent of angel investors were women. She created a six-month program that trains a group of angel investors who contribute to a communal pot of $50,000, which is then awarded to a female-led social enterprise startup. The Pipeline Fellowship's training aims to build a community of diverse angel investors and to deliver much-needed capital to women leading social enterprises. Launched in New York City, the Pipeline Fellowship is now in more than twenty cities across the country and has supported thirteen women-owned social enterprise ventures.

Access to Capital Goes Global

On a global scale, the International Finance Corporation (IFC), an arm of the World Bank that is focused on the private sector in developing countries, is putting its resources to work helping women gain access to capital. In 2013, for example, it launched a $100 million, three-year project with Coca-Cola to provide financing and business skills training to women entrepreneurs in Eurasia and Africa. It began with an initial loan to Access Bank in Nigeria, an early adopter that has worked with female entrepreneurs for years. In 2013, the IFC also issued $165 million in "women's bonds," to raise funds for businesses owned or run by women in developing countries, which it will distribute to local banks and other financial institutions that can lend to businesses majority-owned by women, or businesses in which women own at least 20 percent of a company and occupy senior leadership positions.

Goldman Sachs has also recognized that women's business success is an avenue to prosperity. As a global investment bank that requires growing, stable economies to do business, it has made investing in women a central part of achieving that wider goal. In 2008, Goldman Sachs took its core competency — getting deals done — and sought to spread it far and wide, enrolling ten thousand promising women entrepreneurs running small to medium-sized enterprises in comprehensive training as part of its well-known program named, naturally, 10,000 Women.

First launched in Nigeria, with a local university as a partner, 10,000 Women was the first worldwide corporate venture to comprehensively support female entrepreneurs with business training, access to finance, and a network of mentors and peers. Dina Powell, president of the Goldman Sachs Foundation, designed 10,000 Women with the strong support of CEO Lloyd Blankfein and John Rogers, executive vice president and a key architect of the program. John's passion for the program may stem in part from his birthplace, Seneca Falls, the site of the first women's rights convention. Dina and Melanne, who was then at Vital Voices, spoke often during the conceptual period of the program, concentrating on how best to design it in order to reach women on a global scale.

The business training concentrates on core skills like finance and accounting, marketing, and human resources. Live events and mentoring with local senior executives helped create the supportive business networks that are often scarce for women. Goldman Sachs's data-driven approach also meant that the program included extensive monitoring and evaluation of results, including metrics on revenue, job creation, and use of technology.

A Lagos businesswoman, Ayodeji Megbope, has seen tremendous success since graduating from the 10,000 Women program. Her catering business in the Nigerian city has grown dramatically, from serving 20 guests at a time to regular 750-person orders. She went from cooking in her own apartment to leasing a separate apartment with a large kitchen, and she has bought a delivery truck and hired ten permanent staff members. And she's using her catering skills to help the less fortunate: once a month, she and her staff cater a free meal for prisoners.

Ayodeji was not alone: an evaluation showed that eighteen months after participants graduated from the program, their business revenues had increased by an average of 480 percent. Their success was replicated in a number of countries, from Afghanistan to Liberia, from Brazil to China.

In March of 2014, Goldman Sachs also announced its own partnership with the IFC to raise $600 million to help close the global credit gap for women-owned SMEs. One of its first big initiatives was launched in China in early 2015: a loan of RMB500 million (approximately $80 million), destined to offer online loans to Chinese women entrepreneurs administered through Ant Credit, a financial services company affiliated with Alibaba, China's largest e-commerce company. Because Ant Credit uses a potential borrower's transaction history to evaluate her loan application, many women entrepreneurs already selling on Alibaba's online marketplaces can point to a track record of consistent sales in lieu of collateral, which facilitates approval of a loan.

Henriette Kolb, head of the IFC's Gender Secretariat, noted that many traditional banks are wising up to women's growing economic power, responding with lending programs and banking services aimed at women as clients and as entrepreneurs. Filling these gaps makes for a surefire business opportunity. A Lebanese bank called BLC Bank, a member of the Global Banking Alliance for Women, for example, has built up a new clientele by targeting women entrepreneurs through its We Initiative. With the expertise of the IFC, the BLC Bank has developed one of the first women-focused SME lending units, providing non-financial services like mentoring, training, business toolkits, and networking resources in addition to banking services. "Women's access to financial services is a market opportunity for financial institutions and not charity," Kolb told us.

Scaling Up

Once businesses are off the ground, the next step is growth. This is where business expansion skills and later-stage capital becomes imperative. One telling statistic demonstrates how difficult it is for women to scale up: although women-owned businesses represent nearly 30 percent of all American firms, they generate less than 4 percent of total revenue. Women-owned businesses, on average, are much smaller and generate only about a third of the revenues of the average privately held business.

That's where Pauline Brown thought she could make a difference.

Pauline, who currently is chairman of North America for LVMH Inc., had enjoyed a career of more than two decades in the consulting, corporate, and private-equity worlds, at companies such as Bain, Estée Lauder, Avon, and the Carlyle Group, but she was ready for something different. She decided to take a sabbatical, to reconnect with herself, her passions, curiosities, and nature. She always had been a strong advocate for women's issues, thanks in part to the influences of her two grandmothers, both of whom ran their own businesses and supported their families through difficult times, as well as an aunt who was a contemporary of Gloria Steinem's and taught and wrote about feminist issues.

Pauline clearly had a gift for business and deal-making, but she was at her happiest when working with creative types, as she had during her time at Estée Lauder. She realized she could use her business acumen and experience to mentor and guide female entrepreneurs in creative industries on how to grow and scale up their businesses.

"Little by little, things started to come back to me that gave me joy," Pauline says of her sabbatical. "One of them was working again with creative people. Not running their businesses, but mentoring them and helping shape their strategies. You don't often have serious executives talking to women who are creative entrepreneurs, maybe with the exception of the tech industry — and there are not many women in technology."

This kind of mentorship is essential to helping women-owned small and medium-sized enterprises expand. But expansion also requires later-stage capital, such as private-equity financing and venture capital. "In my experience," Pauline told us, "women business owners are as deserving of funding as their male counterparts, but these women oftentimes do not understand the codes, culture, and formulae of the more male-oriented investment community. While mentoring these women, my primary goal was to demystify the process as well as to bolster their confidence. In the end, the best investors follow the best opportunities, and the best opportunities are built on sound logic and strong leadership."

A 2014 survey of *Inc.* magazine's top 500 and 5,000 firms showed that male founders were more than three times as likely — 14.4 percent versus 3.6 percent — as women to tap equity financing, from angel investors or venture capitalists. Men also had greater access to financing from networks of friends and business acquaintances. Their ability to tap into multiple sources for capital explains why men start firms with, on average, almost twice the capital of women founders. Even the twenty-five largest female-owned firms (by employment), as well as those identified as having high-growth potential, started with significantly less capital than highly ranked male-owned firms.

Theresia Gouw and Jennifer Fonstad launched Aspect Ventures, an early-stage investment fund specializing in mobile technology, with an eye toward investing in entrepreneurs traditionally overlooked by the mostly male Silicon Valley venture capitalists. Aspect was founded on the premise that diversity creates value.

"We think as women we bring a different perspective to the board-room and these companies in how they approach problem-solving and strategic thinking," Jennifer told the *New York Times*. "It's clearly not an industry that puts a lot of women in it, and we're trying in our own way to illustrate how diversity makes a difference."

Women-owned companies like Solera, a private-equity firm, are changing the ratio. Founded in 1999 by Molly Ashby, a buyout veteran with sixteen years' experience at JPMorgan Chase, Solera has so far invested in a number of women-led companies. Success stories include Annie's, the organic natural-foods brand whose initial public offering put its market capitalization at $721 million (making Solera's $81 million investment worth more than $530 million), and YOLO Colorhouse LLC, a line of environmentally friendly, nontoxic paints now carried at the Home Depot.

Access to Markets: Sourcing from Women

One effective way to support women entrepreneurs is through sourcing. Increasingly, companies large and small are using supplier diversity and inclusion programs to provide women and other underutilized entrepreneurs with access to larger markets, through which they can scale up their businesses.

In 2011, Walmart announced the Women's Economic Empowerment Initiative, one of the largest and most ambitious corporate women's initiatives to date. Under this program, Walmart aims to empower nearly one million women through diversity and inclusion and comprehensive training programs, as well as through sourcing from women-owned businesses. "We asked ourselves, 'How can we use our business assets and our philanthropy in concert to accelerate improvements on social issues?'" recalls Kathleen McLaughlin, president of the Walmart Foundation. "Women's economic empowerment is a great example of where we're using both."

As part of its initiative, the company pledged at least $20 billion of spending on products and services from women-owned businesses for its U.S. stores and aimed to increase sourcing from women's businesses in its international operations by 2016. In 2013, it created a dedicated section of Walmart.com that featured products exclusively from companies owned by women.

To achieve its goals, Walmart partnered with the Women's Business Enterprise National Council (WBENC) and WEConnect International, two nonprofits with experience in bringing women-owned enterprises up to global market standards. These organizations identify and certify such enterprises and provide training in areas like accounting, quality control, and scaling up production.

Walmart's senior director for corporate affairs, Sarah Thorn, said the organizations' expertise was invaluable in ensuring that the massive retailer could partner with small-scale enterprises. "Women-owned businesses tend to be smaller, and we're a big retailer that is premised on scale," she explained. WBENC and WEConnect International helped verify and train those suppliers so that they provide the quality and consistency necessary to work successfully with a company like Walmart.

"We have had to change how we look at sourcing," Sarah said. "But also, what are the barriers for these women externally, whether it's access to finance or mentoring or networks, many of the systems that have quite frankly been in place for men for many years. By using our scale and our voice and putting very big, ambitious goals out there for the public, we'll hopefully help women break through these really persistent barriers. This is just one part of our commitment to take steps to respond to the needs of women in our workforce and around the world, in this case through our supply chain."

Walmart also worked with WBENC and WEConnect International to establish a unique "Women Owned" logo for certified businesses, which is displayed on their products' packaging. While it's too early to tell how the new logo is affecting sales, Elizabeth Vazquez of WEConnect International said initial research showed that female shoppers had a preference for products made by women-owned firms because of assumptions of higher quality. "Women are controlling or influencing around $20 trillion in purchasing power," Elizabeth told us. "If we decided tomorrow to spend just 10 percent of that on other women, it's a $2 trillion impact going into the hands of women. You can imagine what that would do to our global economy if women had an additional $2 trillion in their hands to aspire to new heights, create new businesses, and invest in their communities."

The Power in Her Hands

In 2010, fashion icon Donna Karan visited Haiti after an earthquake destroyed much of its capital, Port-au-Prince, and took thousands of lives. Amid the destruction, though, Donna found cause for hope. She saw the extraordinary crafts and artistry of the Haitian people, and decided to use her experience to build an international fashion brand, to help those gifted artisans find a wider market for their wares. Through her Urban Zen store in New York and retailers around the world, Haitian artists working with local materials, such as tobacco, bone, and horn, sell jewelry and home goods to "conscious consumers" globally.

The artisan market is a powerful arena of women's entrepreneurship. According to the Alliance for Artisan Enterprise, artisanal activity is one of the largest economic sectors engaging women in the developing world, second only to agriculture. But women artisans often face challenges in getting their products to wider markets, which is where companies and coalitions like the alliance can help.

The Alliance for Artisan Enterprise was launched by Hillary Clinton and the State Department in 2012, to help provide skills training and access to markets so that artisans around the world can realize their full economic potential. The alliance, a public-private partnership hosted at the Aspen Institute, has more than fifty-five members, ranging from nonprofits, SMEs, companies like Kate Spade and West Elm, and committed individuals, who work together to share best practices on elevating artisans' visibility and helping them enter new markets while maintaining their craft traditions.

Each year in July, the International Folk Art Alliance, one of the founding members of the Alliance for Artisan Enterprise, stages a unique market in Santa Fe, New Mexico, which features about 150 artists' groups and collectives from dozens of countries. In 2014, they sold more than $3 million worth of goods at the market, with the proceeds going to support some 250,000 people worldwide, including the artisans and their extended families around the world. Some of the artisans have told us that they sell as much in their few days in Santa Fe as they do in a year in their home countries, highlighting the importance of exposure and access to buyers.

The Next Wave: Social Enterprise

Entrepreneurial women around the world are using their networks and creating new ones to launch and support the next generation of entrepreneurs. And increasingly, these entrepreneurs are coming to the table with purpose, inventing products and services that solve social problems just as much as they address needs or gaps in the market.

Kavita Shukla came up with the idea for Fenugreen FreshPaper when she was still in middle school. FreshPaper is paper infused with spices and botanicals that keep perishable foods fresh; the blend Kavita uses is based on a tea prepared for her by her Indian grandmother to prevent food poisoning when Kavita accidentally drank some tap water on a visit to New Delhi. FreshPaper not only can prevent food spoilage and waste for grocery shoppers, but has applications all along the supply chain. In Haiti, for example, a woman-owned catering company uses the product so that it can increase the amount of food it can prepare and create new dishes that feature cut fruits and vegetables. Nonprofits around the world order it for areas where refrigeration is scarce.

But Kavita said she had spent many years between her adolescence and the eventual success of her award-winning idea accumulating doubts. "Even as a child, I had this firm conviction that I had created something that could help a lot of people," she told us. "But looking back, when I was younger I kept being told I needed more experience, more degrees, more money, and I started to really believe that."

She reached a turning point with her appearance at Women in the World in 2013, when she was awarded a Toyota Mothers of Invention prize and interviewed onstage by the journalist Rula Jebreal. She credits the experience with helping her realize that it was possible for her to dream really big — far beyond the Cambridge, Massachusetts, farmers' market stall where she once sold her product herself.

"It made me realize it was possible to think about building a global social enterprise, that it was possible for me, as a woman, to go into an industry like the food industry, which is very male-dominated," Kavita said. She encourages more women to allow themselves the time, the space, and, most important, the confidence to execute their ideas. "Women are actually often really inventive. We're naturally looking for simple solutions in our lives," she said, citing her own grandmother, who was full of ideas and solutions but never had the opportunity to turn them into action.

Today, FreshPaper is mass-manufactured in a plant outside Washington, D.C., and the rapid scaling up of production is allowing Kavita to lower costs and get more of the product into the hands of food banks, school lunch programs, and nonprofits.

It's no surprise that so many women gravitate to and succeed in entrepreneurship. When women have the support and the opportunity to pursue that goal, it's clear they can put us on track to fast-forward to a world of growth, opportunity, and progress. Often, they innovate with purpose, finding new, socially conscious solutions to old problems. Yet barriers persist, from legal restrictions that hinder women's ability to open a bank account to the subtle biases that disadvantage women founders looking for loans. Together, we can tackle these and other obstacles that stand in women's way.

9

Unfinished Business

JEFF MEER, A CAREER FOREIGN service officer, winced as a loud noise erupted from the Beijing International Convention Center, where inside, then First Lady Hillary Rodham Clinton was due to address a crowd of delegates from 189 countries in September of 1995.

As the sound rippled through the chilly autumn air, he raced toward the building. His anxiety mounted when he realized it was around the time Hillary would be giving her speech. What was that noise?

Inside the convention center, Melanne was watching history unfold. Hillary had been asked by the UN secretary-general to give the keynote address. Her speech started off slowly, and Melanne, standing offstage with Lissa Muscatine, Hillary's talented speechwriter, was growing anxious. The road to Beijing had been fraught with advocates on both ends of the political spectrum vocally expressing their opposition to her participation. However, when Hillary recited the litany of human rights violations suffered by women around the world, the audience came alive. She prefaced her examples by noting, "These abuses have continued because, for too long, the history of women has been a history of silence. Even today, there are those who are trying to silence our words."

On this day, though, "the voices of this conference and of the women at Huairou [in northern Beijing, where the NGO companion conference was occurring and where Hillary would travel the morning after her speech] must be heard loudly and clearly." Then, loudly and clearly, she declared:

> It is a violation of human rights when babies are denied food, or drowned, or suffocated, or their spines broken, simply because they are born girls.
>
> It is a violation of human rights when women and girls are sold into the slavery of prostitution for human greed — and the kinds of reasons that are used to justify this practice should no longer be tolerated.
>
> It is a violation of human rights when women are doused with gasoline, set on fire, and burned to death because their marriage dowries are deemed too small.
>
> It is a violation of human rights when individual women are raped in their own communities and when thousands of women are subjected to rape as a tactic or prize of war.
>
> It is a violation of human rights when a leading cause of death worldwide among women ages 14 to 44 is the violence they are subjected to in their own homes by their own relatives.
>
> It is a violation of human rights when young girls are brutalized by the painful and degrading practice of genital mutilation.
>
> It is a violation of human rights when women are denied the right to plan their own families, and that includes being forced to have abortions or being sterilized against their will.

As she spoke, delegates who had struggled against those violations clapped and cheered. The first lady had given voice to what everyone in that hall knew to be true: "That human rights are women's rights and women's rights are human rights — once and for all." That sentence further electrified the crowd and has resonated with women around the world in the two decades since.

Since Beijing, that idea, that women's rights are human rights, has helped propel changes in laws and policies to advance the status of women and girls. Women's increasing power to claim their rights — to be free from violence, to take their place in classrooms, boardrooms, and courtrooms — has swept across the globe. Women's voices have erupted on the agendas at high-level political conferences, on the pages of newspapers, and in rural village councils. For those who were there, and for many others, the word "Beijing" stands for an unapologetic vision for women's equality. It has been an inspiration to activists and scholars, politicians and executives, journalists and artists, and countless others who are working hard to help make women's equality a reality.

Alyse Nelson was one of the women inspired by Hillary's words and the network of extraordinary people she met in Beijing as a determined college student. That spring, she was beginning to find her purpose and had been researching how she might start a women's group on her campus. She placed a call to the general phone number of the United Nations, vaguely aware that it worked on women's issues. After being transferred several times, she spoke with a woman who mentioned the Fourth World Conference on Women, and told Alyse she could attend the NGO forum if she was part of a nonprofit organization.

Alyse decided to wing it, finding her way to Beijing as a campus delegate. She didn't know where she would stay, but by the last leg of her dirt-cheap, three-layover plane ride, a flight from Singapore to Beijing, she recalls, "It was electric. The plane was so full of all these women going to this conference, and you could feel this amazing energy." Over the next few days, her purpose crystallized. She was moved by the discussions and by the first lady's call to action. She knew there and then she wanted to use her own voice to lift the voices of others.

When she got home from China, committed to heeding the call to support women and girls, Alyse finished college and joined the State Department as an intern, working nights at a health club and tutoring students to support herself. Eventually, she got a full-time job at the State Department, where she helped to organize the 1997 conference in Vienna where the seeds of Vital Voices were planted. When Vital Voices became an independent nonprofit, she was one of the two employees on Melanne's staff. Today, nearly two decades later, she's the president and CEO.

Despite the extraordinary progress of the past twenty years, the promise of Beijing is yet to be fully realized. Atrocities committed against women continue in all parts of the world. Violence against women in all its forms remains an epidemic. Girls continue to be underfed, under-educated, and undervalued. While women's legal status has improved in the past century, in 90 percent of the world's countries, women still face discriminatory laws that, depending on the country, prevent them from inheriting or owning property, opening bank accounts, divorcing, or obtaining custody of children. This *de jure* discrimination reinforces the everyday biases that permeate society, restricting women's movement, hindering their economic activity, and rendering them vulnerable to violence and abuse. In some countries, married women are required by law to obey their husbands. In others, women are prohibited from applying for a passport. In fifteen countries, husbands can legally prevent their wives from working. In all countries, the glass ceiling, while showing cracks, remains intact across all sectors.

Although the United States has made enormous progress on women's rights over the past century, it has not joined the world community in ratifying the Convention on the Elimination of All Forms of Discrimination Against Women, standing with only seven other nations that have not done so, including Sudan, Somalia, and Iran. Violence against women continues to permeate every level of society. In the United States, even though women earn the majority of university degrees, their rate of participation in the workforce remains around 57 percent, compared to men's workforce participation rate of 70 percent. The gender pay gap in the U.S. has narrowed for unmarried women and women without children, but widens once women begin having children. The midterm elections in 2014 brought the total number of women serving in the House and Senate to 104 — just over 19 percent. Progress on closing the pay gap between women and men has been glacial. Women who work full-time are still paid 78 cents per dollar of men's pay over their lifetimes; women of color earn even less. The cumulative losses can total more than $435,000 over the course of a forty-year work life.

What follows is by no means an exhaustive list of unfinished business on our path to full equality. Rather, it is an enumeration of just a few of the intractable and salient problems facing women today, in the United States and abroad. It is also a snapshot of some of the strategies and tactics that are being employed to solve these problems. Along the way, you'll meet a few of the resourceful women who, with ingenuity and grit, are working to address them.

The Care Conundrum

Care.com founder Sheila Marcelo, whom you met in chapter 5, created a tactical solution to the problem of juggling personal and professional responsibilities. But her experience, and that of millions of women like her, highlights the degree to which the working world is still generally not designed to accommodate women.

The lack of affordable day care, which nearly derailed Sheila's college education, should be one of our most important priorities. The United States is one of only two countries in the world (the other is Papua New Guinea) that offer no paid maternity leave. Unsurprisingly, the lack of governmental support for new mothers affects the rate of female participation in the labor force, which hovers near the bottom of the group of developed countries: in a recent 22-nation study, the United States ranked an unimpressive 17.

Beyond the obvious U.S. policy challenges, we also face a host of structural design flaws. We live and work in institutions and systems designed to reflect a bygone era, one that assumes that all families have one stay-at-home parent. These outdated systems have produced mismatches between working people's lives and expectations at the office, creating a square peg–round hole syndrome — as was well articulated by the late Sandra Bem of Cornell University, in *The Lenses of Gender*.

Today, roughly 60 percent of married-couple households have two parents in the workforce. Nearly a third of households are headed by single parents, most of whom are mothers. Why, then, should we be satisfied with a school day that typically runs from 9 a.m. to 3 p.m. when the average workday stretches to 5 p.m. or later, making it impossible for many people to maintain full-time work and be able to pick up their children from school? Not to mention the fact that from near the end of June through August, school's out. These design flaws can weigh more heavily on women, who tend to be the primary caregivers.

Women still do the vast majority of our nation's — and the world's —

care work. How much more, exactly? Nancy Folbre, an economist and expert on care work, calculated that in 2012, women performed twice as much unpaid child care as men. Beyond its fundamental social value, care work does have economic value. Taken together, women's *and* men's unpaid household work, were it accounted for and compensated as labor, would have boosted America's GDP by 26 percent in 2010.

Care responsibilities can weigh on women's careers. Working mothers are more likely than working fathers to take a "significant amount" of time off work to care for a family member or child. These additional responsibilities penalize women twice: at work, where they are perceived as less committed to the job, and later, in retirement, since time spent out of the labor force reduces overall pension and retirement contributions.

The latter impact can be at least partially countered by acknowledging and valuing care work for what it is, rather than treating it as a gap in a woman's work history. Many countries use what is sometimes referred to as "pension crediting for caregivers," to compensate caretakers (who are usually women) during periods when they are out of the formal labor force. "They improve pension adequacy by compensating for periods of unpaid work during which the care provider makes limited or no pension contributions," according to one 2011 analysis, which also noted that the United States was one of four OECD countries, out of thirty, that did not have such a system in place.

In the meantime, families struggle to pay for quality child care when both parents work outside the home. In 2013, the cost of child care for one infant in the United States consumed anywhere from 7 to 19 percent of a median married couple's household income, depending on the state, and that percentage rises with the number of children. And for too many others, like the 2 million American women working minimum-wage jobs, paid help was far beyond their reach.

It doesn't have to be this way. In fact, seventy-five years ago, it wasn't. In 1940, the government operated a network of child care centers to assist women who had entered the workforce while their husbands fought in World War II. Writing in the *New Republic* in 2013, Jonathan Cohn describes how it came to pass:

Arguably the best child care system America has ever had emerged during World War II, when women stepped in to fill the jobs of absent soldiers. For the first time, women were employed outside the home in a manner that society approved of, or at least tolerated. But many of these women had nowhere to leave their small children. They resorted to desperate measures — locking kids in the car in the factory parking lot, with the windows cracked open and blankets stretched across the back seats. This created the only moment in American politics when child care was ever a national priority. In 1940, Congress passed the Lanham Act, which created a system of government-run centers that served more than 100,000 children from families of all incomes.

After the war, children's advocates wanted to keep the centers open. But lawmakers saw them only as a wartime contingency — and if day care enabled women to keep their factory jobs, veterans would have a harder time finding work. The Lanham Act was allowed to lapse.

In the decades since, there has been no comparable legislative action to alleviate the child care burden. This lack of affordable, quality child care damages — and can even end — the careers of women who have neither the flexibility to bring their children to work nor the economic cushion to take extended unpaid time off after giving birth. A 2011 report by the U.S. Census Bureau found that slightly more than one out of five American women reported that their chosen "leave arrangement" before or after giving birth was to quit their jobs.

Even women with the resources to pay for child care can suffer career setbacks attributable to motherhood: a recent survey of nearly seven thousand graduates of Harvard's MBA program found that very few women voluntarily left the workforce to care for their children. The survey's authors reported that contrary to popular belief, women were not "opting out" to rear children full-time. Rather, they wrote, "the vast majority leave reluctantly and as a last resort, because they find themselves in unfulfilling roles with dim prospects for advancement. The message that they are no longer considered 'players' is communicated in various, sometimes subtle ways: They may have been stigmatized for taking advantage of flex options or reduced schedules, passed over for high-profile assignments, or removed from projects they once led." This experience has been called getting "mommy-tracked," and reflects unspoken and outdated assumptions about women's and men's social roles.

Many professionals can find it difficult to return to the workforce after a period of maternity leave. Cathy Benko at Deloitte saw it happen to her classmates from Harvard Business School, over 60 percent of whom left the workforce after the birth of a second child. She and her Deloitte colleagues saw the same attrition rates mirrored in their own workforce. While around half the company's new hires were female, their numbers dwindled over time. When Deloitte launched its women's initiative in 1993, women made up only 7 percent of the company's partners.

Where had those women gone? They had fallen victim to the "up or out" culture common in demanding workplaces: work harder and sacrifice more to get promoted, or give up and go elsewhere. In fact, to the surprise of Mike Cook, Deloitte's CEO at the time, a study he commissioned found that more than 70 percent of new mothers who left Deloitte were working full-time a year later—just not at his firm. Cathy and her colleagues came up with a third path, through a program designed to off- and on-ramp new mothers, which was later expanded to all Deloitte employees.

In 2005, the company launched Personal Pursuits, a program that allows senior-level employees up to five years off for child rearing, or any other personal reason, while providing them with mentoring, training, and ad hoc work assignments to keep them in the loop. The employees, while not guaranteed their jobs, maintain a connection with the company and can ensure that their skills and technological edge won't lapse. It's a win for Deloitte: in 2006, the company estimated the cost of replacing an employee to be at least twice a person's salary, compared with $2,500 per employee spent on the Personal Pursuits program.

Shaun Budnik, Deloitte's national director for the retention and advancement of women, explained why the program was also a bottom-line booster: "We know we have people we don't want to lose touch with," Shaun told the *Stamford Advocate*. "The cost of rehiring and retraining is so much higher than just keeping in touch with them."

Over the past decade, dozens of other firms have caught on. Leading global corporations, like PwC, Sara Lee, JPMorgan Chase, Morgan Stanley, and the law firm Sidley Austin, offer "returnships" for professionals — mostly but not exclusively women — who have taken an extended and intentional career break. In a 2012 article for the *Harvard Business Review,* Carol Fishman Cohen, a consultant on return-to-work programs, explained why they are such sound investments: "Returning professionals offer enlightened employers a rare opportunity: They allow them to hire people who have a level of maturity and experience not found in younger recruits and who are at a life stage where parental leaves and spousal job relocations are most likely behind them. In short, these applicants are an excellent investment. Using a returnship program as a screening tool lets employers skim the top talent from this pool."

At Vodafone, the global telecommunications firm, women make up roughly 35 percent of employees but only 21 percent of its international senior leadership. The company commissioned the auditing firm KPMG to analyze its internal data, and found that 65 percent of female employees who left the firm did so in the first year after maternity leave. In March 2015, Vodafone announced a new policy that guarantees sixteen weeks of fully paid maternity leave, followed by six months of thirty-hour workweeks at full pay. Vodafone realized its "pipeline problem" was actually more an issue of child care, and used its data to ensure that its thousands of female employees don't feel they have to choose between a fulfilling career and financial security and their obligations to a newborn child. In May 2015, Orrick, Herrington & Sutcliffe became the industry leader among big law firms for parental leave, announcing a new program that will offer its U.S. lawyers paid primary caregiver leave of twenty-two weeks, with the option of taking a total of up to nine months before returning to work.

Workplace flexibility varies by industry. Harvard economist Claudia Goldin has found, unsurprisingly, that less flexible professions, like law and finance, which place a premium on face time in the office, had the highest rates of women dropping out or working part-time after giving birth. By contrast, professions that permit more flexibility without incurring costs or penalizing workers (Goldin gives high marks to pharmacists) tend to retain more women after they give birth. This is not just about mothers, though. All employees, and society at large, stand to benefit from work environments in which caretaking and professional performance are not mutually exclusive.

Mind the Gap

On October 25, 2010, around fifty thousand Icelandic women and their supporters walked out of their offices or homes and poured into the streets of the capital, Reykjavík, to march for equal pay. The protest was scheduled for exactly 2:25 p.m., or 66 percent of a regular nine-to-five workday — and since Icelandic women earned only 66 percent of their male counterparts' pay, they should, in theory, be done with work for the day.

The problem has been clearly identified, yet women around the world still do not earn as much as their male counterparts, even after controlling for factors like education and time out of the workforce. In 2013, fifty years after the enactment of the Equal Pay Act, American women on average earned 78 cents to the male dollar for full-time, year-round work, earning a median salary of $39,157, which is over $10,000 less than men's median earnings of more than $50,000. Although slightly more women have reached the very top of the pay scale — women made up 16 percent of the top 1 percent of earners for the years 2008 to 2012, versus 3 percent twenty-seven years earlier — the overall gap has barely budged in a decade: in 2004, women earned 77 cents to the male dollar, according to an analysis by the National Women's Law Center.

The pay gap widens for women of color, many of whom work full-time for paychecks that put them dangerously close to the poverty line. Average weekly earnings for black women, who earn just 64 cents for every dollar that white men are paid for the same work, stood at $611 in 2014, while Hispanic women, who earn just 56 cents for every dollar of what white men are paid for the same work, take home $548 a week, only a little above the poverty line of $466 for a family of four. The gap also widens for mothers — unmarried women earn 96 cents to the un-married man's dollar, but married mothers with at least one child under eighteen take home just 76 cents of a married father's dollar. Women were the sole or primary breadwinners in 40 percent of households with children in 2013, up from just 11 percent of households in 1960, according to data from the Pew Research Center, which means whole families are living on women's unequal pay.

Transparency helps. In 2014, Gap Inc. received the results of a study that analyzed pay data for its 130,000 employees around the world. The analysis, done by a workforce diversity consultancy, found that regardless of seniority or country, women and men were being paid equally. Senior Vice President of Human Resources Dan Henkle told a reporter that the exemplary showing was due to the company's vigilant attention to merit and performance, as well as the presence of female leaders at Gap since its inception, when Doris Fisher and her husband, Donald Fisher, each invested 50 percent of the equity that launched the company's first clothing store, in San Francisco in 1969.

The Many Faces of Violence

Katherine Chon was a senior at Brown University, living off campus in an attic apartment on Providence's Angell Street. Slavery, to her, was an institution of a bygone era, an academic issue, something she had studied in an elective class and debated with her friends over dinner. "What would you have done in the days of slavery?" they had asked one another. Of course, she had said, she would have been firmly on the side of the abolitionists. One day, she and her friend Derek Ellerman read an article in the *Providence Journal* about a massage parlor down the street from her apartment. In fact, it was a brothel, in which women were held in debt bondage to traffickers who burned their arms with cigarettes.

She was shocked to learn that slavery was alive and well in America — and was just down the street. That the women were Korean and approximately her age struck a chord with Katherine, herself a Korean American.

She and Derek vowed they would do everything they could to prevent these kinds of abuses from taking place again. From their efforts came the Polaris Project, now known as Polaris. One of the leading anti-trafficking organizations in the United States, Polaris operates on the premise that modern-day slavery, like that of the antebellum period, is an economic enterprise. By helping to train law enforcement agencies and pass legislation, Polaris hopes to change the economic calculus, turning debt bondage from a low-risk, high-profit criminal undertaking to one in which the risks are high and the profits meager.

As chairman and CEO of Carlson, a global travel and hospitality company, Marilyn Carlson Nelson has been another trailblazer in the fight to end sex trafficking. Demonstrating the difference that leaders in the business community can make, Carlson, under her direction, signed a global code of conduct that seeks to protect children from exploitation in travel and tourism. The commitment includes training employees to identify and report perpetrators of child sex tourism. Carlson became the first company to win the Presidential Award for Extraordinary Efforts to Combat Trafficking in Persons.

Gender-based violence takes many forms. It stems from shortsighted economic constraints and long-held traditions. It haunts the life cycles of women and girls, starting even before they're born, when female fetuses are aborted in families with a preference for sons. This human rights violation has skewed the demographics of China and India, breeding new social ills and related human rights violations, such as trafficking and other crimes.

Gender-based violence manifests itself in child marriage, in female genital mutilation, and in domestic abuse. Sexualized violence and intimate partner violence follow women and girls from the home to primary school, high school, and university. Rape continues to be a heinous weapon of war, wielded with virtual impunity. And, of course, it persists in peacetime. Its specter haunts offices, streets, public transportation, army bases, college campuses, living rooms, and bedrooms. In the form of acid violence, it disfigures and maims; as cyberbullying, it silences and dismisses. To the extent we permit gender-based violence to go on, it attests to how little we value the life and potential of a girl, the ideas and the voice of a woman.

There are costs, too, in letting this violence continue, above and beyond the lost lives, the missing girls, and the pain and trauma of survivors. When girls don't go to school, we all miss out on their unfulfilled potential. When women can't work because they are stalked, harassed, or abused, the entire economy suffers. In the United States, one estimate put the costs in health care and lost productivity from intimate partner violence at more than $5.8 billion a year, not including the costs incurred by the criminal justice system. Survivors often experience depression, low self-esteem, and post-traumatic stress disorder, preventing them from living full, productive lives.

Legislation can help. Passed in 1994, the Violence Against Women Act began by acknowledging the inadequate response of law enforcement to crimes like stalking, intimate partner violence, and rape. It then stressed the importance of the "three P's": prevention through education, awareness training, and jobs; protection of survivors through shelters and victim services; and prosecution, with steeper penalties for the violent perpetrators.

The act established new provisions on rape and battering that emphasized prevention, created funding for victim services, and recognized new offenses, becoming the first federal criminal law against battering. Crucially, it provided $1.6 billion of funding over six years, which helped local, state, and federal agencies set up shelter services for victims, create training programs for law enforcement personnel, and establish the National Domestic Violence Hotline, which receives more than twenty-two thousand calls each month. By making the state accountable for the well-being of its female citizens, the law transformed what had largely been dismissed as a private matter into a public concern and a government responsibility.

And it has largely worked. The incidence of intimate partner violence has fallen by 64 percent between 1994 and 2010, according to an analysis by the Department of Justice's Bureau of Justice Statistics. In its first six years, the Violence Against Women Act's prevention programs have saved taxpayers as much as $14.8 billion, according to a 2002 cost-benefit analysis. In an increasingly polarized political climate, the act has enjoyed a measure of bipartisan support, having been reauthorized three times since its initial passage, most recently in 2013.

Despite the progress made, violence against women is far from extinct. In the United States alone, more than one in three women have experienced some sort of intimate partner violence, such as sexual assault, stalking, or physical abuse, in their lifetimes. College campuses have been seared by reports of frequent sexual assaults on female students, which are often met with inadequate administrative response. The Department of Defense estimates that tens of thousands of instances of unwanted sexual contact occur in the armed services every year, although only a fraction are reported.

And while across the globe women's rights activists have made great strides getting laws on the books that prohibit violence against women, it continues to be an epidemic, with one in three women in the world experiencing violence at some point in their lives. This is in part because ending violence against women takes more than the passage of laws; it also takes enforcement and implementation, two areas where we continue to see significant gaps. This is an area where female judges, working together, have had an impact, through programs like the International Association of Women Judges and Cornell Law School's Avon Global Center for Women and Justice, which has worked with 185 female judges from more than forty countries since its inception.

At the center, Kim has seen how critical it is to have people with diverse experiences serving as judges. One prominent example is Justice Elena Inés Highton de Nolasco, vice president of the Supreme Court of Argentina. In 2004, Justice Highton de Nolasco helped create the first Domestic Violence Office of the court, following more than three decades as a public defender and later a judge. To address the challenges that domestic violence survivors faced in seeking help from the legal system, she staffed the office with people from the legal, medical, psychological, and social work fields. The office operates 24 hours a day, 365 days a year.

Through these international networks, women judges act as peer mentors to each other and share best practices and ideas on how to effectively implement laws that protect women from violence. A frequent participant in these international training and mentoring programs is U.S. Circuit Judge Ann Claire Williams, the first woman of color to be appointed to the Seventh Circuit Court of Appeals and the district court in that circuit. She has been using her power for purpose since the earliest days of her legal career. Her initiatives range from helping students of color pass the bar exam to finding ways in which judges around the world can better apply the laws of their land to protect human rights.

Judge Williams has spent the past ten years traveling to Africa with organizations like Lawyers Without Borders to train judges and attorneys on issues as diverse as domestic violence, human trafficking, and corruption. Women judges — and men who understand women's experiences — are critically important to ensuring that the rule of law is fairly applied.

"We all take an oath to apply the law impartially and fairly," Judge Williams said, countering the assumption that a woman judge will automatically rule in favor of a woman in a case. "What we do bring, though, is our background, our experiences as women, and those experiences have an impact on the way we view issues related to women," she said, adding that having women on the bench increases "the confidence that the public has in the system," by better reflecting the society at large.

Ending violence against women will require a multipronged effort, including more economic opportunities for women and changes in cultural attitudes toward women and their worth.

Changing Cultures from Within

Economic deprivation contributes to other forms of violence against women, such as child marriage, the trafficking of women and children for sexual servitude, domestic labor, and other forms of exploitation. These are often interwoven with cultural factors, including beliefs about women's proper role in society. The notion that women bear their family's "honor" on their bodies leads to women being punished for perceived sexual transgressions that bring shame to the family. Often, when a woman is raped, she is blamed for dishonoring her family, and the perpetrator is not punished.

Melanne once met an Afghan girl in a women's shelter in Kabul who, at age five, had been raped. In this case, her father turned her over to the local police instead of subjecting her to an honor killing. Fortunately, the police knew of a shelter, a safe haven where the girl was protected and supported by the women staying there. These acts cannot be justified on the grounds of cultural norms or privacy; they are criminal acts and deserve to be treated as such.

Fortunately, these destructive notions are not fixed or immutable. In India, for example, the culture of silence around sexual harassment and sexual violence was breached in 2012 by the gruesome gang rape and murder of a young student on a minibus in Delhi. Her death led to massive protests and the start of a national conversation and legislative change. In Pakistan, Mukhtar Mai was gang-raped in 2002 on the orders of a village council for an alleged indiscretion by her brother and a woman from another village. According to local custom, she would ordinarily have to kill herself, because the rape had rendered her "dishonored." Instead, she drew strength, as she told Melanne, from her mother's faith in her and her belief in a more loving God. Though illiterate, she took her case to court; ultimately, she was awarded the equivalent of $8,200 by the national government. With the damages she received, and with donations from around the world, she built a school for girls and boys. She was one of the first to enroll. When asked what motivated her, she said, "Only education will change my village."

Such extreme cases shocked not only the nations involved, but the world. But cultural change can happen on a local level too, and doesn't necessarily have to spring from tragedies like that of Mukhtar Mai. One program funded by the Nike Foundation, to combat child marriage in Ethiopia, a country where the rate of child marriage is estimated to be 41 percent, shows how cultural and economic factors can influence each other. According to Girls Not Brides, an initiative of the Elders, child marriage affects every part of the world, although most of the countries with the highest rates are in Africa. In Niger, for example, the United Nations Population Fund (UNFPA) estimates that three out of four women aged twenty to twenty-four had been married before they were eighteen. In Chad and the Central African Republic, the rate is close to 70 percent.

According to the UNFPA, 14.2 million girls had their childhoods stolen from them by being forced into underage marriages in 2010; if present trends continue, that number is projected to reach more than 15 million by 2030. In 2012, Secretary of State Clinton called on a group of leaders, including officers of the Ford Foundation — which made a $25 million commitment to help end child marriage — to confront this challenge, which keeps so many girls from fulfilling their potential and deprives the world of their talents. Darren Walker, the president of the

Ford Foundation, has been deeply committed to continuing the foundation's leadership in ending child marriage and, more broadly, in furthering progress for women and girls.

One way to prevent child marriage is to use incentives to keep girls in school. Nike's incentive program in the Amhara region of Ethiopia, whose child marriage rate of 50 percent is even higher than the national average, begins by deeding a goat to a young girl, with the condition that her family make a commitment to send her to school. In one case, a young girl's father had tried to marry her off to a husband many years her senior. She refused, saying she wanted to stay in school. Her father insisted. After some back and forth, she relented. "Fine," she said, "but if I go, I'm taking my goat with me." Faced with the prospect of losing the goat, her father backed off—the family was too dependent on the milk it provided.

Nike Foundation director Swan Paik described in an interview how the program combined financial assets with what she called "human assets" to subtly increase girls' value in that Ethiopian community. "Over time that incentive [the goat] became less and less important, as the community itself embraced a new norm," she said. "Once the community does that, then that's sustainable development and you don't need the incentives, because the community has decided that they don't want child marriage, and they find all kinds of interesting and creative ways to enforce their own value system."

The program resulted in the near-total eradication of very early underage marriage in the villages where it was implemented. Girls aged ten to fourteen in those villages were 90 percent less likely to be married off than girls in control villages, although girls aged fifteen to nineteen were still likely to be married by the end of the program.

Similarly, in Senegal, Molly Melching founded a community-led program, this time to address the practice of female genital mutilation, or cutting. Now a nonprofit called Tostan, it has been instrumental in providing education, good health practices, and other means to empower communities based on human rights. These empowered communities debated whether the practice of female genital cutting should be abolished. It was painful and degrading to women and often led to health complications, even death.

Molly, who had been an American exchange student and former Peace Corps volunteer in Senegal, was working in the village of Saam Njaay there, teaching in an educational program based on human rights called the Community Empowerment Program, when Hillary Clinton visited in 1997. Hillary later learned from Molly that the program she'd witnessed had sparked a social movement among the women of Senegal and eventually led to their abandonment of genital mutilation, and that the program had become the foundation for Tostan's work. In 1997, in Malicounda Bambara, a village in western Senegal, thirty-five women, who had learned about their rights to health through the Community Empowerment Program, took their case to the local imam, who assured them there was no Koranic justification for the practice. They went on to have discussions with the village chief, and in the end, after many meetings with all members of their community, the village voted to renounce cutting. The women had succeeded in changing the norm from the entrenched harmful practice to one of better health for women and girls.

Since Tostan began its work in 1991, more than seven thousand communities in eight African countries have publicly renounced female genital cutting and child marriage. One village chief, Imam Demba Diawara, has been particularly instrumental. He alone has visited more than 375 communities, where he works with both men and women to end genital mutilation. "It is working," he has said. "But we still have a lot left to do. I am an old man. I need replacements." By ensuring that communities themselves are empowered with information and make the decisions about their own customs, Molly has developed what has become a model program for social change.

In Somalia, Dr. Hawa Abdi, once described as "equal parts Rambo and Mother Teresa," has protected more than 100,000 people from chaos, privation, and terrorism over the past twenty years while at the same time changing a culture from within. In 1983, Dr. Hawa, as she is known, opened a one-room clinic for women on farmland belonging to her family, as recounted in her memoir *Keeping Hope Alive*. Dr. Hawa had dreamed of becoming a doctor since she was twelve, when she saw her mother die from complications of childbirth. At seventeen, she won a scholarship to study medicine in Kiev, in what is now Ukraine. As famine and civil strife cannibalized Somalia throughout the 1990s, she became one of the country's first female gynecologists and took in thousands of Somalis with nowhere else to go. Her small clinic grew into a four-hundred-bed hospital, which her daughters help run. Its surrounding farm acreage evolved into something like an unofficial refugee camp, with as many as 90,000 residents seeking care and shelter at any one time, many of them suffering from malnutrition and the violence of the civil war.

In 2010, members of the militia Hizb al-Islam showed up to demand that she shut down the hospital, angry that an older woman was in charge of such an institution. They put her under house arrest for five days and did their best to destroy the hospital, trashing medical records and equipment. Then the women of her camp rose up: hundreds of them began to protest, compounding the disgust of thousands of Somalis around the world who were following the siege and registering their discontent through social media and other channels. Eventually the militiamen backed down and left — but not before handing over the written apology that Dr. Hawa insisted they owed her.

"I told the gunmen, 'I'm not leaving my hospital,'" Dr. Hawa said to the *New York Times*. "I told them, 'If I die, I will die with my people and my dignity.' I yelled at them, 'You are young and you are a man, but what have you done for your society?'"

Certainly nothing like what Dr. Hawa has done. In addition to providing free medical care and medicines, Dr. Hawa opened a school on the premises for girls and boys, with support from Eliza Griswold, Claire-Lise and Jean-Jacques Dreifuss, and Amanda Lindhout. Dr. Hawa also keeps violence off her premises in other ways. Her daughter, Dr. Deqo Mohamed, helps her run the hospital and surrounding village. At a recent Seneca Women event, she explained that as conflict and chaos spread throughout Somalia, the existing problem of domestic violence worsened. But Dr. Hawa has a strict "no domestic violence" policy: the farm's offenders are locked up in a small room, the onsite "jail" to which she holds the key.

Dr. Mohamed observed that after years of her mother's strictly upholding this zero-tolerance policy, the older generation has finally internalized the importance of respecting women's rights. But, she said, "It took twenty-four years to change the mentality."

Dr. Mohamed has hopes for the next generation. She notes that by their very existence, she, her mother, and other women on the farm are able to model strong, compassionate female leadership for the younger residents, including a generation of boys who she hopes will grow up to treat women as their equals. "The children growing up, the boys, they are seeing women as leaders."

Women, Peace, and Security

In 2009, Melanne visited Kabul, on her first trip to Afghanistan as the U.S. ambassador-at-large for global women's issues. One evening, she sat in on a panel discussion with a group of women who fully intended to give her their perspectives on American engagement in their country and what it could mean for Afghanistan's future. The first one who spoke said, "Stop looking at us as victims, and look at us as the leaders that we are." She was right. Women are targets for violence, but they are also leaders, and their participation is critical to achieving sustainable peace — as has been demonstrated in conflict areas from Northern Ireland to Liberia.

Women bear the consequences of violence and conflict disproportionately. They comprise more than three-fourths of the refugees and displaced persons resulting from wars, famine, natural disasters, and persecution. They are the targets of mass rape in times of war and ethnic cleansing, and often they are the ones left behind to rebuild a society.

Jimmie Briggs saw firsthand how women suffer during war. As a war reporter in the 1990s, he had interviewed numerous child soldiers in various conflicts across the African continent. He began to see that girl soldiers experienced what he called a "double trauma," first by fighting alongside the boys, then by being raped by their adult commanders. Even for girls who managed to escape, such trauma was hardly addressed in reintegration programs.

"I wanted to honor the experiences, the trust, of the women, of the survivors, of the children who told me their stories," Briggs said. "They told me their stories in the faith that I would do something with them besides write an article, so Man Up was born out of that understanding."

Man Up Campaign is a global, youth-led organization active in twenty-four countries, including the United States, that gives young leaders support, advocacy training, and networking opportunities to design and disseminate culturally sensitive and age-specific campaigns, often incorporating sports, music, and entertainment, to raise awareness about gender-based violence.

In June 2014, former British foreign secretary William Hague and actress and activist Angelina Jolie brought together more than 70 ministers and representatives from more than 120 countries with NGOs and gender-based-violence survivors in London for the largest-ever summit on sexual violence in armed conflicts. The year before, William and Angelina had urged the UN Security Council to get serious about ending rape in war. William reminded the members of the Security Council that "as an international community we curbed the development of nuclear weapons, heading off a once threatened and unstoppable wave of insecurity. We have binding Conventions against the use of torture, and on the treatment of prisoners. We have outlawed the use of chemical weapons, and imposed a global ban on cluster munitions. We have made progress in choking off the trade in conflict diamonds that undermines many fragile countries ... It is time to say that rape and sexual violence used as a weapon of war is unacceptable, that we know it can be prevented, and that we will act now to eradicate it."

What is less widely recognized — and what needs to be understood — is how essential women are to all aspects of peace-building, including their participation in peace negotiations and postconflict reconstruction. Launched in 2013, the Georgetown Institute for Women, Peace, and Security, which Melanne directs, supports research, scholarship, global conferences, and strategic partnerships to advance policies that close the gender gap in peace and security. Just as the role women play in the economy has recently been well documented, we need to better understand the vital role women play in advancing peace and security.

Making women central to the peace process and to security has recently become a priority of America's foreign policy. On January 23, 1997, Madeleine Albright was sworn in as the first female secretary of state in the Oval Office, surrounded by her family. Her first stop after the ceremony was the White House's private residence, where she met with Hillary Clinton, a gesture that underscored her commitment to continuing their work on global women's issues, which had begun two years earlier, during preparations for the Fourth World Conference on Women in Beijing.

Less than two months after Albright's swearing-in, the first lady and the secretary of state stood together at the State Department in front of a standing-room-only audience on International Women's Day. Hillary wore a pink suit; Secretary Albright was clad all in red. When Hillary had arrived at the State Department, Secretary Albright leaned in and whispered, "We clash." The two burst out laughing — but then went on to deliver a message that was unified and anything but frivolous. In consecutive speeches to the crowd of ambassadors and diplomats, career foreign service aides and policy buffs, each outlined why America's foreign policy must integrate the lives and concerns of women and girls in its pursuit of a more peaceful and prosperous world.

Before then, the State Department and its embassies rarely tracked information on the status of women. In 1997, one staffer read thousands of cables looking for information on women. She found barely a mention. When Melanne's office would call the department to gather relevant data on women and girls in preparation for a trip or a meeting by the first lady, that information was rarely available. It seemed that tracking half the population wasn't an important part of country-level information gathering. But with Hillary becoming a global voice for women's rights, with the impact of the Beijing conference, and with Albright providing leadership on the inside, the institutional culture slowly began to change.

In October 2000, the Security Council adopted Resolution 1325, recognizing "the important role of women in the prevention and resolution of conflicts and in peace-building." It was the first time the UN body responsible for upholding peace and security officially acknowledged how women experience conflict and how vital they are to ending it. Several additional resolutions have been adopted over the past fifteen years to strengthen the original Security Council action.

In June 2008, under Secretary of State Condoleezza Rice's leadership, Resolution 1820 was adopted by the Security Council. The resolution formally recognized that sexual violence was not just a byproduct of war, but also a deliberate tool of warfare that "demands a security response." This marked an important stage in the development of the women, peace, and security agenda by affirming that this type of violence, when directed at civilians, "can significantly exacerbate situations of armed conflict and may impede the restoration of international peace and security," and that rape and other forms of gender-based violence can constitute a war crime, a crime against humanity, or an element of genocide.

The following year, under the leadership of Secretary Clinton, the Security Council adopted Resolution 1888, which called for the appointment of a special representative of the secretary-general to oversee the UN's efforts to combat sexual violence in armed conflicts. Today Zainab Bangura is playing a strong leadership role in that position. Among its many provisions, it also called for the need to end impunity, noting that prosecution of violators not only promotes "individual responsibility for serious crimes, but also peace, truth, reconciliation and the rights of the victims." Yet all these years later, women are still largely shut out of the negotiations to end conflicts and the decisions that are made in postconflict reconstruction. By one estimate, over the past two decades, women have made up just 9 percent of all peace negotiators in major peace processes. Unsurprisingly, about half of peace agreements fail within five years of being signed.

But the law and public policy can only go so far in addressing discrimination and violence faced by women. Laws can punish and deter, but they can't address the larger culture that feeds these scourges. For that, we need to change the culture and attitudes that lead to bias, discrimination, and violence against women. We need to expand opportunities for women and girls, and ensure that they can take their rightful place in the economy, at decision-making tables, and in the community. We can pull on many different levers of change to close the gender gaps that still remain, and fast-forward to the world we all want to see. As we will see, three of those critical levers for change are education, technology, and media.

Regina Maria Silva Gomes, with support from Coca-Cola's Coletivo program, helped clear the once trash-strewn streets of her Brazilian favela and organized local women artisans to transform plastic bottles and other debris into charming bird feeders, toys, and decorative items that are sold for cash.

Instituto Coca-Cola® Brasil

On a visit to the White House, teen girls in ANNpower — a national mentoring program that is a partnership between ANN INC. and Vital Voices — met with Hillary Clinton and other notables, including ANN INC. CEO Kay Krill (center, with sunglasses). *ANN INC./photo by Micky Wiswedel*

After surviving U.S. Airways' "Miracle on the Hudson" landing — thanks to Captain Chesley "Sully" Sullenberger (right) — Pam Seagle, a Bank of America senior marketing executive, rethought her priorities. "I wanted to live with purpose," she recalls. Her goal: to help other women.

Chuck Burton/AP Images

In 1993, her first year as first lady, Hillary Clinton broke precedent by setting up her own office in the West Wing of the White House, where she helped shape administration policy on health care and other domestic issues. On May 2, when this photo was taken, Hillary and Melanne traveled to Baltimore to participate in an event with working women.

White House Photo Office

A survivor of gang rape, Sunitha Krishnan (right) of Hyderabad now helps India's victims of sexual slavery through the school she founded, Prajwala. Diane von Furstenberg (left) is a passionate supporter of her efforts.

Courtesy of Sharon Farmer/ sfphotoworks.com

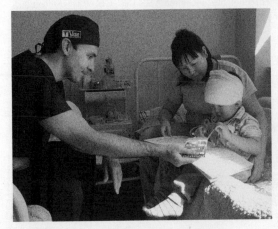

Dr. Ebby Elahi, an oculofacial surgeon and director of global health at the Virtue Foundation, examines a patient on a medical expedition. His extensive work with the youngest-known victim of acid violence spurred important legal reforms in Cambodia.

Virtue Foundation

Ann Claire Williams, the first woman of color to be appointed to the U.S. Seventh Circuit Court of Appeals, addresses a conference hosted by Cornell Law School's Avon Global Center for Women and Justice, which assists women judges from more than forty countries in preventing violence against women. *Virtue Foundation*

In a rare public appearance together, all four women ever to sit on the U.S. Supreme Court gather to honor Justice Sandra Day O'Connor (second from left), the first woman to serve on the Court. From right, in photo, are Justices Elena Kagan, Sonia Sotomayor, and Ruth Bader Ginsburg. Kim, seated at the far left, is the cofounder of Seneca Women, which hosted the tribute. *Kevin Wolf/Invision for Seneca Women/AP Images*

Two of the most powerful women in the world, Christine Lagarde, managing director of the International Monetary Fund, and Hillary Clinton, former secretary of state, high-five each other while being interviewed onstage at the 2014 Women in the World Summit in New York City.

Women in the World/Tina Brown Live Media

The upper ranks of America's regulatory agencies and boards are increasingly populated with women. Among them is Sharon Bowen (at podium), the first African-American woman on the Commodity Futures Trading Commission, who also acts as a mentor to many women lawyers, including Kim.

U.S. Commodity Futures Trading Commission

When Zainab Salbi (second from left) read about the so-called rape camps in Bosnia in 1993, she took the money she'd been saving for her honeymoon and used it to start what became Women for Women International, which works with women in war-torn countries.

Courtesy of Zainab Salbi

Microcredit pioneer Muhammad Yunus, founder of Grameen Bank, Melanne, and Kim celebrate the appointment of Andrea Jung (far left) as president and CEO of Grameen America, which provides microloans to women in the United States.

Courtesy of Clayton Collins

Give a woman a loan, and the next thing you know she's lifted her whole family, and her village, out of poverty. And odds are she'll swiftly pay back the borrowed sum. That's what Muhammad Yunus learned when he launched Grameen Bank's now much-copied program of microloans. Melanne saw that multiplier effect firsthand when she visited Grameen clients in Bangladesh in 2012. *Nurjahan Chaklader, Grameen Bank, Bangladesh*

CERTIFIED BY
WBENC/WEConnect INTERNATIONAL

W☺MEN™
OWNED

WWW.WOMENOWNEDLOGO.COM

The nonprofits Women's Business Enterprise National Council and WEConnect International created the Women Owned logo to alert consumers to products made by women-owned companies. *WBENC*

"Human rights are women's rights and women's rights are human rights": First Lady Hillary Clinton's ringing words at the United Nations Fourth World Conference on Women in Beijing in 1995 helped inspire an international wave of activism and legislation.

National Archives and Records Administration

Described as "equal parts Rambo and Mother Teresa," Dr. Hawa Abdi has protected more than 100,000 people from Somalia's rampant violence, chaos, and privation, sheltering them at her farm near Mogadishu.

Vital Voices/G. Court

More than 7,000 communities in eight African countries have publicly renounced female genital cutting and child marriage. Some credit goes to Tostan — a nonprofit that arms communities with health and hygiene information and encourages them to make their own decisions — and its founder, Molly Melching, seen here with Tostan clients and Hillary Clinton in 1997.

White House Photo Office

After becoming the first woman in her Kenyan village to attend college in the United States and earn a doctorate, Kakenya Ntaiya returned and started the Kakenya Center for Excellence, the first primary boarding school for local girls.

Kakenya Center for Excellence

In her films and TV shows, America Ferrera portrays realistic Latina characters that young women can identify with. For crusading journalist Nicholas Kristof's documentary series *Half the Sky,* she traveled to India to visit a shelter that provides schooling for children of sex workers.

Courtesy of Jamie Gordon and Mikaela Beardsley/photo by David Smoler

The star of *Thelma and Louise* and *A League of Their Own,* Geena Davis is also the founder of the Geena Davis Institute on Gender in Media, dedicated to original research into how women are portrayed on TV and in film.

Toby Canham/Getty Images

One of the world's bravest and best-known schoolgirls, Nobel Peace Prize winner Malala Yousafzai is a living symbol of the importance of universal education.

Nigel Waldron/Getty Images

"We hold these truths to be self-evident: That all men and women are created equal." Deliberately echoing the language of the Declaration of Independence, the groundbreaking Declaration of Sentiments issued by the Seneca Falls Convention in July 1848 — the first national convention for women's rights — was signed by 68 women, including organizer Elizabeth Cady Stanton (depicted here in a later engraving), and 32 men, among them abolitionist Frederick Douglass.

Eminent Women of the Age, *1868*

Malak Jân, a revered sage and influential thinker, at home in her rural village of Jeyhounabad in western Iran. Blind from the age of twenty, she revolutionized the role and value of women and girls in her community. At great personal risk, she led reforms that included the equal feeding of girls and boys, access to education for girls, and equal inheritance and property rights.

© 2015 The Nour Foundation

10

Levers for Change: Technology and Education

IT WAS A BARGAIN NO GIRL should have to make. Kakenya Ntaiya was fourteen years old, living in a remote Masai village in the Kenyan bush, when she struck a pact with her father, who wanted her to undergo female genital mutilation, which he thought would increase her chances of getting married. She said she would acquiesce if he let her continue her schooling.

Kakenya held up her end of the bargain, missing school for two weeks on account of the pain. As soon as she healed, she made her way to Sosio Secondary School, where she blossomed. She studied hard, excelled, and won a scholarship to Randolph-Macon Women's College in Lynchburg, Virginia, in 1999. She wanted to go.

Men from her tribe, the Masai, had left before. Some had gone to big cities in Africa, others to America or the United Kingdom. Few came back. Women — women were different. They married, and they stayed. But Kakenya had hope and a strategy. She needed the permission of the elders in her community and knew that a Masai tradition held that visitors who arrive before sunrise bring good news, and it is bad luck to tell them "no." Every morning, she woke up in darkness and visited the elders one by one until she had everyone's consent for her to go to college. "Getting an education was very important to me," Kakenya told us. "I knew it was the only way I could get a different life than the one my mother was living. I knew it was going to enable me to avoid getting married at a younger age, it was going to get me a job and earn an income that would enable me to support my family, and it was going to enable me to be a role model for other girls and to give them an opportunity to access quality education."

With the support of her fellow villagers, who sold pumpkins and goats to raise the $3,000 she needed for the plane ticket, she made her way to Virginia, and later to the University of Pittsburgh, where she received her doctorate in education. But before she left home, she made a promise: she would return, and bring with her the thing her community needed most — education.

Thanks to the generosity of so many who came to know Kakenya in the United States, including the philanthropist Vicki Sant, ten years later, she delivered. In 2009, the Kakenya Center for Excellence opened for business; it was the first primary boarding school for girls in her village. Since it opened, more than two hundred girls have enrolled. The students take classes in English, Swahili, math, science, geography, history, religion, the arts, and physical education.

The school also encourages leadership, and is developing a curriculum that will empower students to resist community pressures and stand up for their rights. Parents who enroll their daughters sign a pledge to spare them from undergoing genital mutilation. At the same time, girls learn the skills important to the traditional life of the villages, such as agriculture and animal husbandry, so that even as their horizons expand, they will maintain their connection to their families and communities.

"Education is very important for girls because it allows them to learn their legal rights, it liberates them, and gives them an opportunity to realize their full potential by avoiding FGM [female genital mutilation], early marriage, and early childbirth," Kakenya said.

In Kenya, as in too many other countries, girls from poor families are less likely than boys to go to school. In the northeast of the country, 55 percent of poor girls have never been to school, versus 43 percent of poor boys. According to UNESCO, as of 2007, 33 percent of Kenyan girls fifteen years of age and older were illiterate. At the Kakenya Center for Excellence, Kakenya told us, not only can the students read and write; they can also speak English with confidence.

In 2014, the inaugural class of thirty-two girls graduated from the eighth grade. Today, the same village chief who had once said that educating girls was a waste, since they were destined only for marriage, now sits on the school's board as a dedicated supporter of girls' education. Kakenya said that the fathers, many of whom were at first reluctant to send their daughters away to school, are tremendously proud, and she's starting a second school to keep up with demand.

Kakenya's story is a clear-cut illustration of the importance of education in accelerating women's progress toward equality. Investing in quality education, particularly for girls and women, has ripple effects that go beyond building human capital. Girls' education can lead to decreases in unplanned pregnancies, lowers the spread of disease, and increases earning power. As the former chief economist of the World Bank and later U.S. Treasury secretary Lawrence Summers once said, "Investment in the education of girls may well be the highest return investment available in the developing world."

Ensuring girls' and women's access to education is a necessary precondition for us to fast-forward to the more egalitarian world we want to see. Education, as we will see, has been key to closing the gender pay gap and helping women like Kakenya unlock their potential. Equal access to technology is today another precondition: new information technologies, and especially mobile innovations, have the potential to bring millions of women into the global economy, yet the current gender gap in access to tech threatens to leave them behind. Without these two levers, progress for women and girls — and consequently all of society — will be hampered. Made equally accessible to all, education and technology can accelerate our global community forward.

Education is a basic human right. In recent years, developing countries have made steady progress toward closing the gender gap in primary education. In those countries, the scaling up of access to education will be essential to getting more women into the workforce and boosting GDP. In developed economies, higher education has unlocked women's earning potential, raising productivity and increasing economic growth.

In all regions of the world, the gender gap in education is closing. Nations in North America, Latin America and the Caribbean, Europe, and central Asia have closed over 99 percent of the education gender gap; the Middle East, North Africa, eastern Asia, and the Pacific region have closed about 93 percent; and sub-Saharan Africa has closed 82 percent of the gap. But political unrest, war, poverty, and discrimination still keep girls out of school. In some parts of the world, girls can even face a bullet for wanting to exercise their right to education.

Malala Yousafzai was on her way to school in Pakistan's Swat Valley in October of 2012 when a Taliban gunman boarded the school bus and shot the fifteen-year-old in the head, then fired at two of her friends. Malala barely survived, but the attack only emboldened her: she became an outspoken activist for the right to education, especially for girls.

Malala's fight for survival and her relentless advocacy for the right to an education has captivated the world, drawing attention to the incredible challenges some girls face in exercising their fundamental right to learn, and inspiring more young Pakistani women to become courageous education activists as well. In 2014, the same year Malala was awarded the Nobel Peace Prize, she donated the $50,000 she received from the World's Children's Prize to rebuild a United Nations school in Gaza, which had been damaged during a conflict between Israel and Hamas. "Without education, there will never be peace," she said.

Even where girls can freely attend school, often their schools are places where bullying, harassment, or violence is common. Forty-four percent of the respondents in a 2004 survey of Malawian schoolgirls said they had been touched in a sexual manner, without their permission, by teachers or male classmates. In Zimbabwe, an astonishing 92 percent of schoolgirls surveyed in a 2000 research study reported being propositioned by older men, and 50 percent had been assaulted by male strangers or experienced unwanted sexual contact at the bus stop or walking home from school. A 2012 survey by Cornell Law School's Avon Global Center for Women and Justice, of schoolgirls in Zambia, found that 84 percent of students interviewed had personally experienced some form of sexual harassment or violence by a teacher, fellow student, or other man while traveling to and from school, or knew of classmates who had experienced such behavior.

Schoolgirls have also become targets of violence in Nigeria. In April 2014, the militant group Boko Haram, whose name has been loosely translated as "Western education is forbidden," kidnapped hundreds of girls from a boarding school in the town of Chibok. The terrorist group has said that some of the girls would be forced to become "wives" to the militants, while others would be treated as slaves or used as suicide bombers. In March 2015, the group kidnapped another 500 women and children from the town of Damasak, reportedly killing 50 of them before leaving the town. In May 2015, reports emerged that Boko Haram has perpetrated the mass rape and forced pregnancy of hundreds of women and young girls.

Despite the risks in some parts of the world, girls and their families continue to fight for safe access to schools. Why? It is clear that primary schooling is essential, and the paybacks on girls' education only accelerate in secondary school. Unfortunately, girls' enrollment in secondary school is still inconsistent. In 2009, over 50 percent of girls were enrolled in secondary school in southern and western Asia (compared to nearly 60 percent of boys), and barely more than 30 percent in sub-Saharan Africa (compared with 41 percent of boys). In all regions of the world, girls' enrollment trails that of boys. And even where education is free and accessible, quality varies widely and girls face other barriers. Girls living in rural areas are prone to drop out of school once they begin menstruating, because of a lack of sanitary products and bathrooms. Only 23 percent of underserved, rural girls in sub-Saharan Africa make it all the way through primary school.

Anand Mahindra, the chairman of the international corporation Mahindra & Mahindra, had been approached by one his top female employees, Sheetal Mehta, a product manager for some of the company's flagship projects. She told her boss that as much as she loved working for the company, she wanted to derive more meaning from her work. At the same time, Anand was contemplating making a greater corporate commitment to social responsibility. Inspired by his mother, whose positive influence had instilled strong values in him, he decided to launch a non-profit dedicated to girls' education. He asked Sheetal to take charge of the initiative. Anand knew that schooling for girls would be a boon to Indian society, contributing to the decline of social customs like child marriage and the dowry system, in which the bride's family contributes money or household items to the groom's family, which predisposes parents to think of their daughters as a financial burden.

Project Nanhi Kali, which means "little bud" in Hindi, does not seek to replace the national education system. Instead, it provides a comprehensive educational support program to girls in some of India's most economically disadvantaged areas, from the Mumbai slums to the nation's eastern states that had been racked by Maoist uprisings. Working through nearly two dozen local NGO partners on the ground in eight states, Project Nanhi Kali ensures that the girls get academic tutoring before or after school, using innovative and proven teaching methods, and provides them with all of the supplies and clothing they need — pens, paper, a backpack, and school uniforms — to attend school with dignity and pride. The NGOs visit with the students' families and reinforce the importance of educating their daughters and keeping them in school. As a result of the success of the program, absent teachers are returning to the classroom, the girls are winning state-funded scholarships, and more parents are taking pride in their daughters' education and achievements. Melanne visited one of the Nanhi Kali–supported schools in Mumbai and was impressed by the quality of the instruction and the excitement of the children, who were eager to learn. Today Nanhi Kali is supporting the education of 110,000 girls.

Giving Girls the Support They Need

Tammy Tibbetts first became interested in Liberia while writing a profile of a Liberian refugee, living in her New Jersey hometown, for a college journalism class. As she learned more about the country and the many challenges facing its girls, she became more and more convinced that education — and in particular educating girls — was the solution. Tammy, the first in her family to graduate from college, was passionate about education and felt that reaching girls in their teens was critical.

After graduation, she began building her career as a social media maven at Hearst magazines. When she started to volunteer after work for a foundation that supported Liberian refugees, she soon realized that she could use her job skills to achieve the same impact, and at the same time inspire women of her generation to get involved. She envisioned her friends, colleagues, and peers using video and social media marketing to raise funds to sponsor girls overseas to become the first in their families to graduate from secondary school. "I started to see new models of philanthropy emerging that empowered communities," Tammy said, "and I saw how young people could do more with less."

In 2009, she posted her concept on Facebook. To her surprise, an acquaintance named Christen Brandt wrote back offering to help. They gathered a few more friends and created the first "She's the First" You-Tube video. She's the First soon earned the support of the powerful women who themselves had been the first in their family to graduate from college — women like Christine Osekeski, the publisher of *Fast Company*, which featured Tammy in 2011, and Laura Davis, a managing director at JPMorgan Chase. In 2012, a grant enabled Tammy to leave her job at *Seventeen* to work full-time on She's the First. "That bond," she said, "creates an empathy and a fire to pay it forward."

The She's the First model begins with a nationwide network of chapters, most based at a college or high school. Each chapter leverages its own social networks to raise money through bake sales and other events. Rather than contribute to a particular institution or group of girls, She's the First fully supports individual scholars as they pursue their education in the developing world. Working with local partner organizations, each sponsored student is assigned a mentor, who talks to her family to ensure they're on board with their daughter's academic career. Sixty girls have graduated so far; many go on to college, others start businesses.

The seeds for Ann Rubenstein Tisch's work on girls' education were sown in 1988 when, as a national correspondent for NBC network news, she interviewed a group of teenage mothers from an inner-city high school in Milwaukee. The high school had opened a day care center on the premises, so students who were also parents could stay in school. But when Ann asked the students what their vision for the future was, some of them started to cry.

"They knew that even though this was wonderful, they were stuck. Stuck dead in their tracks. They really didn't see themselves anywhere in five years," Ann told us. "At that moment, I remember saying to myself that we are not doing enough for these kids. We need to figure something out. I've got to get this story done, but I need to file this away for future action."

Several years later, her mind turned back to those students in Milwaukee, hardworking young women for whom life held too little hope for the future. What if she could bring the best education possible to girls with the least opportunity? What if she could offer them a completely different path? Ann began researching the notion in depth, exploring partnerships with other institutions and planning what the ideal school would look like. In partnership with her husband, Andrew Tisch, she cofounded the Young Women's Leadership Network. The first school, the Young Women's Leadership School of East Harlem, opened in September 1996, in an office building on 106th Street in East Harlem.

By any standard, the school has been a huge success: its students go on to earn four-year college degrees at three times the rate of their peers, according to the school's data. The Young Women's Leadership Network now has five schools in New York City, which collectively serve approximately three thousand girls. The model has inspired more than a dozen affiliates in four other states, and has been credited with sparking a renaissance in single-sex education across the nation. But it is the original school in East Harlem, where it all began, that holds a special place in Ann's and Andrew's hearts.

Guna, a Sri Lankan immigrant who did not finish elementary school, was hired as the East Harlem school's custodian when the school first opened in 1996. He saw how the students were going off to college with sizable financial aid packages, and decided to transfer his own daughter to the school. Several years later, Ann and Andrew were delighted when their daughter received a letter saying that she had been accepted for early admission to Brown University. That same day, Guna's daughter got the same letter. "Guna and his wife, and Andrew and I, are now proud Brown parents together, and our daughters are classmates," Ann said. "If anyone ever forgets that education is the great equalizer, and really the only equalizer, that story says it all."

Andrew agrees. He was particularly moved when he and Ann were able to bring Malala to the East Harlem school, where she addressed more than two hundred girls from the Young Women's Leadership schools. The experience was life altering for the girls, who gained a broader perspective and became grateful for the fact that, for them, going to school every day was not a life-threatening experience. "Malala has been an inspiration and catalyst for so many," Andrew said. "Education used to be a cottage industry, but now the world is waking up to the fact that girls' education is a global imperative, as more and more people realize the benefits of giving a girl an education. When you educate a girl, you educate a generation." In addition to the Young Women's Leadership Network, Andrew holds leadership positions at Harvard Business School and Cornell University. He also believes that women's leadership in education is essential and recently helped identify and recruit Cornell University's first woman president, Elizabeth Garrett.

Ann and Andrew are happy to see that beneficiaries of high-quality education are paying it forward at every level. Students and administration from Cornell and many other colleges have partnered with the Young Women's Leadership schools to mentor high school girls, and recently Ann and Tammy Tibbetts have joined forces, so the girls of the Young Women's Leadership Network can support girls' education in the developing world. In December 2014, the students at the YWLN school in Astoria, Queens, sent a check for $890.57 to She's the First after raising the money through bake sales. On the memo line of the check they wrote, "For: helping send a girl to school."

It's hard to understand what's stopping countries from investing more in educating their girls, given how clearly it pays off. One study estimated that Kenya stood to gain $3.4 billion in additional gross income each year — the equivalent of the income of the country's entire construction sector — if all 1.6 million of its adolescent girls finished secondary school and its more than 220,000 adolescent mothers were gainfully employed. The same study, which surveyed fourteen countries in southern Asia, Africa, and Latin America, concluded that investing in the next level of education for today's cohort of girls would yield lifetime earnings equivalent to more than 50 percent of GDP, or 1.5 percent each year.

The Blind Spot: Girls in STEM

It's unfortunate that we still see too few women majoring in the STEM disciplines: science, technology, engineering, and math. Reshma Saujani is one woman trying to change this, by targeting girls in high school.

Girls Who Code, the nonprofit she launched in 2012, aims to get girls hooked on computer coding while they're still young, through classes that take place after school and during summer sessions.

Reshma was inspired to start Girls Who Code after observing a troubling pattern while touring her congressional district during an unsuccessful campaign for Congress in 2010. The Fourteenth District of New York encompasses the East Side of Manhattan, home to some of the wealthiest people in the country, as well as parts of Queens and the Bronx, where some of New York's poorest reside. She saw how inequality translated into a vast disparity in access to computers. And she was equally struck by the wide gender gap in technology.

Girls Who Code reached approximately three thousand girls between its launch in the spring of 2012 and the end of 2014; the organization has set an ambitious goal of reaching one million students nationwide by 2020. Reshma told us that her students are particularly keen to use their newfound skills to change the world: "In 2012 I basically put twenty young girls together and we put them in a conference room at a technology office and said, 'All right, let's see what happens when we teach them how to write a computer program.' The results were just tremendous. Not only did they learn how to code, but they were building things that were about making their communities a better place."

The participants are mentored by women from leading technology firms, and companies like Google, eBay, and Twitter contribute funding. Girls Who Code recently announced a new partnership with Accenture, the global consultancy and technology service provider, whose employees volunteer to train the next generation of IT talent.

The National Center for Women and Information Technology, cofounded in 2004 by Lucinda (Lucy) Sanders, aims even younger, creating programs that target girls starting in kindergarten and continuing through college. In 2007, NCWIT launched a small awards program, the NCWIT Award for Aspirations in Computing, to recognize girls in high school who show an aptitude for computer science, and invite them to NCWIT meetings. Since its inception, the program has reached more than twenty-one thousand girls. The girls have found the experience transformative. It provides much-needed validation to counteract the discouragement they often experience at school, where they are a small minority — or sometimes the only female student — in advanced placement computer science classes. The winners support each other, and young women are giving back by mentoring middle school girls in a near-peer mentoring program called AspireIT. At the beginning of the school year, one girl posted on the group's Facebook page that she was the lone female in her programming class. The others jumped in with encouragement: "Don't worry!" "Hang in there!" "You can talk to us."

With the resources of such firms as Google and Motorola, Lucy has scaled up the Aspirations in Computing Award to become NCWIT's signature nationwide program, with regional and local events that recognize girls in their own communities. The program added an Aspirations in Computing Educator Award, in a nod to the inspirational and dedicated teachers whom many women now in the tech field credit with putting them on the path to success. Apple was the most recent to sign on in support of the organization, making a commitment of about $10 million over the next four years.

"Young women who self-identify as technical are a priceless group," Ruthe Farmer, NCWIT's chief strategy and growth officer, said. "Their skills are very attractive to everybody."

Paula Stern knows the value of women's networks and how helpful they can be when you're a trailblazer in a new field. She was one of the first female commissioners of the U.S. International Trade Commission and was at one point the second-highest-ranking woman in the U.S. government. Today, she pays it forward by working with organizations like NCWIT. "In this digital economy, America's future competitiveness in trade relies on creating technology," she told us. "We know diversity in any field creates better results and has always been the hallmark of America's success. Without women and girls in technology, we risk having technology which is not as creative, and can diminish our ability to compete globally."

Fixing the Pipeline

As we have seen, engaging girls in science and technology when they're young is key, but it's equally important to keep them engaged as they advance through high school and college. A 2012 study by the Girl Scouts of America found that over 80 percent of girls are interested in a STEM career, but only 13 percent cite a STEM field as their top career choice; most choose medical practitioner jobs over scientific careers. Often, the cause is not a lack of interest or aptitude, but rather a pernicious phenomenon known as stereotype threat, in which girls confronted with difficult subject matter or the occasional setback drop out for fear they will confirm negative (and unfounded) stereotypes about girls' inability to compete in math and science. This suggests a need to affirm girls' confidence in their abilities, since high school girls currently earn *more* math and science credits in many courses than their male peers and perform better in those classes (although not necessarily on standardized tests).

By college, only 20 percent of freshman women in the United States planned to major in a STEM field, compared with 50 percent of freshman men. At the bachelor's degree level, women represented only 18 percent of computer science graduates in 2014, *down* from 23 percent a decade earlier. As of 2013, women held only 29 percent of the jobs in the science and engineering fields. One 2007 study by the Society of Women Engineers found that nearly one in four women engineers leaves the profession after the age of thirty, while only one in ten men do.

Given the paucity of women in these areas, young girls are less likely to have female role models they can look up to. Role models matter: two sociologists found that in communities in which large numbers of women worked in STEM disciplines, high school girls were just as likely as or more likely than boys to take physics courses. Another survey found that only 4 percent of 368,000 high school girls who said they wanted to pursue STEM careers had a mentor to encourage them.

Dr. Carla Shatz, a world-renowned neurobiologist and professor of biology and neurobiology at Stanford School of Medicine, knows the importance of role models, especially when one is a pioneer breaking into a new field. She was the first woman to receive a PhD in neurobiology and to chair the department at Harvard Medical School, and she was the first woman to be given tenure at Stanford School of Medicine in the basic sciences. As the first, she did not have any female role models in her professional life, but found male role models who helped her achieve her goals. Dr. Shatz has said, "Looking back, I had wonderful mentors but no role models about how to combine a work life and a personal life . . . Being among the first women to be successful in science, it would have been nice to have had some other role models." In fact, Dr. Shatz accepted the position as chair of the neurobiology department at Harvard Medical School in part because she wanted to serve as a visible role model for other women in science. "I had many offers of chairs but when I was offered [the] position at Harvard it came with enough resources so that I could give back to the next generation. I saw that in this position I could act as a role model," she has said. "There were no other women as chairs at that time of the basic science departments at Harvard Medical School (there was one chair of health policy), and I knew that if I declined, the next person to be asked would be a guy!"

Finding role models in the tech industry is particularly important for women pursuing careers in that field. The industry itself is known to have a culture that is unfriendly, even hostile at times, to women. Anita Sarkeesian, a blogger and feminist pop-culture critic, received death and rape threats for documenting misogyny in video games and the wider "gamer" culture. Online harassment of women has been called "the next civil rights issue" of our time, pushing some women offline altogether.

Why does this matter? With so few women in the pipeline for these jobs, we are missing out on a huge reservoir of untapped human capital at a time when there's a critical need for STEM talent. Furthermore, a dearth of women at the top, where important research and design decisions are made, means that innovations and policies may fail to address the needs of a large swath of the population. An ongoing lack of diversity at senior levels can translate to business strategies — and ultimately products — that serve the needs of a small sector of consumers. We need an educational system that encourages everyone to claim a space in this emerging economy, because technology, like education, is critical to advancing women and girls.

Women and Tech: The Backstory

The tech industry was not always this lopsided, notes Megan Smith, the first female chief technology officer of the United States and a former vice president of Google. The history of computing is, in fact, a women's story. Ada Lovelace, the daughter of the Romantic poet Lord Byron, was a mathematician with a poetic soul, "who embodied the combination of the arts and sciences," writes the historian Walter Isaacson. In the 1840s, Lovelace envisioned the creation of a general-purpose machine capable of being programmed and reprogrammed to execute a wide range of tasks and operations, beyond simple mathematical computations. (She also raised the question, still unanswered, of whether a machine could ever "originate anything" — that is, think for itself.)

A century later, during the Second World War, the American war effort called for additional "computing" power. Betty Jean Jennings Bartik, a math whiz from Missouri, eschewed a career teaching calculus and passed over recruitment letters from the likes of IBM, which was seeking to hire "system service girls." Instead, she took a computing job at the U.S. Army's Aberdeen Proving Ground, calculating ballistics trajectories by hand, until she heard of an opportunity to work on the ENIAC, a machine designed to compute the same sorts of artillery firing tables she was figuring out with pencil and paper. She and five other women worked on the ENIAC, helping to program what became the first electronic, all-purpose computing machine.

"They invented computer science," Megan Smith points out. "We don't know exactly how they chose these six women for the ENIAC project. And they weren't even allowed to see the machine at first because of the security clearance, so they were given diagrams."

The future of computing can and should be a women's story too. Megan, in her role as CTO, is trying to make this future a reality through initiatives to recruit top technologists, particularly women, to build digital and mobile services for the government and tell the "untold stories of women in science and technology."

Megan was lucky. As a girl in middle school she loved her science class, thanks to a gifted teacher, Mrs. Salizman, who linked the history of scientific discovery to the process of innovation — "doing something that you actually didn't know the answer to," in Megan's words. The next year, for the eighth-grade science fair, she and a classmate tackled the solar system, building a model with simple construction materials. The experience taught her the importance of doing — not just reading and absorbing, but getting her hands dirty.

"It was the first time I understood you could take a principle of something and design something related to the principle — like invent or innovate something. That's an essential thing in tech," Megan told us. "We read and write in language arts, but we have this read-only for science, which makes it really inaccessible."

Melinda Gates, who majored in computer science and economics at Duke University, had a similar experience as a high school student in the early 1980s. She credits her math teacher Susan Bauer, an early computer science enthusiast, with persuading the school principal to buy computers so the students at her all-girls school could learn coding.

"That inspired me to major in computer science in college, and I'm *still* inspired by the enthusiasm that drove her to learn and to share what she learned with us," Melinda Gates told us, adding that the single-sex environment smoothed the way for her and her classmates to embrace computer science. "Nobody had a sense that this was an area for the boys, because there were no boys. The usual roadblocks weren't there."

Maria Klawe is trying to replicate Megan Smith's and Melinda Gates's experiences at Harvey Mudd, a small, science-focused private college in California with around eight hundred students. Maria arrived at Harvey Mudd from Princeton, where she was dean of the engineering school, and had previously been dean of science at the University of British Columbia. She is adamant that more women and minority students can excel in computer science, but it's up to the institutions to create a level playing field and make everyone feel welcome. She insists that entry-level computer science classes need not be daunting, even to students with no prior experience. And most of all, they should be fun.

It's worked. In 2013, around 47 percent of Harvey Mudd's computer science majors were female, more than two and a half times the national average for coed colleges; the proportion of women among engineering students at Harvey Mudd was more than half.

Increasing the number of women in the tech field is also critical to driving social progress. Many senior-level women in tech we spoke with observed that women often use their engineering power for purpose. Ann Mei Chang spent eight years as a senior engineering director at Google and currently serves as executive director of the U.S. Global Development Lab at USAID. Ann Mei worked in Melanne's office at the

State Department as a Franklin Fellow and led the work to address the gender gap in mobile technology and the Internet. In her experience, women are increasingly likely to use technology to tackle societal ills.

"One of the things I noticed in the technology field is that men tend to be drawn to technology because they like to fiddle with things, because they are fascinated by the technology itself — it's kind of a puzzle to solve," Ann Mei said. "Whereas women tend to be drawn more to technology because it's a powerful tool that can actually solve real problems in the world and can make the world a better place. They can create something and use it as a creative tool. I absolutely see more women looking at ways they can take their skills and resources and apply them to improve the world, although certainly many men do as well."

Leila Janah is another woman who is using technology for good — to close the digital divide and bring women in developing countries into the global economy. She believes that despite limited access to computer equipment and sometimes to education, women can and should be able to work in the tech field. And she's convinced some of the biggest names in Silicon Valley — Google, LinkedIn, and Intuit, to name a few — that she's right.

She began thinking about the links between developed and emerging economies when she was a seventeen-year-old student, teaching English as a volunteer in Ghana at a school for the blind. Her smart, motivated students taught her a valuable lesson of their own.

"I spent a lot of time in former British colonies in Africa and South Asia, where there are a large number of unemployed young people with the skill and will to work and with access to technology," Leila told us. "It may not be the most cutting-edge technology, but they have computers that work and Windows software." But despite the infrastructure and their work skills, they still could not get jobs. These willing workers were being excluded from global markets.

After graduating from Harvard and working at the World Bank and as a management consultant in India, Leila founded Samasource in 2008, a nonprofit that connects major technology companies with women, refugees, and young people who perform "microwork."

The company's proprietary software, the SamaHUB, breaks down tasks like transcription and data-tagging into smaller pieces, which are then distributed to workers in high-poverty countries. From her home base in San Francisco, Leila now oversees an operation of nearly 6,500 workers, from Pakistan to Haiti and a dozen other countries in between, and Samasource has paid out more than $4.7 million in wages and benefits to date.

In 2012, Leila's work won the Secretary of State's Innovation Award for the Empowerment of Women and Girls. The award, created in 2010, was made possible through a collaboration between the Rockefeller Foundation, under Judith Rodin's leadership, and the Secretary's International Fund for Women and Girls. "We must do more and we must do more with more urgency to empower women," Judith said.

Justice Sandra Day O'Connor understands the transformative power of using technology for good. That is why, when she retired from the Supreme Court and wanted to revive civic education in the United States, she helped design a video game to engage students in civic participation. Justice O'Connor, who has since twice delivered the keynote speech at the annual Games for Change conference, launched iCivics in 2009, which provides a suite of role-playing video games that teachers can incorporate into their curriculum to encourage students to learn the basics of American citizenship. Players can take the role of a Supreme Court law clerk, a legislator, even the president of the United States.

As Justice O'Connor has said, "Games, like iCivics, are about navigating a system. You learn rules, make choices, and have to engage with the world in which you are playing . . . If you said the phrase 'delegate authority to an executive agency' to a seventh-grader, you can imagine the look you'd get. But when they are doing it in the context of a game, it becomes both real and compelling." So far, thanks to this important legacy of Justice O'Connor, more than seventy thousand educators and seven million students have used iCivics lessons, and the games are used in schools in all fifty states.

We've seen the extraordinary advances that come about when women have access to technology. The Hollaback! app, for example, lets users report incidents of street harassment in real time, using location-based technology. Emily May, Hollaback!'s executive director, told us that when women are able to aggregate their stories on a site like Hollaback, it provides a sense of relief (the sense that "it's not just me") and enables a collective consciousness to arise. "People can move outside these stories as just individual experiences that they had, and move toward looking at these stories as a more systemic part of our culture," she said.

Technology propels social media campaigns and activism as never before. With the help of technology, women played a key role in political uprisings during the Arab Spring through their use of social media in Tunisia, Yemen, and Libya. In Egypt in 2011, a young woman's powerful call to her nation, delivered on YouTube and shared on Facebook, led to mass protests in Cairo's Tahrir Square. In Tunisia, activist Lina Ben Mhenni documented protests across the country on her blog, building awareness and connecting people in different parts of the country to the revolution. Technology is changing how women connect with one another and with the wider world, helping them fight for their rights and do business.

Over the past few decades, technology, and mobile technology in particular, has rippled through industries such as health care, education, and the media, connecting individuals to causes, companies, communities, and each other. In the developing world, technology (when accessible) has the potential to transform women's lives by providing critical access to information, addressing health needs, and offering opportunities to save income safely and engage in financial transactions. Ring the Bell, an online multimedia campaign based in India, has reached 130 million people with its public service announcements, encouraging them to stand up and denounce violence against women with a text message or SMS. The simple cellphone is being used to protect women from violence, as Melanne learned in the Democratic Republic of Congo, where text messages serve as an early-warning system in a place where conflict has raged for more than a decade and rape is a tool of war. Cellphones are also being used to provide small entrepreneurs and farmers with real-time access to market information and weather forecasts, and to help them predict the supply and demand for goods and crops.

The greatest impact of the cellphone will be in mobile banking. Among people living in poverty globally, women are 28 percent less likely than men to have a bank account — an estimated 1.3 billion women remain outside the formal financial sector. Through cellphone banking, they are able to keep their income secure and engage in financial transactions, even if they have too little money for a formal bank account. In its 2015 annual letter, the Bill and Melinda Gates Foundation predicted that "mobile banking will help the poor radically transform their lives."

The Miracle of Mobile

As most of us who have benefited from mobile technology know, smart-phones, when and where they're available, can be weapons of mass empowerment. Apps and services are now designed specifically to lower the barriers to entrepreneurship, allowing women to start and manage their own businesses and get real-time market information, even from rural or remote areas. Research by the Cherie Blair Foundation and GSMA, a mobile operators' association, found that in the developing world, nine out of ten women said their mobile phones made them feel safer, eight out of ten felt more independent, and four out of ten enjoy enhanced economic opportunity thanks to their phone.

Muhammad Yunus, the Bangladeshi economist, told us, "More and more health services will be provided through the mobile phone. We keep saying that very soon, all the diagnostic services for every single person will be delivered at home by the mobile phone. Nobody will have to come to a clinic."

MasterCard is using mobile payment technology to promote financial inclusion. You might think of MasterCard as a piece of plastic in your wallet. It's actually a technological system that safely transmits information between merchants and banks, so buyers and sellers can make transactions quickly and with confidence. Governments, too, are taking advantage of this technology. The MasterCard Center for Inclusive Growth is leveraging learnings from hundreds of MasterCard's public-private partnerships to enable women's economic growth. For example, in South Africa, the government — in one year — registered more than twenty million citizens, opened bank accounts, and distributed ten million MasterCard debit cards, mostly to women, allowing them to access government and social subsidy programs safely. Without the worry that the funds, which had been coming in cash, would be taken away and used for things unrelated to caring for the family, women are using their purchasing power in new and powerful ways.

Shamina Singh, executive director of the MasterCard Center for Inclusive Growth, is also working to bring women into the banking sector. "The thing that we hear over and over again when we are talking to women in India or Mexico is 'We need a way to obtain capital for our small businesses,'" Shamina told us. "But mostly these women don't even call them small businesses. They'll say, 'My husband is a farmer but I sell salsa,' or 'I pickle and I do other things and I sell that on the side,' and meanwhile they are bringing in 70 percent of the household income from this informal work. So this economic opportunity with women cannot be overestimated. We are focusing on the ways we can help these business owners grow. With 85 percent of transactions still being done in cash, we have an enormous opportunity to combine their smarts and ambition with our data and technology to transform economies and change lives. I'm so grateful to be in a place where doing well and doing good is not just an aspirational notion, but a corporate ethos that is actionable." Right now, she noted, one of the biggest obstacles for women is their lack of a credit history that lenders can use to evaluate their ability to repay. With the technology MasterCard is developing, women business owners can use their transaction histories as a proxy for credit, enabling them to build credit scores that can make it easier to get loans.

Women no longer have to travel to processing centers hoping to pick up orders of vegetables that may not be available. They don't have to scramble for child care before they make those trips. They have more money to save and invest in their children's education. "Mobile technology enables women to access the information, networks, and capital they need to grow their businesses, become financially independent, and play a stronger role in their societies," Cherie Blair told us.

The Kenyan mobile payment service mPesa, for example, allows users to send and receive money via an SMS message. Widely used across the country for commercial transactions and remittances, mPesa has the added benefit of allowing women to save and keep their money safe from husbands or family members who might try to take or borrow it. Mobile phones also offer a path to entrepreneurship in and of themselves, as with the "mobile phone ladies" of Bangladesh, the half million village women throughout the country who sell airtime to their neighbors.

The Qatari telecom giant Ooredoo sees vast potential for mobile phone ladies. While building a mobile phone market in a new country is never a straightforward proposition, it's even harder when that country is Myanmar, where roughly 30 percent of the population has no access to safe drinking water, where decent roads are scarce, and where per capita GDP is the lowest in its region. But Ooredoo is confidently diving in, with the help of thirty thousand women whom it is training to distribute its phones and sell prepaid phone cards with airtime to the 90 percent of the population who do not yet own a cellphone. It's modeled on a similar program in Iraq, where its business has doubled since partnering with women vendors.

Thanks to initiatives like these, women's access to technology is poised to grow. But bridging the digital gender gap in the developing world will provide more than just an earnings boost for phone companies. In a ceremony at the State Department in October 2010, Kapilaben Vankar, an Indian microentrepeneur in SEWA, described how access to the simple cell phone had transformed her fledgling enterprise. The occassion was the launch of mWomen, a partnership among GSMA, the Cherie Blair Foundation, and USAID to reduce the gender gap in mobile technology. Indeed, a 2010 report by the Cherie Blair Foundation and GSMA found that bringing mobile phone technology to an additional three hundred million women in low- and middle-income countries would also provide "significant social benefits to women and their families," in addition to $13 billion in incremental revenue for mobile operators.

A maternal-health app called maymay, for example, is one such mobile technology that brings clear social benefits to women. Part of Ooredoo's strategy to help drive the market for 3G data services in Myanmar, maymay is also a tool to get health information to expectant mothers in a country with a maternal mortality rate of around 200 deaths per 100,000 live births, one of the worst in the region. Users enter their expected due date, or the date of their last period, and the app sends three messages a week with health advice timed to the stage of the pregnancy. In addition, the app contains a database of health professionals and uses GPS technology to link the mother with nearby medical care.

Bridging the Tech Gender Gap

Despite all the promising advances, women for the most part have failed to benefit equally from the wave of prosperity unleashed by the technological revolution. Women make up a relatively small percentage of leaders at prominent technology firms, and historically women are underrepresented in the direct creation of technology, making up only 10 to 20 percent of the engineering workforce. In the developing world, there is also a gender gap in access to mobile phones and the Internet. If the gender technology gap isn't closed, women will likely fall further behind in realizing the full benefits that technology can provide.

Shelly Esque joined Intel as its head of public affairs for Arizona, quickly rising to become the U.S. and then global head of corporate affairs. In this role and as president of the Intel Foundation, Shelly engaged her team and others across the company to look at Intel's portfolio of social investments and corporate responsibility programs to determine how Intel and its foundation could have the greatest impact. One answer that came up over and over in these discussions: invest in girls and women. Given Intel's position as a global technology company, the topic of technology access and empowerment came to the forefront. Shelly and her team engaged with key stakeholders and partner organizations to identify where the key gaps — and opportunities — existed. Their research led to the commissioning of the first *Women and the Web* report, released in 2013. As Shelly noted in the report's introduction, "The Internet gender gap reflects and amplifies existing inequalities between the sexes."

This gap has several implications. For companies, it means that women are a huge, untapped pool of talent and potential customers. For countries, it means that a large portion of the population is missing out on the myriad benefits of connectivity: in South Asia, the Middle East, and North Africa, the gender gap stands at nearly 35 percent, while in sub-Saharan Africa, Intel estimates the gap is nearly 45 percent. For individual women, it means less access to entrepreneurship, to important health, weather, and financial information, and less independence. The report estimates that doubling the number of women online over the next three years, bringing an additional 600 million women online, would contribute between $13 billion and $18 billion in annual GDP across 144 developing nations.

Intel is addressing the gap through a program called Intel She Will Connect. Launched in 2013 in Kenya, Nigeria, and South Africa, Intel She Will Connect trains girls and women to be digitally literate, offering onsite training sessions at community centers and other shared spaces; connects girls and women to gender-specific online content and game-like learning experiences on topics such as health, finance, and jobs; and engages girls and women through the online media site and web community WorldPulse.com. "Making the Internet relevant and compelling is key for the program," Renee Wittemyer, Intel's director of social innovation, told us. "Our research showed that when women connect to other women online, they see the relevance of technologies and feel supported. Based on that, we wanted to integrate a peer network into our program, so that the women could connect to one other as part of their digital literacy training." The program aims to reach millions of women across Africa with its digital literacy training and content.

"We treated it as we would treat any problem at Intel: do some research, bring back solutions, and, through iterations, try to find the place where our impact can be most effective," Shelly Esque told us. "That brought us to focusing our efforts on women's access to technology, and then through this empowerment we can positively impact economic and social development. I truly believe that technology can make a difference for women, especially in education and in access to opportunity. In cultures where they don't have many opportunities, I believe technology can be that bridge." In 2015, Intel announced that it was making a $300 million investment to encourage diversity, both within the company and in the industry at large.

Education and technology are two of the most critical levers we can pull to advance women's economic potential. Both are key to enabling full participation in the global economy. Although women are making strides in both fields, without a strong push forward we risk watching women fall behind. Governments and private-sector companies must come together to ensure that women and girls everywhere can gain access to quality education and play an equal role in the emerging technology revolution.

11

Media Matters

BY THE TIME SHE REACHED COLLEGE, America Ferrera almost abandoned acting, even though she'd been pursuing it since she was five years old. The youngest of six siblings, she had reluctantly gone with her family to watch her eldest sister perform in a school play, and had come away with a sure idea of her life's vocation. But education was everything to her mother, a Honduran immigrant who was raising the kids singlehandedly. During high school, America babysat and waitressed to earn money to attend an acting workshop, where she landed her first agent, all while maintaining straight A's.

"Every single audition was an obstacle," America said. "How was I going to get there? Who was going to take me? My mother worked every day, so it was either beg a sibling or beg a relative or get on a bus or whatever it was. I had this blind faith that I was just going to keep on moving and eventually something would open up."

America was accepted to the University of Southern California, but unlike other aspiring actors on campus, she didn't only major in theater. Instead, she threw herself into international relations, where she studied issues that, to her, "were urgent and needed attention." Her early college years followed soon after 9/11, and the events being played out on the world stage made acting seem less than urgent. She wanted to make a difference — how could she find purpose in Hollywood?

"But at the same time," America said, "I knew my deepest passion was acting, so how was I going to reconcile those things? Being the dramatic teenager I was, I thought my only option was to quit acting and do something that meant more in the world." She took her dilemma to a trusted adviser, a professor of conflict resolution, appropriately enough. He was a white man in his seventies, with a successful corporate career behind him. In the second semester of her freshman year, she burst into his office one day, tears streaming down her face.

"I said I didn't know what I was supposed to do with my life," she explained, "because I realized how important these issues in the world were, and I really wanted to do something that made a difference. But my passion was acting, and how could I just give up the thing I loved?"

Her professor calmed her down. He shared details of his own life, describing a mentoring relationship he had struck up with a young Latina woman from a low-income immigrant family. Although he had been mentoring her for years, she had never fully opened up to him, because, he thought, of the gulf between their life histories. One day his mentee told him, "If you really want to understand my life, come watch this movie with me." The movie was *Real Women Have Curves,* in which America herself played a starring role as young Latina caught between her college ambitions and her duty to help provide for her family (and for which she won an award at the Sundance Film Festival). After they watched the movie together, he said, they went to talk to his mentee's parents, and asked them to watch it too.

"They decided they would support their daughter's dream of going to college," America explained. "So he helped me see that I didn't have to give up what I loved doing to have an impact on the world — that in fact it was heading straight for the thing that I love and choosing it as a tool in the world that gave me power. That was really a big shift for me — that moment when I realized I didn't have to be two separate things. I didn't have to give anything up."

America went on to win Emmy and Golden Globe awards for her portrayal of Betty Suarez, an aspiring fashionista in the ABC series *Ugly Betty.* And, in 2013, she graduated from USC with a degree in international relations; it had taken her ten years to complete. Just as her mother dreamed, all six Ferrera children were now college graduates. America found her purpose through acting, portraying realistic Latina characters with whom young women everywhere could identify.

Patricia Harrison, president and CEO of the Corporation for Public Broadcasting (CPB), is similarly committed to inspiring women and girls—in her case, using real-life stories as inspiration. Patricia also chairs the leadership council of Women and Girls Lead, an organization that commissions educational documentary programs which profile women in history who have long been overlooked and female activists who fight issues ranging from sexual assault in the U.S. military to child marriage in Afghanistan. Since taking over at the CPB in 2005, Patricia has made diverse programming her top priority, launching the first-ever Diversity and Innovation Fund for all forms of public media.

Her tenure has also seen the commissioning of groundbreaking documentaries, including *MAKERS,* a six-part series that looks at how the women's movement affected traditionally male-dominated fields, from moviemaking to lawmaking; *Women, War, and Peace,* a series by producer and philanthropist Abigail Disney, which highlights how women experience conflict and help rebuild their societies; and *Half the Sky,* Nicholas Kristof and Sheryl WuDunn's documentary based on their best-selling book about the oppression and courage of women and girls worldwide.

"People are listening to each other's stories," Patricia told us. "And I thought it would be important to tell the stories in a way that could inspire, especially young girls, and also provide hope to some of the women who are meeting unconscionable, terrible challenges." After serving as assistant secretary of state for educational and cultural affairs under President George W. Bush, she views her work at the CPB as giving her a "media megaphone," extending the important work she began at the State Department to educate and build tolerance and respect.

Thanks to influential figures like Nicholas Kristof, Sheryl WuDunn, Patricia Harrison, and others, what were once deemed "women's issues" have taken their rightful place in mainstream public discourse. And entertainment powerhouses like America Ferrera, Geena Davis, and Shonda Rhimes, the creator of the television shows *Grey's Anatomy* and *Scandal,* are portraying women in a whole new light. Emma Watson, Meryl Streep, Angelina Jolie, and other actors are using their star power to bring these issues to the fore. Matthew Winkler, the cofounder and longtime editor in chief at *Bloomberg News* (now the editor in chief emeritus), sought to integrate women into the company's hard-hitting financial and economics coverage, on the premise that women were an important part of the economy and their stories should be told.

Nicholas Kristof has been especially effective in delivering the stories of women and girls, thanks to the wide reach of his regular columns in the *New York Times* and his million and a half Twitter followers. Through his work, he has brought greater awareness to the challenges facing women and girls around the world, while casting light on some of the darkest places that we would rather not see: women suffering from sexual exploitation by traffickers and the unspeakable pain caused by rape as a tool of war. There is nowhere he will not travel to capture the human rights stories of our time. He raises our collective awareness of the consequences of gender inequality and calls on us to help transform the lives of women and girls. In *Half the Sky*, Nicholas reminds us what's at stake: "In the nineteenth century, the central moral challenge was slavery. In the twentieth century, it was the battle against totalitarianism. We believe that in this century the paramount moral challenge will be the struggle for gender equality around the world."

His and Sheryl's most recent book and documentary film series is called *A Path Appears*, which examines hard issues like human trafficking in the United States and the cycle of poverty in Haiti. Nicholas and Sheryl, joined onscreen by celebrity activists like Ashley Judd and Jennifer Garner, offer readers and viewers inspiration and examples of how to get involved in solving these problems, sometimes in small but meaningful ways. Visitors to the website apathappears.org can contribute to the organizations featured in the films, find ways to volunteer, sign petitions, and share their own stories of promoting change.

Since the invention of the printing press in the fifteenth century, the written word has been instrumental in the spread of ideas, images, and information. The media's reach and power has grown exponentially in our age of digital connectivity and content delivered on mobile devices. In addition to Nicholas and Sheryl, other documentarians, like Sharmeen Obaid Chinoy, whose Oscar-winning *Saving Face* followed Pakistan's acid violence victims and a reconstructive surgeon who operates on them, are using digital platforms to combine storytelling with activism. On savingfacefilm.com, you can watch the trailer and join the fight against acid violence through the nonprofit organization Project SAAVE (Stand Against Acid Violence). *Miss Representation*, a documentary about the media's portrayal of women and girls, offers tools for discussing the film's issues among teenagers and families.

Chime for Change (chimeforchange.org) is another online and offline campaign that combines the power of storytelling, celebrity reach, and corporate support for far-reaching impact. Founded by Gucci, Chime for Change is a multimedia crowdfunding and digital storytelling platform. One of its lead spokeswomen is Salma Hayek, the actress and outspoken advocate against gender-based violence, whose husband, François-Henri Pinault, is the CEO of Kering, Gucci's parent company. François-Henri himself is a leading voice on the topic within the European business community; the Kering Foundation supports forty-seven NGO partners working on issues like domestic violence, sexual violence, and female genital mutilation, and also works with employees to train them and raise awareness about these issues. As Marie-Claire Daveu, Kering's chief sustainability officer, told us, solidarity with women is in the company's DNA.

"For every level of society, if you are rich, if you are poor, you have violence," Marie-Claire said. "We have to bring something very operational, because a lot of our employees are women. Our customers are women and we also have so many women in the supply chain. We try also to sensitize our own employees, because we think that our assistants, our bosses, our women managers can have this kind of problem. They also understand that there is no shame to speak about it."

A social action campaign called Girl Rising, led by executive producer, cofounder, and CEO Holly Gordon, documents young women worldwide on their quest to get an education and realize their potential. To accompany its groundbreaking films, Girl Rising has created innovative ways to get involved with girls' education through its website, girlrising.com. The Girl Rising movement is going global, beginning in India and the Democratic Republic of Congo, where local-language versions of the film *Girl Rising* will be screened to encourage communities to embrace the importance of educating girls. By opening viewers' eyes to the challenges and triumphs of the lives of women and girls, these and other media makers are shifting perspectives and moving people to action.

Many of these media maestros are gathering women together offline too. We have seen how Women in the World and the *Fortune* Most Powerful Women Summits connect leaders in real life. Arianna Huffington, founder of the *Huffington Post* news site, is also using her platform to help women redefine success by putting well-being and compassion at the center, with her new book *Thrive* and a related conference series. Mika Brzezinski, the popular cohost of the MSNBC show *Morning Joe*, is encouraging women to know their worth and is launching a Know Your Value live events tour for women, based on her 2011 book *Knowing Your Value*, with panels on topics like negotiating a raise, and prizes for women who can best articulate their value. Moira Forbes, the American journalist and daughter of Steve Forbes, is the publisher of *Forbes-Woman*, and each year she gathers an impressive group of women from a variety of sectors at the *Forbes* Women's Summit. Recent topics have included redefining power and transforming the roles of engagement.

Oprah Winfrey is perhaps the best example of a woman who has used her media power for purpose. One of the most successful and influential television personalities of all time, Oprah went from a poverty-stricken childhood in Mississippi to receiving the Presidential Medal of Freedom. At every stage of her career, she has been dedicated to opening doors for other women and girls. She started a girls' boarding school in South Africa, encouraged viewers to donate and volunteer their time to worthy causes, and mobilized millions of dollars from philanthropists and other generous individuals through the charity Oprah's Angel Network. Zainab Salbi, the founder of Women for Women International, whom we met in chapter 6, told us that her numerous appearances on Oprah's show were essential to her organization's success. Today Zainab herself is embarking on a media venture that aims to tell positive, inspiring stories of women in the Middle East which can be reflected back within the culture to men and to the women themselves.

Oprah understands the value of partnering for purpose with women from corporate and nonprofit realms, multiplying their reach and power. She recently joined forces with one of Starbucks's most senior executives, Annie Young-Scrivner, who now heads the company's recently launched tea retailer, Teavana.

Annie's background and philosophy made her an ideal candidate for the job. Born in Taiwan to Chinese parents, who moved the family to Seattle when she was seven, Annie has worked in more than two dozen countries, honing her ability to relate with people around the globe. Like Oprah, Annie believes in creating community and connection — and one way to do that, of course, is over a cup of tea. Teavana invited Oprah, a tea lover, to work with the company's chief teaologist to create her own blend of spicy chai, the sale of which helps fund girls' education. Launched in April 2014, Teavana Oprah Chai raised $5 million for the Oprah Winfrey Leadership Academy in its first year. They are also partnering with other organizations, such as Girls Inc., the goal of which is to give girls the tools and support they need through training and peer networks.

"I think it's really about living what your company value is," Annie told us. "Our mission is to inspire and nurture the human spirit, one person, one cup, and one neighborhood at a time." For Annie, living those values means using her power for purpose wherever she can.

Lan Yang, known as "the Oprah of China" and one of the country's most popular television hosts, hopes her enormous media power can help support a generation of Chinese women experiencing their country's profound socioeconomic changes. Lan Yang is an accomplished journalist and the founder of a women's talk show, *Her Village,* which she's grown into an online community for Chinese women that reaches three hundred million people a month through both television and online content. She, like a growing number of successful Chinese women, including real estate developer Zhang Xin of SOHO China, are encouraging others to pay their good fortune forward through philanthropy, which is nascent but developing in China. Through her foundation, Lan Yang is actively growing and training China's philanthropic community, and played an instrumental role in bringing Bill Gates and Warren Buffett to China to meet with some promising charitable donors. She is excited about the role that Chinese women will play in its new economy — and especially how they will use their power for purpose.

Katie Couric is another example of a woman using her influence in the media industry to make a lasting impact. An award-winning journalist with thirty-five years in the news business, Katie has built an impressive career as a reporter, television host, and author. After fifteen years as the popular host of the *Today* show on NBC, she went on to be the first solo woman news anchor of the *CBS Evening News* and then host her own daytime talk show, *Katie.* She is now the global news anchor for Yahoo.

Off the screen, Katie is a dedicated mother and passionate advocate for cancer awareness. Following the tragic deaths of her husband John Paul "Jay" Monahan to colon cancer and, four years later, her sister Emily Couric to pancreatic cancer, Katie has gone on to cofound several organizations that have raised awareness and significant funds for cancer research, including Stand Up to Cancer, the National Colorectal Cancer Research Alliance, and the Jay Monahan Center for Gastrointestinal Health.

Meryl Streep has used her star power to champion female leaders and the rights of women everywhere. She has lent her voice and support to myriad women's organizations and has played strong female roles on the screen. She won an Academy Award in 2012 for her portrayal of British prime minister Margaret Thatcher, and is set to play the British feminist Emmeline Pankhurst, a founder of the Women's Social and Political Union, in the film *Suffragette,* about British women's fight for the right to vote. Streep has also become an advocate of the National Women's History Museum, which is in the making.

"History until the 20th century was written by one member of the human family and it wasn't the mother," Streep has said. "It was dad. That's who wrote history and . . . what was important? Movements of armies, sovereignty of nations, all sorts of things. But women were there all along and they have incredible stories that we don't know anything about."

One key part of that history is *Ms.,* "the first periodical ever to be created, owned, and operated entirely by women." By 1971, the growing feminist movement in the United States was ready for its own mainstream magazine. Gloria Steinem, then a budding journalist and feminist organizer — who would go on to be recognized as the leader of the movement — and Brenda Feigen, an attorney and activist, held two packed meetings in their respective apartments, with interested writers, feminists, and reporters. Out of those meetings came *Ms.*

The first issue sold out of its 300,000-copy press run within days. Mail from readers poured in, much of it grateful letters from women who felt their lives, concerns, and challenges were finally being addressed. Now eighty-one years young, Steinem continues to speak about feminism, its history, and its future. She encourages women to form networks and communities with others working for social change, including allies in the environmental movement, those advocating for health care and domestic workers, and those in the civil rights movement. "We need to move from dependence to independence to interdependence," she admonishes.

While all of these women and men have used their platforms to tell and commission diverse stories about the lives of women, bringing topics like acid violence, sex trafficking, and girls' access to education to the fore, women's voices are still the exception, not the norm. In 2012, women made up only 36 percent of newsroom staffers in papers across the United States, a figure that has hardly budged since 1999.

Entertainment Takes the Lead in Depicting Women Leaders

The television industry has already managed to elect a female president in 2005 (Geena Davis, in *Commander in Chief*) and vice president in 2012 (Julia Louis-Dreyfus, in *Veep*), well before we've seen the real thing. Just as real-life stories of heroes like Sunitha Krishnan and Leymah Gbowee can inspire us, entertainment, too, can allow us to envision a more equitable future and provide role models for girls and young women.

By one analysis, it will take more than a century for the U.S. Congress to reach gender parity at its current rate of progress; by contrast, actor and media advocate Geena Davis notes, entertainment is "the one hugely imbalanced sector of society where we can make the change overnight."

"In the time it takes to make the next movie or create the next TV show, we can achieve parity," Geena told us. "Yes, there are woefully few women CEOs in the world, but there can be lots of them onscreen. The same can be true with girls and women in STEM. How long will it take to achieve gender equality in boardrooms and C-suites in the real world? A boardroom scene can be half women in a TV show or movie that shoots *tomorrow*. It's progress that can be accomplished with the stroke of a pen in the screenplay and would make a huge impact on how we view women in the world."

As proof, in the past decade, we've seen the "*CSI* effect" take hold: young women who've grown up watching female heroes of crime-scene television dramas have entered the forensics departments of top universities in large numbers, accounting for between 75 and 80 percent of students in accredited programs across the United States, according to several analyses, about twice the percentage of women in nonforensic STEM fields. "Women are the future of forensic science," Virginia Commonwealth University's forensics program director Bill Eggleston told a reporter from the Associated Press. "It's not just evolving, it's a revolution."

Detoxifying Our Media Diet

Unfortunately, depictions of strong female leads are still the exception, not the rule. Geena put numbers behind this by launching the Geena Davis Institute on Gender in Media, which is led by Madeline Di Nonno. The institute studies how women and girls are portrayed on television and in film and has now sponsored the largest amount of research ever done on gender depictions in media. Its widely cited original research is shocking: a 2012 analysis of gender stereotypes determined that male characters accounted for over 70 percent of speaking parts in family films from 2006 to 2011. A 2014 global report showed that female characters are often cast in a sexualized light — they are more than twice as likely as male characters to be thin, wear revealing outfits, or appear in the nude.

The onscreen marginalizing and devaluing of women happens even when they're not in the spotlight. Only 17 percent of actors in crowd scenes in film are women. Seeing these depictions over and over creates the false assumption that a group in which women constitute 17 percent is "normal," Geena observed. That might be one more explanation for why we're stalled at 16 percent of women in leadership. "You get up to about 17 percent women, whether it's tenured professors or law partners or military officers or Congress, and because the vast amount of media we consume has trained us to see that as the normal ratio, you feel done," says Geena.

Research has confirmed that audiences internalize these imbalances and provocative stereotypes. Media scholar Ethan Zuckerman of the MIT Center for Civic Media often discusses the "media diet," or what we watch and read, and points out that simply tracking people's media intake may influence them to make "healthier choices." Just as a steady flow of junk food will increase the likelihood of illness, the consumption of popular culture can affect young women's psychological health. For example, one study found that "messages and images that focus on the value of appearances and thinness for females have a significant negative impact on body satisfaction, weight preoccupation, eating patterns, and the emotional well-being of women in western culture." Although the poisonous effects of an unhealthy media diet aren't limited to women, it takes an especially heavy toll on their self-esteem. When girls absorb the prevailing stereotypes on television shows, it can impact not only their confidence but also their life choices.

Unfortunately, the pernicious effects of American entertainment culture extend beyond its borders. Movies and TV shows are among its chief cultural exports: one estimate found that American films and other entertainment media can account for over 90 percent of market share in some countries. To give you an idea of how deeply Hollywood movies and TV shows can penetrate a foreign culture, consider what happened to Geena Davis following a talk she gave in Washington, D.C., a few years ago.

A woman came running after her as she was leaving the event. She begged Geena, "Please, please. I am from Congo, you have to help us."

What the woman said next startled her: "Please make them stop sending *Real Housewives of Beverly Hills* to the Congo. It is so awful and damaging for us."

"Well, I can't control that," Geena told us. "But to a large extent, we in the U.S. are responsible for sending a very negative view of women and girls around the world."

Geena had been both smart and lucky throughout her career, landing groundbreaking roles like Dottie, the catcher in *A League of Their Own,* and Thelma, the runaway housewife in *Thelma and Louise.* "Because I played some parts along the way that really resonated with women, I became keenly aware of how few opportunities we give audiences to feel excited and inspired by the *female* character," she told us.

Today, Geena is using a combination of research and her power as a Hollywood insider to advance her goal to "dramatically increase the percentage of female characters—and reduce gender stereotyping—in media made for kids." She was inspired to launch the institute after watching children's shows and G-rated videos with her then two-year-old daughter. While she wasn't keeping an exact count, it seemed as though there were nearly three times as many male characters as female. Wondering if she was hallucinating, she brought up this imbalance with female friends, who were shocked to realize they hadn't noticed this until she pointed it out. The institute sponsored the first research on G-rated films. Sure enough, for every female speaking character in children's movies, there were two male characters with speaking roles.

"That was interesting, so I started bringing it up with people in the industry," Geena recalled. "If I had a meeting set up with someone already—say, a studio executive or producer—I would casually bring it up: 'Have you ever noticed how few female characters there are in entertainment made for kids?' And to a person, they would say, 'Oh, no, no, that has been fixed!' Often they would cite a movie with pretty much one female character as proof that things had changed and the problem was fixed."

Geena is also a fan of the bottom-line argument: films starring women are a profitable investment. A 2014 analysis by the statistics website FiveThirtyEight.com examined thousands of films for whether they passed the "Bechdel test," a three-part rule devised by the cartoonist Alison Bechdel in partnership with her friend Liz Wallace, which specified a movie should feature (1) at least two named female characters (2) who have a conversation with one another that is (3) not about men.

The analysis found that films that passed the Bechdel test—only about half of the 1,794 films released from 1970 to 2013—were, on average, smaller-budget films than those that didn't (think major Hollywood action movies). Yet the films that passed the test had a higher gross return on investment, dollar for dollar, than films that failed it. Furthermore, FiveThirtyEight found no evidence that movies with female characters did not "travel well," an excuse often given by Hollywood studios, which rely heavily on international earnings. Recent hits like *Bridesmaids* and *The Hunger Games,* not to mention the $1 billion-plus-grossing children's animated hit *Frozen,* are also making the case.

"Hollywood pretty much operates under the assumption that women will watch men, but men will not watch women, and they apply that to kids too," Geena told us. "But that is not true—research shows that movies starring a female character or directed by a woman are absolutely equally profitable as movies starring or directed by men. We've seen it over and over again—movies that appeal to women or teen girls can be wildly successful."

In recent years, possibly due to increasing demand, we are beginning to see a shift in some forms of media. Mainstream women's magazines, for example, have expanded their coverage of more serious women's issues. Titles like *Cosmopolitan, Marie Claire, Elle, Vogue, More, Harper's Bazaar,* and *Glamour* now regularly feature content about human rights, women making a difference, politics, career advice, and female role models. Advertising has also followed suit, with brands like Dove and Always winning female consumers with empowering images. Dove's "Real Beauty" campaign celebrates healthy bodies of all shapes and sizes, encouraging a positive body image. One of Always's "Like a Girl" commercials asks what it means to do something like a girl. It contrasts teenagers who, when asked to "run like a girl," prance around and pretend to worry about their hair, with fearless pre-adolescents who throw imaginary baseballs, run vigorously, and throw punches when asked to "fight like a girl." It asks, "When did doing something like a girl become an insult?" and reframes "like a girl" as shorthand for performing a task with drive, energy, and ferocity.

The children's show *Sesame Street* is doing its part to promote messages of female empowerment. In 2011, it featured a song and video that reinforces that girls can become anything, depicting a lead girl Muppet singing, "I'm a girl who's going to change the world." The video then shows her as an astronaut, a judge, and a doctor. Her backup Muppets sing, "She's going to change the world. She's going to make the world a better world."

Sherrie Westin, the executive vice president for global impact for *Sesame Street,* is working to make sure its programs are a tool for development around the world, all while teaching valuable lessons and enhancing girls' education. *Sesame Street,* through culturally sensitive curricula and various media, uses its lovable, engaging Muppets to teach and inspire — especially girls who are still too often marginalized and kept out of school.

Girls are introduced to the Muppets, who can serve as compelling role models: Raya, for example, is a smart and empowered Muppet who teaches good health and hygiene habits. Kami, who lives with HIV, provides vital health information and also shows children afflicted with HIV that they have nothing to fear. Khokha, a Muppet in Egypt, wants to be an engineer or a doctor, and the program emphasizes the education of girls. In Afghanistan, the Muppet Gulguly works hard on her schoolwork, showing all the girls in her country that they belong in school. And equally important, the characters demonstrate to little boys that it is okay for girls to get an education and pursue nontraditional roles and responsibilities, planting the seeds for societal change.

At different levels of the media and in new digital channels, women are redefining whose stories are told and whose voices are heard. Whether taking part in grassroots social media campaigns or rising through the ranks of America's top newsrooms or wielding insider influence in Hollywood, women are leveraging their voices to push for better, more realistic representations of their lives, their leaders, and their looks. We believe the media can and will be instrumental in changing perspectives on the value and role of women and girls.

12

Moments in History:
Our Moment Is Now

IN 1848, CHARLOTTE WOODWARD was earning a pittance stitching gloves in her home in Waterloo, New York. Like other women of her era, the former schoolteacher, not yet twenty years old, had been denied property ownership rights, citizenship, and political representation. In some states, if a woman married, everything she owned or earned belonged to her husband. That July, Woodward was intrigued by an announcement she read in the newspaper about a meeting of women to be held in a chapel forty miles away in the town of Seneca Falls. Looking for an opportunity to better her life and that of her family, she did what women have done throughout history and to this day: she joined a network.

Earlier that month, over tea one Sunday, Elizabeth Cady Stanton, Lucretia Mott, and three other women came up with the idea for the Seneca Falls Convention. Stanton and Mott recalled their journey to London, where, as women, they had been relegated to the sidelines at an international abolitionist gathering. They agreed then and there to organize a women's rights convention when they returned to the United States. Back home, they discussed their frustration with their second-class status, and together they drew up an announcement for an assembly "to discuss the social, civil, and religious condition and rights of woman." Their resulting campaign to reform child custody, divorce, property laws, equal pay, and suffrage gained steam from the moral outrage and organizational channels of the abolitionist movement.

Stanton and Mott also drew inspiration from the writings of Sarah Moore Grimké. The erudite daughter of a plantation owner, Grimké was one of the first women to espouse women's rights and perhaps the earliest proponent of equal pay for women in the United States. Her revulsion at slavery moved her to join the abolitionist cause, but her energies shifted to women's rights when, working as a schoolteacher, she learned that her male colleagues earned three times as much for the same work.

Charlotte Woodward longed for connection to such a purposeful sorority. She tentatively approached her neighbors to see if anyone might like to join her on the trip to Seneca Falls, which would take more than two days. She was met with mixed reactions when she knocked on doors. Undeterred, she set out early on July 19 by horse and carriage, accompanied by the handful of fellow travelers she had mustered. If they formed a dishearteningly thin procession at first, they were joined at each crossroad by other women, gaining heart and strength.

Also traveling to Seneca Falls were abolitionists, including the former slave Frederick Douglass, who found common cause with women's emancipation and would prove to be an important male ally of female suffrage. Years later, at a speech before the International Council of Women in Washington, D.C., he would state:

> There are few facts in my humble history to which I look back with more satisfaction than to the fact, recorded in the history of the woman-suffrage movement, that I was sufficiently enlightened at that early day, and when only a few years from slavery, to support your resolution for woman suffrage. I have done very little in this world in which to glory except this one act — and I certainly glory in that. When I ran away from slavery, it was for myself; when I advocated emancipation, it was for my people; but when I stood up for the rights of women, self was out of the question, and I found a little nobility in the act.

Others on the road to the gathering included pacifist Quakers from Philadelphia, wives and mothers who had never had the opportunity to work outside their homes, and teenage girls, including one who had started going door to door at age twelve with antislavery petitions. When Woodward reached the hot, packed Wesleyan Methodist Chapel in Seneca Falls, she found a diverse crowd, bound together by a shared purpose, moved to further action by the inspiring speeches.

To be sure, not everyone was moved. The convention was widely derided in the press. A Philadelphia newspaper editorial huffed, "A woman is nobody. A wife is everything." An Albany newspaper warned that equal rights would "demoralize and degrade" women. The convention was condemned as "the most shocking and unnatural event ever recorded in the history of womanity."

By the end of the momentous two-day gathering, one hundred signatures — those of sixty-eight women and thirty-two men — were dry on the Declaration of Sentiments, which demanded basic civil, economic, and political rights, including the vote, for women. The negative press fueled publicity, as word of mouth traveled and spurred women's rights activists to form regional groups. By 1850, a national event held in Worcester, Massachusetts, drew about a thousand attendees. In 1851, Susan B. Anthony would join Elizabeth Cady Stanton in her efforts, spending the next fifty years of her life advocating for women's suffrage. Each year, Anthony traveled around the country, giving up to one hundred speeches, in an effort to educate her fellow citizens.

Given the pace of transportation and communication in the mid-nineteenth century, but mostly the momentous shift in thinking that would be needed to secure the vote, the early women's movement was a slow-burning phenomenon. It would take more than seventy years from the date of the Seneca Falls Convention before women would secure the right to vote, when the Nineteenth Amendment, also known as the Susan B. Anthony Amendment, passed on June 4, 1919. Neither she nor Elizabeth Cady Stanton would live to see women cast their votes. Indeed, Charlotte Woodward, the young glove maker, was the only participant of the Seneca Falls Convention who lived to see their dream achieved.

One year after the passage of the Nineteenth Amendment, in 1920, halfway around the world in Jeyhounabad, a small village in western Iran, a fourteen-year-old girl was beginning to feel the first painful signs of losing her sight. Malak Jân Nemati, born in 1906 into a family of notables with an ancient mystical lineage, would prove instrumental in transforming the mindset of a male-dominated community toward a more egalitarian view of the role and value of women and girls.

Located near Mount Bisotoun, Jeyhounabad is an agricultural village whose climate is marked by harsh winters and blistering summers. With no electricity (that would come only in the 1980s), the rustic living conditions of Jeyhounabad during Malak Jân's time have been likened to those of premodern life in the West. The simple clay houses formed a small and intimate community that was isolated, dependent wholly on the surrounding agricultural land.

Jeyhounabad and the nearby villages, however, were not isolated from the regional and national patriarchal view of the role of women and girls. Rooted in age-old tradition, females were deemed subservient to males in every way. Women were not entitled to express a point of view, and under the law, their statements would be considered as having half the value of men's. The birth of a girl was not a celebrated occasion, but rather one for which people would frequently offer their condolences. Girls did not go to school, and often they were fed less than boys. From a young age, girls were assigned household chores with the goal of preparing them for marriage and the bearing of children.

Malak Jân's father, an influential mystic and poet, had a different vision for his young daughter. Contrary to the customs of the time, Malak Jân was offered an education akin to that of her elder brother; she studied classical philosophy, theology, Persian language and literature, and music. This would provide the basis for her lifelong pursuit of knowledge, which would include far-ranging subjects such as mathematics, biology, law, history, and geography. Her teenage years, however, would begin a life of physical frailty and health challenges, as she began to feel the effects of a chronic and acutely painful ocular condition that would render her completely blind by the age of twenty. As a blind, frail young woman in an environment that rewarded physical strength, Malak Jân would clearly suffer social and material disadvantages.

Yet despite these obstacles, the strength of Malak Jân's character and convictions would lead her to become a revered sage and powerful leader in her region, an influential thinker who would later be recognized well beyond the fields of Jeyhounabad. Equipped with uncommon courage, wisdom, inner strength, and generosity, she would become a champion for the rights of women and girls, often at great risk to herself. Her power would stem not from her physical strength, material position, or status, but rather from the depth of her conviction — the power of her perspective.

For Malak Jân, acquiring the correct philosophy of life, shaped by one's intellectual and moral development, was fundamental to the pursuit of a meaningful life. She emphasized that service to others in the midst of tending to one's daily affairs provided the fuel for self-knowledge and ethical progress. She firmly believed that each person had a duty to use his or her positive traits for the benefit of others.

It was with that mindset that Malak Jân sought to improve the lives of her fellow villagers, from providing daily meals to those in need to introducing much-needed innovations to her community. "Though hardly leaving her native surroundings, her social initiatives were downright revolutionary," her biographer, Leili Anvar, wrote. "She was instrumental in bringing electricity to the village and encouraged villagers to grow fruits and vegetables by introducing new irrigation techniques." She also instituted a system of microcredit whereby villagers could borrow on the honor system to improve their own livelihoods. Her wisdom, generosity, and unwavering attentiveness to everyone — from the peasant villager to the educated urbanite, including many who had traveled from the West to seek her counsel — captured the hearts and minds of all.

But Malak Jân understood that progress for her community would require more than just modernizing infrastructure and farming techniques. Progress would also demand a change in mindset about the value and role of women and girls. Under her leadership, gender reform in her community meant feeding girls and boys an equal amount of food, allowing girls to go to school and women to attend classes, equal inheritance and property rights, and full economic participation and financial independence for women. Malak Jân's insistence on the equal participation of women was not, however, limited to civic and familial life. She also insisted on their full participation in the moral, intellectual, and spiritual life of their community, for which she was subject to severe criticism and even threats on her life.

Yet her patience, perseverance, and generosity of spirit ultimately won out. "The stunning contrast between these rugged tall men and this frail woman who spoke in a soft and composed voice has left a great impression on those who witnessed their willful submission to her authority," Anvar wrote. Ultimately, Malak Jân believed the education of both men and women would be the most powerful catalyst for progress. She would often say if you alter people's thinking, their actions will follow.

> By facilitating the emancipation of women, she naturally led an entire community steeped in tradition toward a more modern and equitable conception of the rights and duties of human beings towards one another. She encouraged them to challenge their own cultural, social and religious heritage and to become aware of the negative impact of prejudice and cultural determinism. In short, the transformation of an entire culture may be one of her greatest enduring legacies.

Malak Jân's presence and wisdom has had an impact on people around the world, an achievement marked by the centennial celebration of her birth at the Asia Society in New York City in 2006. Her life serves as a powerful example for those who want to help shift perspectives on the value of women and girls. "She was well aware," her biographer wrote, "that during her own lifetime she would not see a world in which women were equal to men. Yet, she was hopeful that on the scale of human history, each individual struggle would count toward establishing this equality."

In 1995, two years after Malak Jân passed away, some forty thousand people converged in Beijing for the Fourth World Conference on Women, the largest conference in the United Nations' 50-year history. Nearly 150 years after Elizabeth Cady Stanton and 99 others inked the Declaration of Sentiments, 189 nations signed the Beijing Declaration and Platform for Action, a document that Phumzile Mlambo-Ngcuka, the executive director of UN Women, has called "the most comprehensive global policy framework and blueprint for action for equality and human rights of women and girls everywhere."

In early 2015, with the twentieth anniversary of the Beijing conference fast approaching, Secretary-General Ban Ki-moon called for a renewed commitment to its goals. In a foreword to a republication of the Beijing Declaration, Ban wrote, "When we empower women and girls, we will realize a better future for all." In March of 2015, Hillary Clinton, Chelsea Clinton, and Melinda Gates presented the *Full Participation Report*, a result of their No Ceilings initiative. The report aggregates and analyzes 850,000 data points on the status of women and girls from more than 190 countries, to better understand the gaps in and progress toward equality.

"Data is a road map to impact," Melinda Gates told us. "Behind every data point is a real person's struggle for a better life. So the data captures the truth of what's going on in communities around the world. But when you add up all the data points, they reveal patterns you can't see by any other method."

What did these 850,000 data points reveal? As Hillary Clinton put it, "Despite all this progress, when it comes to the full participation of women and girls, we are just not there yet."

So how can we get there?

We hope this book has demonstrated that there is an undeniable momentum building, and getting there is within our reach. The data is in, and it is conclusive: advancing women and girls can fast-forward us to that better world we all want for ourselves and for generations to come. Women are not only populating the leadership ranks but, just as important, are increasingly participating in every area of society. And as women are achieving power at every level, they are often using that power for the purpose of advancing other women and girls. They are being joined by an ever-growing number of men, working together across sectors, across nations, and across economic strata to build partnerships for the benefit of all. Education, media, and especially technology are providing unprecedented opportunities for acceleration.

Since Seneca Falls, we have been on a journey to women's full and equal participation, a journey that requires a change in the way we view and value half the world's population. This shift in perspective starts within each of us: knowing our own power, finding our purpose, and connecting with others to turn that purpose into action.

As we have learned from our own personal journeys, by connecting with like-minded people who share our values, we can accelerate not just our own lives, but progress for women everywhere. And we are not on this journey alone: male champions from around the world are recognizing that investing in women and girls is not solely a women's issue.

Progress for women means progress for all. We believe there is a collective shift under way, evidenced by the mounting data, fueled by technology and connectivity, and propelled by emerging women leaders. There are few propitious moments in history when forces converge, creating the potential for a transformative leap — a moment when we can move fast and we can move forward.

Our moment is now.

Appendix A: Toolkit

From Anecdote to Action

WHAT FOLLOWS IS A TOOLKIT based on research, our own experience, and the collective wisdom of the women and men we have met from around the world, including many of those we have interviewed for this book. It is designed to help you evaluate your own work and life through the lens of power, purpose, and connection, and take action based on the tips and tactics that have worked for us and for others. We have also included a work plan called "Making the Case for Women and Girls." It's a playbook on how to make the case in your own life, in the arena of your choosing—whether it's within your government, company, organization, or community.

To complement the toolkit, we have included a directory of resources that can help you take the practical next steps you need to get involved. This directory includes where to find the latest research and suggestions of a number of organizations dedicated to advancing women and girls. For those who have started or are interested in starting their own company, social enterprise, or nonprofit, we have also included some additional resources. Owing to the space limitations of the printed book, we have created www.senecawomen.com, where you can connect to more inspiring people, ideas, research, organizations, events, and opportunities.

We hope these tools will help you build a better understanding of how you can combine your own power and purpose to achieve success and meaning in your life while building a better world.

I. Know Your Power

We now know the data is in. Women collectively command unprecedented resources, access, and influence. But it's equally important to know the data on yourself and your organization so you can situate yourself within this shifting paradigm, assess your own power, and define what success looks like for you.

Take a few minutes each day, over the next seven days, to assess your strengths, skills, and resources. What skills have you developed? What natural strengths do you bring to the table? What weaknesses do you have? The answers will help you identify where you need reinforcement. If you are finding this exercise difficult, ask a trusted colleague, friend, or loved one to help.

Corporate coaches advise their clients not only to think about what they need to accomplish today's goals but also to think strategically about what problems will need to be solved, or what skills will be relevant, in the future. Set aside the time and think about your own role and how to acquire or upgrade the skills you might need to stay relevant and ahead of the curve. As Wilma Wallace, vice president, global responsibility, business and human rights at Gap Inc., told us, "You need to invest in spending some time reflecting on your past to this moment. What makes you happy? What are you good at? How do you want to show up? Do you want to show up as someone who's a doer? Do you want to show up as someone who is a strategic thinker? What's your brand? What's your value proposition? What makes you distinct? And use that to guide you in what you invest in and how you spend your time, and whom you spend your time with. And follow your inner radar."

We understand it's not easy to carve out time for these extracurriculars. As leadership expert Herminia Ibarra notes, informal meetings, classes, and interactions can feel like "unstructured work" with no clear payoff. But understanding what makes your organization tick, where you fit in, and who and what you need to know are all necessary steps for creating opportunity. "We mostly don't do it because of habit and inertia," writes Ibarra. "Tuning in to the outside is unstructured work — networking, walking the halls, going to lunch — we don't even know where to begin. Value it as much as the required meetings and email duty. The payoff will come in the longer run."

Vishakha Desai, a professor at Columbia University's School of International and Public Affairs and a special adviser on global affairs to the university's president, suggests dreaming big but knowing what the individual steps are toward that dream. "As a dancer, one of the metaphors I've used is that I want to soar like Baryshnikov, but I also want to land like Baryshnikov," she told us. "Soar like an eagle and land like a rock. We have got to figure out both of those: how to break it down, and say what the steps are, and how do you then connect it back together again. Kids don't always get enough training to do that. It's skills-building: break down your big idea into manageable parts, but don't ever forget the big idea. You have to count the trees and you have to see the forest."

CREATING CONFIDENCE AND FIGHTING FEAR

One major obstacle facing women as they seek to achieve their goals is the confidence deficit — even at the highest levels of leadership. Katty Kay and Claire Shipman are two accomplished broadcast journalists: Kay is the anchor of the BBC's *World News America,* Shipman is a reporter for ABC News. Between them, they've interviewed heads of state, Hollywood stars, and senior business executives. Yet after speaking to scores of highly credentialed female power players for their 2009 book, *Womenomics,* they reached a crucial, and surprising, realization: despite their achievements, some of the most successful women they met admitted to lacking confidence. Shipman and Kay described "the power centers of this nation" as "zones of female self-doubt — that is, when they include women at all."

Everyone experiences fear in the face of a challenge, or when one is trying something new. But Kay and Shipman were struck by the persistence and perniciousness of this male-female confidence gap. As they researched it for what would become their second book, *The Confidence Code,* they found study after study that not only proved the confidence gap's existence, but demonstrated how it hampers women's performance on everything from school exams to salary negotiations and promotions. What is confidence, anyway? Kay and Shipman are partial to a description from Richard Petty, a professor of psychology at Ohio State University: "Confidence is the stuff that turns thoughts into actions."

Kay and Shipman trace the roots of men's confidence back to the grade school playground. Boys roughhouse, tease each other, and knock each other down. They play sports, tasting loss with relative regularity. These activities build resilience and comfort with failure, qualities that girls, who at that age typically outperform boys academically and behaviorally, are less likely to learn. By the time high-achieving girls get to college, this fear of failure manifests itself in what has been called "B-phobia," or a fear of getting anything less than an A. Studies have found that B-phobia can deter women from taking challenging courses of study. They shy away from STEM fields and economics and instead pursue humanities courses, where students on average get higher grades. The punch line, of course, is that despite their superior grades, women are often less qualified for the highest-paying jobs, many of which are now in STEM-related fields.

So how can you embrace the risks that bring the biggest payoffs? The first step is to challenge your fears.

GET COMFORTABLE WITH "NO"

Part and parcel of building confidence is getting comfortable with the word "no." All too often, we don't ask for things because we are afraid of getting an answer we don't want to hear. But as many will attest, it often takes many no's to get to yes. Instead of seeing no as failure, one technique is to reframe it as a step to success. Reshma Saujani — Yale Law School graduate, daughter of Indian refugees from Uganda, founder and CEO of the thriving nonprofit Girls Who Code, and the former deputy public advocate of New York City — hardly comes across as a natural cheerleader for failure. But Reshma, who applied to Yale Law three times before convincing the dean in person to let her in, insists that failure is something women should cozy up to — she even suggests throwing "failure parties."

"We don't talk about our struggles enough," Reshma told us. "We learn so much more, I think, from our struggles when they hurt really bad. I think having those failures, throwing parties and having people stand up and share what went wrong in their life and how they got over it, is critical to women's leadership." That also means not expecting a smooth ascent to the top of your profession.

Shamina Singh, executive director of MasterCard's Center for Inclusive Growth, said, "My life has been a series of chutes and ladders — ups and downs — with some roundabouts thrown in for good measure . . . and definitely not linear. I'm always questioning and pushing to find a better way. It's about combining forward movement and momentum with serious reflection and assessment. Inertia is not an option."

EMBRACE FAILURE IN ORDER TO SUCCEED

As we learned in chapter 10, Reshma's greatest accomplishment came on the heels of a blistering failure — her unsuccessful run for Congress in 2010. Her experience campaigning in the Fourteenth District of New York had led her to refocus her purpose and start the successful non-profit Girls Who Code, an organization that targets low-income high school girls and teaches them computer coding.

In her book *The Up Side of Down: Why Failing Well Is the Key to Success*, Megan McCardle argues that failing is not only part of life, but one of the best ways to learn. In researching the book, Megan found that most businesses fail, and the most successful entrepreneurs and executives cite early failures — and the lessons learned — as the key factors in their success. Failure is information: it's advice on what doesn't work, so you can act more strategically the next time.

To get comfortable with the fear of failure, start by imagining what it actually looks like. Visualize it, and ask yourself: What am I afraid of? What is the worst thing that could happen? If you can live with the worst thing that could happen, chances are this is a risk you're ready to take. If you're having trouble visualizing the future, stop and think back to the past. Think of something that you really wanted to happen, but didn't.

Or, conversely, think about something you really wanted, but in hindsight would not have been good for you. Sometimes a no can turn into an unexpected opportunity.

We often evaluate outcomes in the context of very narrow timeframes. You won't always know in the moment what will ultimately lead to success and what will truly count as failure. By putting your best foot forward, making your best effort while letting go of the results, you free yourself from attachment to the outcome and can better focus on the process and the opportunities that may unexpectedly unfold.

Elaine Leavenworth, senior vice president and chief marketing and external affairs officer at Abbott Labs, says she used to hang a sign above her desk bearing the motto "Progress, not perfection," with the word "perfection" intentionally spelled wrong, as a reminder that you can aim for perfection, but there's no such thing. Instead, she says, "you get great progress."

FEAR OF WHAT OTHERS SAY OR THINK

Women are often raised to be people pleasers. The downside of this can be an excessive reliance on external validation. We can come to care too much about how others react to us. While we're not advocating selfish or ruthless behavior, it's important to get beyond pleasing others and start listening to yourself. Not everyone will agree with your opinion, your strategy, or your idea. Don't let yourself be talked out of what you believe is right, and don't be afraid of what other people say.

The higher you aim, the harsher the criticism can get. It sometimes seems that women receive a disproportionate share of criticism as they ascend to leadership positions.

Putting purpose at the core of your leadership is one way to steel yourself against criticism. When you know your actions are guided by a larger purpose, you may have more confidence in your decisions. In the meantime, try to evaluate criticism with objectivity and grace. With confidence in your purpose, you'll be better able to tease out the legitimate and helpful criticism from the unnecessary commentary.

Nell Merlino, founder and president of Count Me In and the creator of Take Our Daughters to Work Day, often says that "fear is a feeling, not a fact." Why let fear calcify into something that hampers your life? Instead, you can transform it into a fuel that pushes you further — to be more creative, to work a little harder, to try something new and innovative. Anything worth achieving requires time and effort. It took the suffragettes of Seneca Falls seventy years of derision, criticism, and pushback before they accomplished their goal of winning the vote for women in the United States.

YOU ARE WHAT YOU THINK

Thanks to the efforts of people like Geena Davis, the data is in: the media has a powerful effect on how we see ourselves and in shaping our ideas of the roles of women and men — and not always for the good. We need to rethink how media is produced and consumed — whose stories are told and who gets to tell them. In recent years, we have started to see a collective shift, with many prominent women and men in the news and entertainment industries using their influence to create a vision of society that better reflects reality and to address the negative gender stereotypes that hold us all back.

But if you're not behind the camera or writing for a news organization, one of the surest ways to make an impact in your own life is by being conscious of what you consume. Just as we choose healthy foods to nourish our physical bodies, the information and media we take in constitute a mental "diet" of sorts — and if it's full of junk, it can harm you. Images of exceptional wealth and unattainable bodies (even top models have their pictures retouched with Photoshop) can leave us feeling inadequate and unable to measure up. One way to cope? Go on a "media detox."

Start with a media journal — track what kinds of news and entertainment you consume. Look at your television habits, scroll through your browser history, check your Twitter and Facebook feeds, your bookshelf and coffee table, the ticket stubs in your wallet. Do you notice any patterns?

Strip it down to the bare minimum. For one week, avoid social media feeds. Read just what you need to in order to keep up with your industry, and with news and current events in general. Dig into a book, into nature, into quality time with family and friends. Notice how it feels. Do you feel better or worse?

After a week, add back habitual media sources, one at a time, starting, perhaps, with a favorite TV show or magazine. Again, notice how it feels. Take stock of those effects and what caused them, and know that just as it is within your power to control what goes into your body, you can take steps to limit your consumption of what feels unhealthy for your psyche.

Ultimately, true power comes from being able to objectively define what success looks like for yourself, design your goals accordingly, and take the steps you need to achieve them.

II. Find Your Purpose

Once you know your power, finding your purpose is the next critical step. "Sense and meaning and purpose are about what you can contribute where you are, and that can take many different forms," says Kathleen Matthews, who, as we saw, was able to find purpose first as a reporter and now in her role at Marriott.

Pam Seagle was forced to think about purpose after she had a life-changing experience on US Airways flight 1549. But there are many other paths by which one can arrive at purpose. We hope that this book is one of them.

What Matters to You: Identify the issues and activities that matter most to you. What ignites your passion? What do you find yourself reading about? Talking about? Are there issues you wish you could change in your own life, on the world stage, or in your community? These issues can range from injustices you've read about in the news to ones you have seen in your own life. Are there passions or interests that you once had that have gotten squeezed out of your life? Are there new activities or opportunities you would like to pursue or participate in? Make a list of your top three.

How to Get Going: Once you have identified your top three issues or interests, first familiarize yourself with the latest research and news on those topics. Next, identify organizations that try to make a difference, and find out how you can get involved. See the resources in appendix B, or visit senecawomen.com.

Once you have identified your purpose, here are three ways you can think about turning that purpose into action.

VOLUNTEER

Is there a volunteer opportunity with a nonprofit organization that aligns with your purpose? Volunteering your time has long been one of the most common ways that people find purpose to anchor their lives. You can volunteer your time to a person or cause of your choice. Volunteering at a girls' school or women's shelter, mentoring a young woman in your profession, or raising money for a nonprofit you believe in are all ways to get started. Studies have found that people who regularly volunteer (a minimum of around two hours per week) have a greater sense of well-being and tend to live longer. A survey of volunteers in the United States found that states with the highest rates of volunteerism had lower mortality and incidence of heart disease. No time to volunteer because of an overcommitted life? Volunteering can be an opportunity to share your purpose with those close to you, if you volunteer with a friend or family member.

"It's easy to get people to write checks," says Sharon Bowen, commissioner of the Commodity Futures Trading Commission. "But to have someone devote the time to adopt a school and to actually go and work with kids who are underprivileged — I found personally that those kinds of experiences enrich my life and make me a better person the next day. I think a lot of people conceive of these activities as a drain on their time. But I can't think of any situation, whether it's pro bono or working in the community, where I didn't get back more than I put into it."

GO PRO BONO

Pro bono work entails donating your professional skills to a cause or outcome that you find meaningful. Lawyers, for example, can represent clients free of charge. But if you're not a lawyer, there are still ways you can extend your services to individuals and organizations on a pro bono basis.

Each of us has valuable skills that can be put to good use to serve a greater purpose. What skills, talents, and resources can you share with others? Are you a gifted event manager? Perhaps you can donate your expertise to host a fundraising event for the organization or cause of your choice. Are you an accountant? Seek out a nonprofit that works on a cause close to your heart and offer your services there. Whether it's for web design or project management or anything in between, there is always a person or organization in need of your services. You can also use pro bono service as a way to hone the skills you already possess, and to build up your own expertise and experience even as you are giving back. As Aaron Hurst notes in his book *The Purpose Economy,* pro bono work combines two innately rewarding activities: the opportunity to improve or master a skill and to have a social impact.

TAKE IT TO WORK, MAKE IT YOUR WORK

There is another way to contribute beyond these more traditional purpose-driven activities, and that's by infusing purpose into your work and daily life. This can mean using your skills and talents to find a career or job that allows you to do that. It may mean rethinking your current role and examining how you can align your own purpose with your organization's goals. We will learn more about this in section IV, "Making the Case for Women and Girls."

GETTING STARTED ON PURPOSE

Now that you're aware of some of the many challenges we face, identify where those intersect with your own life. Are there steps you can take to bring your skills or resources to bear so that you can make a difference? Review the list of organizations you created. Are there ways for you or your organization to get more involved?

If you're short of time, you can always support worthy nonprofits through charitable contributions. Many women's foundations, in the United States and overseas, are chronically underfunded. Your support will make a difference. Another way to contribute is by educating yourself and sharing information on the issues critical to advancing women and girls. Bring awareness to your community.

Every action counts. As the Virtue Foundation put it so beautifully, "True global change must begin within each one of us. One person at a time, one act at a time." In a world in which we are increasingly strapped for time, begin to find ways to integrate the advancement of women and girls into your daily activities.

GIRLS MATTER

Educating girls is one of the most effective things we can do to fast-forward to a more equitable world. How can you get involved? It might mean supporting organizations that advance girls. Perhaps you have an impact on the young people in your own life. Help them think about how gender expectations are built into the toys and books marketed separately to boys and girls.

If you have a daughter, niece, or granddaughter, take the opportunity of gift-giving (on a holiday or birthday, for example) to talk to her about what she wants, and why. There are a range of toys and books that encourage girls to develop critical thinking and build analytical skills, rather than to transform their appearance. It may be just an occasional event, but the gift you give matters. Look for websites that provide resources to parents and caregivers who seek to raise confident girls, or organizations that promote self-esteem in children.

We've discussed the importance of technology in connecting women with one another and providing the job opportunities of the future. It is important to support organizations that encourage girls in technology, like Girls Who Code and the National Center for Women and Information Technology (NCWIT). Today, some women still have a fear of technology, or think of it as a man's game. How can you debunk your own technophobia? Start by thinking of what it is you'd like to be able to accomplish and why. Whatever you're looking to do, know that it is attainable — it's not as hard as you think, whether it's becoming adept at social media or acquiring a seemingly obscure skill like coding. You can enroll in an online class that will introduce you to the basics or help you build on the skills you already have. As Ann Mei Chang, the head of USAID's Global Development Lab, noted, many women she has met in the technology industry came to it later in life. It's never too late, or too early, to pick up another tech skill.

SHOP WITH PURPOSE: SUPPORTING WOMEN ENTREPRENEURS

Supporting women entrepreneurs is an effective way to make an everyday activity, like shopping, part of finding your purpose. There are many ways to do this. One is to think about how your company sources its goods and services. Is there an opportunity to order more materials and services from women-owned businesses?

On a personal level, think about how to leverage your own economic power. It can be as simple as buying a product from a female entrepreneur or business owner. Look for WBENC and WEConnect International's new "Women Owned" logo on products at Walmart and other retailers. Or use your purchasing power to support women artisans around the world who produce beautiful and unique products.

Closer to home, find out which businesses in your community are owned and operated by women, and share this information with your friends and family. Spread the word on social media, or write a positive review on Yelp. With the exponential power of connectivity, these seemingly small steps can have an outsized impact.

Gender-based investing may be another option. The Pax Ellevate Global Women's Index Fund (and other mutual funds) invests in companies that advance the interests of women. If you're unable to invest on a large scale, crowdfunding sites such as Kickstarter, IndieGogo, and Plum Alley offer a great way to invest small sums to support women who are creating new products and companies.

III. Connect with Others

Once you have found your power and know your purpose, partnering with others is one of the best ways to achieve your goals. Purpose-driven partnerships can propel your life, projects, and career in ways you might never expect. Partnering for purpose can open doors, increase your circle of influence, and expand your horizons dramatically.

BUILD A PURPOSE COALITION AT WORK

At any level, if you're going to start something, you need allies. Do your research, and find like-minded individuals who are in a position to support your efforts. Figure out whom you need to connect with and who can help you achieve your goals. Know the leadership of your organization and who is responsible for which functions. Think about how you can build strong relationships with those who can help you get your project off the ground. This network of allies may be the difference between a project that takes flight and one that founders.

You don't need to be at the top of an organization to promote changes or have an impact. Bea Perez of Coca-Cola notes that it's a middle manager's role to raise her hand and deliver new ideas — so be sure to have a plan to execute when your ideas get taken up. Executives above you are depending on you to know what's going on in your area. Let them know that you know, and give them a roadmap on how to get from idea to execution. "Knowing where you are in the organization, and knowing the power you have to influence and the power you have to make recommendations — don't get surprised when your recommendation gets taken," Perez says.

Leadership consultant Bob Frisch uses the term "kitchen cabinet" to describe the informal network of managers that senior executives rely on to give them sound, independent advice. Members of the kitchen cabinet are not necessarily part of the official executive committee, and they may not carry executive titles themselves. Nonetheless, by earning the trust and gaining the ear of senior leaders, they can wield significant decision-making influence.

To join the kitchen cabinet, assess your workplace and find the person in charge who shares your values and whose work you admire. Think about how you might best partner with that person or bring ideas to the table.

OUTSIDE ALLIANCES:
PARTNERSHIPS FOR GOOD

As you think about allies within your organization, don't forget about outside allies. As we saw in the book, sometimes the most powerful programs are partnerships between two or more organizations. Furthermore, showing your own organization that other entities are interested in working together to advance women and girls can be a strong way to make the case. Public-private partnerships are effective because they harness diverse types of expertise and influence. Gathering partners from outside your organization can be a useful way to show how your project can take off and the valuable relationships it can build for your organization. If you can show your organization that its clients or stakeholders are interested in your initiative, you may be halfway there.

As we've seen, these partnerships can be cross-sector, lateral, and vertical. They can form within a community, across a border, or link women globally.

Think of how your organization might work collaboratively with another. If you work at a domestic violence awareness organization, for example, is there an existing network that might be a good partner for distributing valuable information? Or it could be as simple as linking up with a community group — say, your religious institution or a community garden — to share information. If you work at a company, there may be partnerships with these organizations to create a philanthropic or "shared value" opportunity.

Of course, the Internet also offers unprecedented opportunities for collaboration, networking, and the rapid spread of ideas, products, and services. Tap into existing networks related to your industry, professional organizations, and other networks of women on the issues that matter to you.

TIPS

As we have seen, wherever you sit, connecting with others is critical to achieving your goals. Working cooperatively and getting the buy-in of others is essential to the success of leaders — whether they run a company, a nonprofit organization, or a project in their local community. Today, women at all levels of organizations are building important collaborations across industries and sectors with the goal of accelerating change — what is sometimes called the new girls' network.

These partnerships and mutual support networks are the key. Moving from competition to collaboration does not always come easily, especially in environments that have only recently moved beyond tokenism. A female in a predominantly male milieu may feel so lucky to have "made it" that she believes she must focus solely on hanging on to her position, leaving her with little bandwidth to help other women succeed, or fearful that another woman might threaten her position. The media does its part to reinforce this "cat fight at the top" stereotype. But as more and more women reach positions of power, it's clear that success is no longer a zero-sum game. And one thing is certain: leaders who support each other multiply their own success.

Support Women Leaders: Think about how you can support another woman leader, whether in your work or in your community. As we have seen, women leaders often come in for heavy criticism. Remember that if you don't want others to needlessly criticize you, the first step is not to thoughtlessly criticize them. Be honest with yourself if you find that you criticize women more sharply because you put higher expectations on women leaders. Some of the best advice we've received is to try to separate the person from the quality. Few people in this world are all bad or all good. Try to step away and be objective.

Coping with Envy: We all come to the table with insecurities that can be triggered by others' success. But it's important to move beyond feelings of envy and jealousy; these emotions can have lasting and damaging effects on one's performance and team, making one less likely to be open to others' good ideas and more likely to spread negativity. That said, envy can also be an opportunity for personal or professional growth, say Tanya Menon and Leigh Thompson, both professors of management. Provided that you confront it and work through it, envy provides "a useful source of information," they write. "Think of it as data on what you value." In other words, once you've gotten envy's cue, turn it around to see how you can make a difference in your own work. For example, if you notice that a colleague's face time with the boss makes you green, try to understand why she's getting more of it and what you can do to put yourself in front of the boss more frequently. Menon and Thompson also recommend that you affirm yourself by thinking about your own accomplishments and innate strengths.

In our lives and careers, we have, of course, struggled with envy. And we've seen the unmistakably negative effects it can have on ourselves and others. Indeed, jealousy hinders our collective progress, so curtailing it or channeling it into useful information is one way we can all contribute to advancing women and girls, while at the same time improving our sense of self-worth.

Take the time to think objectively about the qualities, advantages, and benefits you have that others do not. Each of us has a unique combination of positive qualities and advantages. When your feelings of jealousy and insecurity arise, remind yourself of those strengths and try to shift your thoughts away from envy and toward a feeling of gratitude. Transform your intentions with "giver" behavior, and try to perform a good act for the person of whom you are jealous. If you find this hard, as we all sometimes do, remind yourself that you're the one who will benefit the most by transforming what could be a toxic environment to a positive one that can foster your and others' growth and development.

IV. Making the Case for Women and Girls

This book has shown you just how and where women fit in today's global environment. Understanding the critical role that women play in driving economic and social progress can help you understand your own significance as an agent of change. You can use the wealth of data we've provided on the importance of including and investing in women to make the case that your organization — whether you work in a company, for a nonprofit, or in the public sector — should be looking to women as a force for progress.

But making the case doesn't just mean walking into the office with an armful of reports. It means working to understand the goals of your organization, how women intersect at various levels of the organization's value chain, and what opportunities exist to make a difference. Equally important, it requires a critical self-analysis to find out how you can use your skills and knowledge to advance your organization's goals while also making the case. Below are some steps you can follow to help you make the case.

1. Take a holistic view of your organization and pinpoint your organization's goals. This may mean understanding the philanthropic goals as well as the brand, customer-facing, and bottom-line goals of your organization.

2. Evaluate the entire value chain of your organization to see where women do or can intersect in a meaningful way, and where there is an opportunity to increase women's engagement. This includes everything from suppliers to human resources to management to customers.

3. Determine what resources are available. Think beyond dollars — some organizations, like nonprofits, may not have enough resources to make a financial commitment. However, every organization has hidden resources that can be targeted toward new, more inclusive practices. If you want to start a women's initiative at your company but find there isn't room in the budget, see if you can begin with an informal mentoring circle that can move forward without company funding but still taps into the essential nature of the program you envisioned. Consider whether an existing program can be reoriented toward a more inclusive or diversity-friendly outcome. Does your company already commit to a day of volunteering every quarter? Perhaps that's fertile ground to propose volunteering at the local women's shelter or offering a day of pro bono services to aspiring or existing women business owners.

4. Evaluate your own position in the organization, and take a close look at what influence you can wield. If you are a CEO, you can, of course, influence a large number of decisions, but at every level, you have the power to promote change — you just need to analyze how and where you can use your position and your skills. Think strategically about what you bring to the table and how you can turn that specific

knowledge and those skills into a plan of action based on the needs and goals of your organization.

5. Build allies. Wherever you sit, it's important to find allies, like-minded individuals who can work with you toward your goal. Identify people inside and outside your organization whose interests might naturally align with your own or who might share the larger vision of what you are trying to accomplish. These allies may not be the "usual suspects." You never know who will be responsive to your ideas, and why. Don't dismiss people who may not seem like obvious cheerleaders. Sometimes broaching your ideas in an informal setting can prompt a more candid and receptive conversation. And don't forget allies outside your organization. Sometimes the most powerful programs are those that involve multiple parties. As mentioned earlier, showing your own organization that other entities are interested in working together to make something happen can be a powerful way to make the case. If you can show your organization that its stakeholders are interested in your initiative, you've won half the battle.

6. Do the work. You can't convince anyone that what you're saying makes sense unless you can show concrete evidence. Draft a plan that takes into account the questions you might have to answer. Arm yourself with the data and confidently make the case.

7. Find your people. Making change happen isn't easy. Get comfortable with being uncomfortable. You are asking those around you to adopt a new perspective, and some people will naturally resist that sort of change. Be patient and persistent, and keep stressing those areas of mutual self-interest to show you have the organization's best interests at heart. One way to keep going is to find your people. By that we mean find the people within or outside your organization who share your vision. In our experience, good things happen when you surround yourself with positive people.

Finally, for more information and resources for how you can make the case, go to www.senecawomen.com, join us, and together we can fast forward!

Appendix B

What follows are research sources and organizations that are mentioned in the book. For additional resources, visit www.senecawomen.com.

Research

ECONOMIC EMPOWERMENT

Access to Credit among Micro, Small, and Medium Enterprises. International Finance Corporation, 2013.

Aguirre, DeAnne et al. *Empowering the Third Billion: Women and the World of Work in 2012.* Booz & Company, 2012.

The Angel Investor Market in 2010: A Market on the Rebound. Center for Venture Research, 2011.

Azevedo, Joao Pedro, et al. *The Effect of Women's Economic Power in Latin America and the Caribbean.* The World Bank, 2012.

Bart, Chris, and Gregory McQueen. "Why Women Make Better Directors." *International Journal of Business Governance and Ethics* 8, no. 1, 2013.

Bem, Sandra. *The Lenses of Gender: Transforming the Debate on Sexual Inequality.* Yale University Press, 1994.

Benko, Cathy, and Bill Pelster. "How Women Decide." *Harvard Business Review,* September 2013.

Blau, Francine D., and Lawrence M. Kahn. "Female Labor Supply: Why Is the US Falling Behind?" Discussion Paper No. 7140, Institute for the Study of Labor, 2013.

The Bottom Line: Corporate Performance and Women's Representation on Boards, 2004–2008. Catalyst, 2011.

Budig, Michelle. *The Fatherhood Bonus and the Motherhood Penalty: Parenthood and the Gender Gap in Pay.* Third Way Next, 2014.

Dawson, Julia, et al. *The CS Gender 3000: Women in Senior Management.* Credit Suisse Research Institute, 2014.

Demirguc-Kunt, Asli, Leora Klapper, and Dorothe Singer. *Measuring Financial Inclusion: The Global Findex Database.* The World Bank, 2013.

The Economic Impact of Women-owned Businesses in the United States. Center for Women's Business Research, 2009.

Ellis, Amanda, et al. *Gender and Economic Growth in Uganda: Unleashing the Power of Women.* The World Bank, 2006.

Ely, Robin J., et al. "Rethink What You 'Know' about High-Achieving Women." *Harvard Business Review,* December 2014.

Fact Sheet: The Wage Gap Is Stagnant for Nearly a Decade. National Women's Law Center, 2014.

Fishman Cohen, Carol. "The 40-Year-Old Intern." *Harvard Business Review,* November 2012.

Folbre, Nancy. *For Love and Money: Care Provision in the United States.* Russell Sage Foundation, 2012.

Frisch, Bob. "Who Really Makes the Big Decisions in Your Company?" *Harvard Business Review,* December 2011.

The Full Participation Report: No Ceilings. Clinton Foundation and Bill and Melinda Gates Foundation, 2015.

Fultz, Elaine. *Pension Crediting for Caregivers: Policies in Finland, France, Germany, Sweden, the United Kingdom, Canada and Japan.* Institute for Women's Policy Research, 2011.

The Global Gender Gap Report, 2014. World Economic Forum, 2014.

Global Wage Report: 2014/2015: Wages and Income Inequality. International Labour Organization, 2015.

Goldin, Claudia. "A Grand Gender Convergence: Its Last Chapter." *American Economic Review* 104, no. 4 (2014), 1091–1119.

Gonzales, Christian, et al. *Fair Play: More Equal Laws Boost Female Labor Force Participation.* International Monetary Fund, 2015.

Groundbreakers: Using the Strength of Women to Rebuild the World Economy. Ernst & Young, 2009.

Hausmann, Ricardo, Laura D. Tyson, and Saadia Zahidi. *The Global Gender Gap Report, 2006.* World Economic Forum, 2006.

Hewlett, Sylvia Ann, and Melinda Marshall. *Women Want Five Things.* Center for Talent Innovation, 2014.

The Human Era at Work. The Energy Project and *Harvard Business Review,* 2014.

Hurst, Aaron. *The Purpose Economy.* Elevate USA, 2014.

Ibarra, Herminia. "Six Ways to Grow Your Job." *Harvard Business Review,* September 25, 2013.

ILO 2014 Global Wage Report, 2014–15. International Labour Organization, 2014.

Kay, Katty, and Claire Shipman. *The Confidence Code.* Harper Business, 2014.

Kelley, Donna J., et al. *2013 United States Report: Global Entrepreneurship Monitor: National Entrepreneurial Assessment for the United States.* Babson College, 2014.

Klepacki, Laura. *Avon: Building the World's Premier Company for Women.* Wiley, 2006.

Kristof, Nicholas D., and Sheryl WuDunn. *Half the Sky: Turning Oppression into Opportunity for Women Worldwide.* First Vintage Books, 2010.

Laughlin, Lynda. *Maternity Leave and Employment Patterns of First-Time Mothers: 1961–2008*. U.S. Department of Commerce and U.S. Census Bureau, 2011.

Liswood, Laura. "Women Directors Change How Boards Work." *Harvard Business Review*, February 2015.

Matsui, Kathy, et al. *Women-omics: Buy the Female Economy*. Goldman Sachs, 1999.

———. *Womenomics: Japan's Hidden Asset*. Goldman Sachs, 2005.

———. *Womenomics 3.0: The Time Is Now*. Goldman Sachs, 2010.

———. *Womenomics 4.0: Time to Walk the Talk*. Goldman Sachs, 2014.

McArdle, Megan. *The Upside of Down: Why Failing Well Is the Key to Success*. Penguin Group, 2014.

Menon, Tanya, and Leigh Thompson. "Envy at Work." *Harvard Business Review*, April 2010.

Mind the Gaps: The 2015 Deloitte Millennial Survey. Deloitte, 2015.

On Pay Gap, Millennial Women Near Parity — for Now: Despite Gains, Many See Roadblocks Ahead. Pew Research Center, 2013.

Parents and the High Cost of Child Care, 2013 Report. Child Care Aware of America, 2013.

Prahalad, C. K. *The Fortune at the Bottom of the Pyramid: Eradicating Poverty Through Profits*. Wharton School Publishing, 2006.

Ramaswami, Rama, et al. *Scaling Up: Why Women-owned Businesses Can Recharge the Global Economy*. Ernst & Young, 2009.

A Roadmap for Promoting Women's Economic Empowerment. United Nations Foundation and Exxon Mobil, 2013.

Robb, Alicia, et al. *Sources of Economic Hope: Women's Entrepreneurship*. Ewing Marion Kauffman Foundation, 2014.

Silverstein, Michael J., and Kate Sayre. "The Female Economy." *Harvard Business Review*, September 2009.

Strengthening Access to Finance for Women-owned SMEs in Developing Countries. International Finance Corporation, 2011.

2014 Catalyst Census: Women Board Directors. Catalyst, 2014.

Wang, Wendy, et al. *Breadwinner Moms: Mothers Are the Sole or Primary Provider in Four-in-Ten Households with Children; Public Conflicted about Growing Trend*. Pew Research Center, 2013.

Women and Mobile: A Global Opportunity. Cherie Blair Foundation for Women and GSMA.

Women in the Boardroom: A Global Perspective. Deloitte, 2013.

Women on U.S. Boards: What Are We Seeing? EY Center for Board Matters, 2015.

World Development Report, 2012: Gender Equality in Development. The World Bank, 2012.

EDUCATION

Generation STEM: What Girls Say about Science, Technology, Engineering, and Math. Girl Scouts Research Institute, 2012.

Riegle-Crumb, Catherine, and Chelsea Moore. "The Gender Gap in High School Physics: Considering the Context of Local Communities." *Social Science Quarterly* 95, no. 1 (2014), 253–68.

Title IX at 40: Working to Ensure Gender Equity in Education. National Coalition for Women and Girls in Education, 2012.

The 2014 State of Women-owned Businesses Report. American Express OPEN, Womenable, 2014.

GENDER-BASED VIOLENCE

Beijing Declaration and Platform for Action: Beijing+5 Political Declaration and Outcome. UN Women (2000).

Catalano, Shannan. *Intimate Partner Violence, 1993–2010.* U.S. Department of Justice, 2012.

Clark, Kathryn Andersen, Andrea K. Biddle, and Sandra L. Martin. "A Cost-Benefit Analysis of the Violence Against Women Act of 1994." *Violence Against Women* 8, no. 4 (2002), 417–28.

Costs of Intimate Partner Violence Against Women in the United States. Centers for Disease Control and Prevention, 2003.

Department of Defense Annual Report on Sexual Assault in the Military: Fiscal Year 2013. Department of Defense, 2013.

Global and Regional Estimates of Violence Against Women: Prevalence and Health Effects of Intimate Partner Violence and Non-partner Sexual Violence. World Health Organization, 2013.

Global Education Digest, 2011: Comparing Education Statistics Across the World. UNESCO Institute for Statistics, 2011.

Mai, Mukhtar. *In the Name of Honor.* Washington Square Press, 2006.

Marrying Too Young: Ending Child Marriage. United Nations Population Fund (UNFPA), 2012.

The Millennium Development Goals Report, 2014. United Nations, 2014.

Molloy, Aimee. *However Long the Night: Molly Melching's Journey to Help Millions of African Women and Girls Triumph.* HarperCollins, 2013.

National Intimate Partner and Sexual Violence Survey: 2010 Summary Report. National Center for Injury Prevention and Control and Centers for Disease Control and Prevention, 2010.

Salbi, Zainab, and Lauri Becklund. *Between Two Worlds: Escape from Tyranny: Growing Up in the Shadow of Saddam.* Gotham, 2006.

UN Security Council, Security Council Resolution 1325. S/RES/1325. October 31, 2000.

UN Security Council, Security Council Resolution 1820. S/RES/1820. June 19, 2008.

UN Security Council, Security Council Resolution 1888. S/RES/1888. September 30, 2009.

Women's Participation in Peace Negotiations: Connections Between Presence and Influence. UNIFEM, 2012.

HEALTH AND WELL-BEING

Abdi, Dr. Hawa, and Sarah J. Robbins. *Keeping Hope Alive: One Woman: 90,000 Lives Changed.* Grand Central Publishing, 2013.

Developing Physically Active Girls: An Evidence-based Multidisciplinary Approach. Tucker Center for Research on Girls and Women in Sport, 2007.

Dreifus, Claudia. "The Smiling Professor." *New York Times,* April 22, 2008.

Gilbert, Daniel. *Stumbling on Happiness.* Knopf, 2006.

Grimm, Robert, Jr., Kimberly Spring, and Nathan Dietz. *The Health Benefits of Volunteering: A Review of Recent Research.* Corporation for National and Community Service, 2007.

Quisumbing, Agnes R., and Chiara Kovarik. *Investments in Adolescent Girls' Physical and Financial Assets.* UK Department for International Development and Girl Hub, 2013.

Schwartz, Barry. *The Paradox of Choice: Why More Is Less.* Harper Perennial, 2004.

The "Science Behind the Smile." *Harvard Business Review,* January–February 2012.

Seligman, Martin. *Authentic Happiness.* Simon & Schuster, 2013.

von Furstenberg, Diane. *The Woman I Wanted to Be.* Simon & Schuster, 2014.

INNOVATION AND TECHNOLOGY

Houck, Max M. "Is Forensic Science a Gateway for Women in Science?" *Forensic Science Policy and Management* 1, no. 1 (2009).

Isaacson, Walter. *The Innovators: How a Group of Hackers, Geniuses, and Geeks Created the Digital Revolution.* Simon & Schuster, 2014.

Kakar, Yana Watson, et al. *Women and the Web: Bridging the Internet Gap and Creating New Global Opportunities in Low and Middle-Income Countries.* Intel, 2013.

Paik, Swan, and Julia Taylor Kennedy. "The Girl Effect: An Innovation Kitchen." *Policy Innovations,* August 30, 2011.

JUSTICE AND THE RULE OF LAW

Maternity and Paternity at Work: Law and Practice across the World. International Labour Organization, 2014.

Women, Business and the Law, 2014: Removing Restrictions to Enhance Gender Equality. International Bank for Reconstruction and Development and The World Bank, 2013.

LEADERSHIP AND POLITICS

Anvar, Leili. *Malak Jân Nemati: Life Isn't Short, but Time Is Limited.* Arpeggio Press, 2012.

Barsh, Joanna, and Susie Cranston. *How Remarkable Women Lead: The Breakthrough Model for Work and Life.* Crown Business, 2009.

Childs, Sarah, and Mona Lena Krook. "Critical Mass Theory and Women's Political Representation." *Political Studies* 56 (2008).

Cott, Nancy F. *No Small Courage: A History of Women in the United States.* Oxford University Press, 2000.

Lawless, Jennifer L., and Richard L. Fox. *Girls Just Wanna Not Run: The Gender Gap in Young Americans' Political Ambition.* American University School of Public Affairs, 2013.

O'Connor, Sandra Day, and H. Alan Day. *Lazy B: Growing Up on a Cattle Ranch in the American Southwest.* Random House, 2002.

Sandberg, Sheryl. *Lean In: Women, Work, and the Will to Lead.* Alfred A. Knopf, 2013.

Stanton, Elizabeth Cady, Susan Brownell Anthony, and Matilda Joslyn Gage, eds. *History of Woman Suffrage: 1848–1861.* Susan B. Anthony, 1889–1922.

Volden, Craig, Alan E. Wiseman, and Dana E. Wittmer. "When Are Women More Effective Lawmakers than Men?" *American Journal of Political Sciences* 57, no. 2 (2011).

MEDIA AND CULTURE

Smith, Dr. Stacy L., and Marc Choueiti. *Gender Disparity On-Screen and Behind the Camera in Family Films.* Geena Davis Institute on Gender in Media, 2010.

———, Marc Choueiti, and Dr. Katherine Pieper. *Gender Bias Without Borders: An Investigation of Female Characters in Popular Films Across 11 Countries.* Geena Davis Institute on Gender in Media, 2014.

———, and Crystal Allene Cook. *Gender Stereotypes: An Analysis of Popular Films and TV.* Geena Davis Institute on Gender in Media, 2008.

The Status of Women in the U.S. Media, 2014. Women's Media Center, 2014.

For more research, visit www.senecawomen.com.

Nonprofits, Foundations, and Campaigns

ECONOMIC EMPOWERMENT

Akilah Institute for Women

Business for Social Responsibility

Catalyst

Cherie Blair Foundation

Clinton Foundation

Count Me In

Diller–von Furstenberg Family Foundation
Ford Foundation
Girl Effect
Global Banking Alliance for Women
Grameen America
Jasmine
Knowledge Institute
Lean In
No Ceilings: The Full Participation Project
Oprah's Angel Network
Rockefeller Foundation
Self Employed Women's Association
Take Our Daughters to Work Day
TechnoServe
30% Club
Tory Burch Foundation
United Nations Foundation
UN Women
WEConnect International
Women Moving Millions
Women's Business Enterprise National Council
Women's Forum for the Economy and Society
Women's Funding Network
Women's World Banking

EDUCATION

Asia Society
Coop's Hoops
Girl Rising
iCivics
Kakenya Center for Excellence
Malala Fund
Project Nanhi Kali

Rajiv Gandhi Foundation
She's the First
Sun Culture Foundation
U.S.-Afghan Women's Council

GENDER-BASED VIOLENCE

A Path Appears
Girls Not Brides
Half the Sky
Hollaback!
Kering Foundation
Man Up Campaign
Mukhtar Mai Women's Organization
National Domestic Violence Hotline
NO MORE
Polaris
Prajwala
Project SAAVE (Stand Against Acid Violence)
Ring the Bell
Tostan
United Nations Population Fund
Women for Women International

HEALTH AND WELL-BEING

Bill and Melinda Gates Foundation
Center for Sport, Peace, and Society at the University of Tennessee at
Knoxville
Dr. Hawa Abdi Foundation
International Center for Research on Women
Jay Monahan Center for Gastrointestinal Health
National Colorectal Cancer Research Alliance
St. Jude's Children's Research Hospital
Stand Up to Cancer

Swasti–Health Resource Center
Virtue Foundation

INNOVATION AND TECHNOLOGY

Center for Talent Innovation
Girls Who Code
Global Development Lab at USAID
National Center for Women and Information Technology
Samasource
TechGirls
TechWomen

JUSTICE AND THE RULE OF LAW

American Civil Liberties Union
Avon Global Center for Women and Justice, Cornell Law School
Cab Riders United
Diane Halle Center for Family Justice
Families for Safe Streets
International Association of Women Judges
International Organization for Migration
Lawyers Without Borders
Ms. Foundation
O'Connor House

LEADERSHIP AND POLITICS

Congress of Women
DirectWomen
The Elders
Eleanor Roosevelt Center at Val-Kill
EMILY's List
Fortune Most Powerful Women
Girls Inc.

Girl Scouts of America
International Republican Institute
Mathare Youth Sports Association
National Democratic Institute
Off the Sidelines
Oprah Winfrey Leadership Academy
Running Start
2020 Women on Boards
Vital Voices
Women and Girls Lead
WomenCorporateDirectors
Women in Public Service Project
Women's Campaign Fund
Woodrow Wilson Center
Young Women's Leadership Network

MEDIA AND CULTURE

Chime for Change
Geena Davis Institute for Gender in Media
International Folk Art Alliance
MIT Center for Civic Media
Rede Nami
Women in the World
World Pulse

PEACE AND SECURITY

Afghan Women's Network
Cooperation for Peace and Unity
Gbowee Peace Foundation
Georgetown University Institute for Women, Peace and Security
International Rescue Committee
Refugees International
Women Peace and Security Network Africa

Social Enterprises

ECONOMIC EMPOWERMENT

The Alliance for Artisan Enterprise

Aspect Ventures

Belle Capital

Care.com

Golden Seeds

Grameen Bank

IndieGogo

Kickstarter

Maiden Nation

Pax Ellevate Global Women's Index Fund

The Pipeline Fellowship

Plum Alley

Solera

Uncommon Union

Urban Zen

HEALTH AND WELL-BEING

Annie's

Fenugreen FreshPaper

INNOVATION AND TECHNOLOGY

YOLO Colorhouse LLC

For more organizations, visit www.senecawomen.com.

Acknowledgments

THIS BOOK IS AN OUTGROWTH of many years of our work to advance women and girls. Countless people around the world shared their insights with us, and many of them continue to provide indispensable leadership on these issues across government, the nonprofit world, and the private sector. They inspire us with their commitment. And there are so many to whom we owe a large debt of gratitude.

To Linda Zecher, president and chief executive officer of Houghton Mifflin Harcourt, for encouraging us to write this book. To the staff at HMH, starting with Bruce Nichols, who freely shared his advice and made this a far better book, and Ben Hyman, for his counsel, enthusiasm, and helpfulness. To Lori Glazer, Stephanie Kim, and Ayesha Mirza for charting our public appearances, and to Larry Cooper and the other members of the HMH team for their unfailing assistance and support. To our agents at ICM, Jennifer Joel and Rafe Sagalyn, for their experienced guidance throughout.

To team Seneca:

First and foremost, to our writing and research partner, Anna Sussman. She is a rare talent with a deep commitment to advancing women and girls. We owe her much gratitude for the many sleepless nights and for her creativity, sense of humor, and exceptional abilities as a journalist.

To Prisca Bae, Elisa Gonzales, and Maithili Pradhan for their tireless work and support throughout this journey, and to Jane Chen for her unsurpassed ability to unfailingly deliver. Each of you, driven by your heartfelt commitment to women and girls, made the impossible possible. We are deeply grateful for the enormous around-the-clock contributions you provided.

To all the leaders and collaborators who agreed to be interviewed for *Fast Forward*. This book is yours. Your efforts on behalf of our common cause are making the world a better place. We can only repay you by remaining committed to progress for women and girls around the world.

We also want to thank the many friends and supporters who urged us to write this book, helped us make important connections, unearthed key sources, and were always there when we needed them. A special thanks to Jane Sambol for her contributions at a crucial moment.

To our families. It is they who sacrificed the most as we birthed this volume. To Kim's husband, Mattia, for his steady, kind manner, support, and generosity of spirit, and to Kim's mother, Paula, for her insightful, substantive contributions and for her everyday loving encouragement of all things concerning this project.

To Melanne's husband, Phil, and children, Michael, Alexa, and Elaina, who provided invaluable advice, encouragement, and the loving support that got us through the long nights, weekends, endless travel, and constraints on our time with them.

To Hillary Clinton, dear friend, colleague, and inspiration, thank you for leading the way: for introducing us over many years to women who are on the front lines of change; for your unstinting commitment to enabling women's economic, social, and political progress; and for inspiring us to continue the journey every day.

This is indeed a journey. It does not end with a book. We hope you, dear readers, will join us on this journey and become part of the Seneca Women community (senecawomen.com), working in whatever way you can to promote progress for women and girls. For, as we hope this book has demonstrated, advancing women and girls can help us fast-forward to the world we want to see.

Notes

1. Why Women, Why Now

page

3 *"If we stop thinking of the poor"*: C. K. Prahalad, *The Fortune at the Bottom of the Pyramid: Eradicating Poverty Through Profits* (Wharton School Publishing, 2006), 1.

In 2012, a leading consultancy estimated: DeAnne Aguirre et al., *Empowering the Third Billion: Women and the World of Work in 2012* (Booz & Company, 2012), 5, accessed March 3, 2015, http://www.strategyand.pwc.com/media/uploads/Strategyand_Empowering-the-Third-Billion_Full-Report.pdf. (Booz & Company is now known as Strategy&.)

4 *From 1997 to 2014 . . . more than 9 million: The 2014 State of Women-owned Businesses Report* (American Express OPEN, Womenable, 2014), 1, accessed March 3, 2015, http://www.womenable.com/content/userfiles/2014_State_of_Women-owned_Businesses_public.pdf.

Women own or lead: Rama Ramaswami et al., *Scaling Up: Why Women-owned Businesses Can Recharge the Global Economy* (Ernst & Young, 2009), www.ey.com/Publication/vwLUAssets/Scaling_up_-_Why_women-owned_businesses_can_recharge_the_global_economy/$FILE/Scaling%20up%20-%20why%20women%20owned%20businesses%20can%20recharge%20the%20global%20economy.pdf.

Women also wield: Michael J. Silverstein and Kate Sayre, "The Female Economy," *Harvard Business Review,* September 2009, https://hbr.org/2009/09/the-female-economy.

"Women already are the most dynamic": Muhtar Kent, "This Century Goes to Women," *Huffington Post,* October 13, 2010, http://www.huffingtonpost.com/muhtar-kent/post_1057_b_762044.html.

Investing in women and girls: T. Paul Schultz, "Mortality Decline in the Low-Income World: Causes and Consequences," *American Economic Review* 83 (May 1993): 337–42; Deon Filmer, "The Structure of Social Disparities in Education: Gender and Wealth," World Bank Policy Research Working Paper 2268 (January 2000), http://elibrary.worldbank.org/doi/pdf/10.1596/1813-9450-2268; Andrew Morrison and Shwetlena Sabarwal, "The Economic Participation of Adolescent Girls and Young Women: Why Does It Matter?," World Bank PREM Note 128 (2008), http://siteresources.worldbank.org/INTGENDER/Resources/morrison_sabarwal08.pdf; Jonathan Blagbourgh et al., *Because I Am a Girl: The State of the World's Girls 2009* (Plan Australia, 2009), https://www.planusa.org/becauseiamagirl/docs/becauseiamagirl2009.pdf.

"Greater gender equality": Ana Revenga et al., *World Development Report 2012: Gender Equality and Development* (World Bank, 2011), xiii, https://siteresources.worldbank.org/INTWDR2012/Resources/7778105-1299699968583/7786210-1315936222006/Complete-Report.pdf.

A 2011 analysis by Catalyst: The Bottom Line: Corporate Performance and Women's Representation on Boards, 2004–2008 (Catalyst, 2011), 1, www.catalyst.org/system/files/the_bottom_line_corporate_performance_and_women%27s_representation_on_boards_%282004-2008%29.pdf.

Credit Suisse has found: Julia Dawson et al., *The CS Gender 3000: Women in Senior Management* (Credit Suisse Research Institute, 2014), 18, https://publications.credit-suisse.com/tasks/render/file/index.cfm?fileid=8128F3C0-99BC-22E6-838E2A5B1E4366DF.

A 2015 analysis found: Pat Wechsler, "Women-led Companies Perform Three Times Better Than the S&P 500," *Fortune,* March 3, 2015, http://fortune.com/2015/03/03/women-led-companies-perform-three-times-better-than-the-sp-500/; Karen Rubin, "Research: An Update to Investing in Women-led Companies," Quantopian, March 3, 2015, https://www.quantopian.com/posts/research-an-update-to-investing-in-women-led-companies.

"Gender equality is smart economics": "The Global View," *Wall Street Journal,* April 11, 2011, http://www.wsj.com/articles/SB10001424052748704013604576246292633371136.

2. Know the Power of Women: Make the Case

10   *In less than two weeks:* Kathy Matsui et al., *Women-omics: Buy the Female Economy* (Goldman Sachs, 1999), http://annazavaritt.blog.ilsole24ore.com/wp-content/uploads/sites/54/files/womenomics2-pdf.pdf.

Sixteen years later: Kathy Matsui et al., *Womenomics: Japan's Hidden Asset* (Goldman Sachs, 2005), http://www.acareerinminingbc.ca/sites/default/files/womenomics_japan.pdf; Kathy Matsui et al., *Womenomics 3.0: The Time Is Now* (Goldman Sachs, 2010), http://www.goldmansachs.com/our-thinking/investing-in-women/bios-pdfs/womenomics3_the_time_is_now_pdf.pdf; Kathy Matsui et al., *Womenomics 4.0: Time to Walk the Talk* (Goldman Sachs, 2014), http://www.goldmansachs.com/our-thinking/outlook/womenomics4-folder/womenomics4-time-to-walk-the-talk.pdf.

11 *Increasing women's workforce participation*: Aguirre et al., *Empowering the Third Billion*, 19.

   "It would be beneficial": Christian Gonzales et al., *Fair Play: More Equal Laws Boost Female Labor Force Participation*, IMF Staff Discussion Note, 2015, www.imf.org/external/pubs/ft/sdn/2015/sdn1502.pdf.

12 *In 2006, the World Economic Forum*: Ricardo Hausmann et al., *The Global Gender Gap Report, 2006* (World Economic Forum, 2006), http://www3 .weforum.org/docs/WEF_GenderGap_Report_2006.pdf.

   From 2000 to 2010: Joao Pedro Azevedo et al., *The Effect of Women's Economic Power in Latin America and the Caribbean* (World Bank, 2012), 7, http://www .bancomundial.org/content/dam/Worldbank/document/PLBSummer12latest .pdf.

   In Brazil, for example, children: *The Effect of Women's Economic Power*, 8.

13 *in excess of $42 billion*: Shamika Sirimanne et al., *Economic and Social Survey of Asia and the Pacific, 2007: Surging Ahead in Uncertain Times* (United Nations Economic and Social Commission for Asia and the Pacific, 2007), viii, accessed March 3, 2015, http://www.unescap.org/sites/default/files /Survey_2007.pdf.

14 *"To achieve the economic expansion"*: "Secretary Clinton's Remarks at the Asia Pacific Economic Cooperation Women and the Economy Summit," San Francisco, September 16, 2011, accessed May 21, 2015, fpc.state.gov/172610.htm.

15 *600 percent increase*: *Title IX at 40: Working to Ensure Gender Equity in Education* (National Coalition for Women and Girls in Education, 2012), 2, www .ncwge.org/PDF/TitleIXat40.pdf.

   1,000 percent increase: Calculated from data in "Women's Sports and Fitness Facts and Statistics" (Women's Sports Foundation, 2009), 31, http://www .womenssportsfoundation.org/home/research/articles-and-reports/athletes/~/ media/PDFs/WSF%20Research%20Reports/WSF%20FACTS%20March %202009.ashx.

16 *Female high school athletes*: *Developing Physically Active Girls: An Evidence-based Multidisciplinary Approach* (Tucker Center for Research on Girls and Women in Sport, 2007), vi, accessed March 3, 2015, http://www.cehd.umn .edu/tuckercenter/library/docs/research/2007-Tucker-Center-Research -Report.pdf.

   The global consultancy EY: "Making the Connection: Women, Sport and Leadership," infographic, EY, October 2014, http://www.ey.com/BR/pt/About -us/Our-sponsorships-and-programs/Women-Athletes-Global-Leadership -Network---Infographic-women-sport-and-leadership.

17 *Studies have shown that girls*: Jennifer L. Lawless and Richard L. Fox, *Girls Just Wanna Not Run: The Gender Gap in Young Americans' Political Ambition* (American University School of Public Affairs, 2013), 10, https://www .american.edu/spa/wpi/upload/Girls-Just-Wanna-Not-Run_Policy-Report.pdf; *Girls' Participation in Physical Activities and Sports: Benefits, Patterns, Influ-*

ences, and Ways Forward (World Health Organization, 2005), https://www
.icsspe.org/sites/default/files/Girls.pdf.

20 *As a result, 90 percent: Coca-Cola 5by20 Women's Economic Empowerment
2012-2013* (Coca-Cola, 2013), 5-6, http://assets.coca-colacompany.com/19
/08/43a5fccf4c2babcfeed17a06c065/5by20-womens-economic-empower
ment-2012-2013.PDF.

21 *By 1995, women made up:* Barbara H. Wootton, *Gender Differences in Occupa-
tional Employment* (Bureau of Labor Statistics, Monthly Labor Review, 1997),
21, www.bls.gov/mlr/1997/04/art2full.pdf.

22 *The result was ANN Cares: Annual Report 2014,* ANN INC., accessed May 7,
2015, 12, http://phx.corporate-ir.net/External.File?item=UGFyZW50SUQ9NTc
0ODI4fENoaWxkSUQ9Mjc4MTY3fFR5cGU9MQ==&t=1.
In the United States, 80 percent: Sylvia Ann Hewlett and Melinda Marshall,
Women Want Five Things (Center for Talent Innovation, 2014), http://www
.talentinnovation.org/_private/assets/WomenWant%20FiveThings
_ExecSumm-CTI.pdf.

23 *A 2014 survey of nearly twenty: The Human Era at Work* (Energy Project, 2014),
9, http://theenergyproject.com/landing/sharehumanera.
For the next generation: Mind the Gaps: The 2015 Deloitte Millennial Survey
(Deloitte, 2015), 3, http://www2.deloitte.com/content/dam/Deloitte/global/
Documents/About-Deloitte/gx-wef-2015-millennial-survey-executivesumma
ry.pdf.
"In most cases, the male team": Cathy Benko and Bill Pelster, "How Women
Decide," *Harvard Business Review,* September 2013, https://hbr.org/2013/09
/how-women-decide.

25 *With the input of experts:* Mayra Buvinić, Rebecca Furst-Nichols, and Emily
Courey Pryor, *A Roadmap for Promoting Women's Economic Empowerment*
(United Nations Foundation and Exxon Mobil, 2013), http://www.women
econroadmap.org/sites/default/files/WEE_Roadmap_Report_Final.pdf.

3. Find Your Purpose

32 *Harvard University researchers:* Daniel Gilbert, *Stumbling on Happiness*
(Knopf, 2006), 17–25.
"We know that the best": Claudia Dreifus, "The Smiling Professor," *New York
Times,* April 22, 2008, http://www.nytimes.com/2008/04/22/science/22conv
.html?pagewanted=all.

34 *"One of the most selfish":* "The Science Behind the Smile," *Harvard Business
Review,* January–February 2012, https://hbr.org/2012/01/the-science-behind
-the-smile.

41 *"Though I've dedicated":* Diane von Furstenberg, *The Woman I Wanted to Be*
(Simon & Schuster, 2014), 115–16.

4. Connect with Others: Partner for Purpose

45 *"curse of social comparison"*: Barry Schwartz, *The Paradox of Choice: Why More Is Less* (Harper Perennial, 2004), 187–217.

46 *"our media 'friends'"*: Juliet B. Schor, *The Overspent American: Why We Want What We Don't Need* (Harper Collins, 1999), 3–11.
   "curse of high expectations": Schwartz, *The Paradox of Choice*, 185–87, 229–30.
   "To paraphrase my grandfather": Ostad Elahi (1895–1974) was a renowned Persian thinker, jurist, and musician. From August 5, 2014, to January 11, 2015, his life and musical accomplishments were the subject of a special exhibition at the Metropolitan Museum of Art: "The Sacred Lute: The Art of Ostad Elahi." For more information on his life and work, see *Encyclopaedia Iranica*, Volume VIII, and www.ostadelahi.com.

47 *Martin Seligman, a pioneer:* Martin Seligman, "The New Era of Positive Psychology," *TED Talks*, July 2008, www.ted.com/talks/martin_seligman_on _the_state_of_psychology/transcript?language=en.
   "your signature strengths": Martin Seligman, *Authentic Happiness* (Simon & Schuster, 2013), 263.

48 *Her experience was backed:* Robert Grimm, Jr., Kimberly Spring, and Nathan Dietz, *The Health Benefits of Volunteering: A Review of Recent Research* (Corporation for National and Community Service, 2007), http://www.national service.gov/pdf/07_0506_hbr.pdf.
   "helper's high": "Helper's High," Allan Luks, accessed May 8, 2015, allanluks .com/helpers_high.

50 *One of its first reports: Combating Acid Violence in Bangladesh, India, and Cambodia* (Avon Global Center for Women and Justice, Cornell Law School, 2011), http://ww3.lawschool.cornell.edu/AvonResources/Combating-Acid -Violence-Report.pdf.

5. Leadership and Networks at the Top

53 *"The women of Liberia"*: Kevin Conley, "The Rabble Rousers," *O, The Oprah Magazine*, December 2008, http://www.oprah.com/omagazine/Leymah -Gbowee-and-Abigail-Disney-Shoot-for-Peace-in-Liberia#ixzz3THMV rZgh.

56 *Women Moving Millions: All In for Her: A Call to Action* (Women Moving Millions, 2014), 4, www.allinforher.org/sites/default/files/ALL_IN_FOR_HER -A_Call_To_Action.pdf.

57 *"Women remain hugely underrepresented"*: Leslie Bennetts, "Women and the Leadership Gap," *Newsweek*, March 5, 2012, www.newsweek.com/women-and -leadership-gap-63689.
   hold 19 percent: 2014 Catalyst Census: Women Board Directors (Catalyst, 2014),

www.catalyst.org/system/files/2014_catalyst_census_women_board
_directors_0.pdf.

3.1 percent of board chairs: 2013 Catalyst Census: Fortune 500 Women Board Directors (Catalyst, 2013), www.catalyst.org/system/files/2013_catalyst _census_fortune_500_women_board_director.pdf.

less than 5 percent of CEOs: Pyramid: Women in S&P 500 Companies (Catalyst, updated January 13, 2015), accessed March 9, 2015, www.catalyst.org /knowledge/women-sp-500-companies.

In both 2012 and 2013: 2013 Catalyst Census.

Worse still: Still Too Few: Women of Color on Boards (Catalyst, 2014), http:// www.catalyst.org/system/files/woc_onboards_print.pdf.

A recent study by EY: Women on U.S. Boards: What Are We Seeing? (EY Center for Board Matters, 2015), accessed March 3, 2015, http://www.ey.com /Publication/vwLUAssets/EY_-_Women_on_US_boards:_what_are_we _seeing/$FILE/EY-women-on-us-boards-what-are-we-seeing.pdf.

58 *Research dating back:* Sarah Childs and Mona Lena Krook, "Critical Mass Theory and Women's Political Representation," *Political Studies* 56 (2008), 725–36, www.mlkrook.org/pdf/childs_krook_2008.pdf.

She made her case: See, e.g., *The Bottom Line: Corporate Performance and Women's Representation on Boards* (Catalyst, 2007), catalyst.org/system/files/ The_Bottom_Line_Corporate_Performance_and_Womens_Representation _on_Boards.pdf; *Gender Diversity and Corporate Performance* (Credit Suisse Research Institute, 2012), https://publications.credit-suisse.com/tasks/render/ file/index.cfm?fileid=88EC32A9-83E8-EB92-9D5A40FF69E66808; *Women Matter 2013: Gender Diversity in Top Management: Moving Corporate Culture, Moving Boundaries* (McKinsey & Company, 2013), http://www.mckinsey .com/~/media/mckinsey/dotcom/homepage/2012_March_Women_Matter/ PDF/WomenMatter%202013%20Report.ashx; *Women Matter: Gender Diversity, a Corporate Performance Driver* (McKinsey & Company, 2007), www .raeng.org.uk/publications/other/women-matter-oct-2007.

One 2012 study, for example: Jasmin Joecks et al., "Gender Diversity in the Boardroom and Firm Performance: What Exactly Constitutes a 'Critical Mass'?," paper, University of Tübingen (2012), papers.ssrn.com/sol3/papers .cfm?abstract_id=2009234.

And another widely cited: Roy D. Adler, *Women in the Executive Suite Correlate to High Profits* (European Project on Equal Pay, 2001), www.csripraktiken .se/files/adler_web.pdf.

A study from 2009 found: Katherine W. Phillips et al., "Is the Pain Worth the Gain? The Advantages and Liabilities of Agreeing with Socially Distinct Newcomers," *Personality and Social Psychology Bulletin* 35 (2009), 336–50.

women lead differently . . . better board directors: Chris Bart and Gregory McQueen, "Why Women Make Better Directors," *International Journal of Business Governance and Ethics* 8, no. 1 (2013), http://www.boarddiversity.ca/sites/default/

files/IJBGE8-Paper5-Why-Women-Make-Better-Directors.pdf, quoted in Julia Thomson, "Women Make Better Decisions Than Men," McMaster University, DeGroote School of Business, March 25, 2013, http://www.degroote.mcmaster .ca/articles/women-make-better-decisions-than-men/; Laura Liswood, "Women Directors Change How Boards Work," *Harvard Business Review,* February 17, 2015, https://hbr.org/2015/02/women-directors-change-how-boards-work; Anita Woolley, "Why Some Teams Are Smarter Than Others," *New York Times,* January 16, 2015, http://www.nytimes.com/2015/01/18/opinion/sunday/why -some-teams-are-smarter-than-others.html.

Helena's evidence-based approach: Jenny Anderson, "Helena Morrissey, Aiming at Britain's Glass Ceilings, Gets Results," *New York Times,* January 26, 2015, dealbook.nytimes.com/2015/01/26/helena-morrissey-aiming-at-britains -glass-ceilings-gets-results/; *2014 Catalyst Census.*

In the United States, where women: 2014 Catalyst Census.

59 *In her 2009 book:* Joanna Barsh and Susie Cranston, *How Remarkable Women Lead: The Breakthrough Model for Work and Life* (Crown Business, 2009).

Many countries, in Europe: Women in the Boardroom: A Global Perspective (Deloitte, 2013), www2.deloitte.com/content/dam/Deloitte/global/Documents/ Risk/gx-ccg-women-in-the-boardroom.pdf.

A 2014 report found: "Electoral Gender Quotas — a Major Electoral Reform," *Atlas of Electoral Gender Quotas* (IDEA, 2014), www.idea.int/publications /atlas-of-electoral-gender-quotas/upload/Atlas-on-Electoral-Gender -Quotas_3.pdf.

60 *"Every country deserves":* "Gender, Women, and Democracy," National Democratic Institute, accessed March 24, 2015, https://www.ndi.org/gender-women -democracy.

panchayats *had made more:* Raghabendra Chattopadhyay and Esther Duflo, "The Impact of Reservation in the Panchayati Raj: Evidence from a Nationwide Randomized Experiment," *Economic and Political Weekly* (2004), 983–85, http://www.jstor.org/stable/4414710.

less likely to pay bribes: Lori Beaman et al., "Women Politicians, Gender Bias, and Policy-making in Rural India," State of the World's Children 2007 Background Paper (UNICEF, 2006), 4, http://www.unicef.org/sowc07/docs/ beaman_duflo_pande_topalova.pdf.

In particular, female village: Mian Ridge, "Women Spreading Political Wings with Help of India's Quota System," *New York Times,* April 27, 2010, http://www.nytimes.com/2010/04/28/world/asia/28iht-quotas .html?pagewanted=all&_r=0.

61 *India's "silent revolution":* George Mathew, *Panchayati Raj: From Legislation to Movement* (Concept Publishing, 1995), 129.

A 2013 study of the U.S. Congress: Craig Volden et al., "When Are Women More Effective Lawmakers Than Men?," *American Journal of Political Science* 57, no. 2 (2011), 326–41.

"based on their experience as women": Liza Mundy, "The Secret History of Women in the Senate," *Politico*, January–February 2015, http://www.politico.com/magazine/story/2015/01/senate-women-secret-history-113908.html.

"I probably will have retribution": Jonathan Weisman and Jennifer Steinhauer, "Senate Women Lead in Effort to Find Accord," *New York Times*, October 14, 2013, http://www.nytimes.com/2013/10/15/us/senate-women-lead-in-effort-to-find-accord.html.

63 *hovers around 50 percent*: "Labor Force Participation Rate, Female (% of Female Population Ages 15+) (Modeled ILO Estimate)," World Bank, accessed May 18, 2015, http://data.worldbank.org/indicator/SL.TLF.CACT.FE.ZS/countries/1W-PL?display=graph.

More than 40 percent . . . 17 percent of equity: Report of the Eighth Annual NAWL National Survey on Retention and Promotion of Women in Law Firms (National Association of Women Lawyers, 2014), 4, 7, http://www.nawl.org/d/do/150.

Women hold 21 percent: Sue Reisinger, "Top Women Lawyers in the Fortune 500," *Corporate Counsel*, March 18, 2014, http://www.corpcounsel.com/id=1202647358761/Top-Women-Lawyers-in-the-Fortune-500.

64 *This evolution is already*: Molly McDonough, "Demanding Diversity," *ABA Journal*, March 28, 2005, www.abajournal.com/magazine/article/demanding_diversity/print; Kenneth Davis, "Consulting Giant Demands Diversity among Outside Counsel," General Counsel Consulting, www.gcconsulting.com/articles/120135/73/Consulting-Giant-Demands-Diversity-among-Outside-Counsel; Roy Strom, "Strengthening the Business Case for Diversity," *Chicago Lawyer*, July 2012, www.chicagolawyermagazine.com/Archives/2012/07/Business-Case-For-Diversity.aspx; Alison K. Jimenez, "Using Supplier Diversity to Attract Corporate Clients," *Law Practice Today*, December 2009, apps.americanbar.org/lpm/lpt/articles/mkt12091.shtml.

who make up one-third: At time of publication, there were three women serving on the Supreme Court: Justice Ruth Bader Ginsburg, Justice Sonia Sotomayor, and Justice Elena Kagan. *Biographical Directory of Federal Judges*, Federal Judicial Center, accessed March 27, 2015, http://www.fjc.gov.

25 percent of judges: Calculated from numbers of sitting female and male judges on district and circuit courts. At time of publication, there were 340 female judges and 1,010 male judges. *Biographical Directory of Federal Judges*.

"Changing it to accommodate": Sandra Day O'Connor and H. Alan Day, *Lazy B: Growing Up on a Cattle Ranch in the American Southwest* (Random House, 2002), 96.

65 *her brief to the court*: Appellate brief for *Reed v. Reed*, 404 U.S. 71 (1971).

opening the all-male Virginia: *United States v. Virginia et al.*, 518 U.S. 515 (1996), https://supreme.justia.com/cases/federal/us/518/515/case.html.

employment discrimination case: *Ledbetter v. Goodyear Tire & Rubber Co.*, 550 U.S. 618 (2007), https://supreme.justia.com/cases/federal/us/550/618/.

"Dissents speak to a future age": Nina Totenberg, "Ruth Bader Ginsburg and

Malvina Harlan," podcast audio, *NPR Morning Edition*, 8:37 minutes, May 2, 2002, http://www.npr.org/templates/story/story.php?storyId=1142685.

68 *Flexibility, the Harvard economist:* Claudia Goldin, "A Grand Gender Convergence: Its Last Chapter," *American Economic Review* 104, no. 4 (2014), 1091–1119, scholar.harvard.edu/files/goldin/files/goldin_aeapress_2014_1.pdf.

69 *Their application rates quickly:* Cecilia Kang, "Google Data-Mines Its Approach to Promoting Women," *Washington Post*, April 2, 2014, http://www.washingtonpost.com/blogs/the-switch/wp/2014/04/02/google-data-mines-its-women-problem/.

70 *"I never dreamed of one day":* "Madeleine K. Albright Commencement Address at University of California at Berkeley," May 10, 2000, accessed May 21, 2015, http://www.state.gov/1997-2001-NOPDFS/statements/2000/000510.html.

71 *New research tracking:* Astrid Kunze and Amalia R. Miller, "Women Helping Women? Evidence from Private Sector Data on Workplace Hierarchies," Institute for the Study of Labor Discussion Paper No. 8725 (2014), 1, 34–35, http://ftp.iza.org/dp8725.pdf.
Or it can be transformational: Sheryl Sandberg, *Lean In: Women, Work, and the Will to Lead* (Knopf, 2013).

6. Why the Middle Matters

74 Gender and Economic Growth in Uganda: Amanda Ellis et al., *Gender and Economic Growth in Uganda: Unleashing the Power of Women* (World Bank, 2006), siteresources.worldbank.org/INTAFRREGTOPGENDER/Resources/gender_econ_growth_ug.pdf.

75 *While men still dominate:* Calculated percent of women in managerial positions and removed women who are "chief executives." "Household Data, Annual Averages: Employed Persons by Detailed Occupation, Sex, Race, and Hispanic or Latino Ethnicity" (Bureau of Labor Statistics, 2014), 1, accessed March 3, 2015, http://www.bls.gov/cps/cpsaat11.pdf.

76 *"American women, Canadian women. . . I had originally envisioned":* Zainab Salbi and Lauri Becklund, *Between Two Worlds: Escape from Tyranny: Growing Up in the Shadow of Saddam* (Gotham, 2006), 221–22.

79 *While motor vehicle–related injuries:* Ariel Spira-Cohen et al., "Understanding Child Injury Deaths: 2003–2012 Child Fatality Review Advisory Team Report," *NYC Vital Signs* 14, no. 1 (2015), 1, http://www.nyc.gov/html/doh/downloads/pdf/survey/survey-2015cfrat-report.pdf.

7. Power at the Base

83 *"When I found out the story":* Tara Lamont-Djite, "Kate Spade Makes Fashion On Purpose," *Harper's Bazaar*, June 16, 2014, http://www.harpersbazaar

.com/fashion/trends/a2574/kate-spade-launches-for-profit-initiative-on
-purpose/.

84 *Women represent the vast:* Mahbub ul Haq et al., *Human Development Report,
1995* (United Nations Development Programme, 1995), iii, http://hdr.undp.org/
sites/default/files/reports/256/hdr_1995_en_complete_nostats.pdf.
*between 4 and 36 percent: Global Wage Report 2014/15: Wages and Income
Inequality* (International Labour Organization, 2015), 49, www.ilo.org/
wcmsp5/groups/public/---dgreports/---dcomm/---publ/documents/publica
tion/wcms_324678.pdf.
half as likely: Julie Ray, "Worldwide, More Men Than Women Have Full-Time
Work," Gallup, October 17, 2014, http://www.gallup.com/poll/178637/world
wide-men-women-full-time-work.aspx.

85 *One 2012 analysis by Strategy&:* DeAnne Aguirre et al., *Empowering the Third
Billion,* 6.
"It's called micro": Elizabeth Moore, "Obama's Mother, Hillary Clinton Shared
a Belief," *Newsday,* December 27, 2008, http://www.newsday.com/news/nation/
obama-s-mother-hillary-clinton-shared-a-belief-1.886994.

87 *A nephew of McConnell's:* Laura Klepacki, *Avon: Building the World's Premier
Company for Women* (Wiley, 2006), 11.

88 *Grameen Bank today:* "Monthly Reports 01-2015," Grameen Bank, accessed
March 22, 2015, www.grameen-info.org/monthly-reports-01-2015/.

90 *In Indonesia:* "Labor Force Participation Rate, Female (% of Female Population Ages 15+) (Modeled ILO Estimate)," World Bank, accessed March 22,
2015, data.worldbank.org/indicator/SL.TLF.CACT.FE.ZS.

91 *In China, for example:* "Girl Power: As the Supply of Female Factory-Workers
Dwindles, Blue-Collar Women Gain Clout," *Economist,* May 11, 2013, www
.economist.com/news/china/21577396-supply-female-factory-workers
-dwindles-blue-collar-women-gain-clout-girl-power.
In apparel manufacturing: Investing in Women for a Better World (BSR HER-
project, 2010), 4, http://herproject.org/downloads/BSR_HERproject_
Investing_In_Women.pdf.
Many of the workers reported . . . Out of a sample of almost: Priya Nanda et al.,
*Advancing Women, Changing Lives: A Comprehensive Evaluation of the Gap
Inc. P.A.C.E. Program* (International Center for Research on Women, 2013), 14,
http://www.icrw.org/sites/default/files/publications/PACE_Report_PRINT
_singles_lo.pdf.

94 *"Rural women face":* Satrajit Sen, "Vodafone Promotes Mobile App for Rural
Women Entrepreneurs," *afaqs!,* January 29, 2014, http://www.afaqs.com/
news/story/39812_Vodafone-promotes-mobile-app-for-rural-women-entrepre
neurs.
Over the past three years: "Cherie Blair Launches Vodafone Connected Wom-
en Report 2014," press release, Vodafone, July 17, 2014, https://www.vodafone
.in/media/press-release-details?mid=1164.

96 *Grameen Bank in Bangladesh:* "Monthly Reports 01-2015," Grameen Bank, accessed March 20, 2015, www.grameen-info.org/monthly-reports-01-2015/.

8. Entrepreneurs and Innovators

97 *"As immigrants without family"*: Michael B. Farrell, "Care.com, the Big Business of Babysitting," *Boston Globe,* August 14, 2014, www.bostonglobe.com/magazine/2014/08/14/care-com-big-business-babysitting/4Fjpf5q3YUSw3rMn9GraOM/story.html.

98 *As of 2014, such firms: The 2014 State of Women-owned Businesses Report.*
    A 2009 study found that: The Economic Impact of Women-owned Businesses in the United States (Center for Women's Business Research, 2009), 1, https://www.nwbc.gov/sites/default/files/economicimpactstu.pdf.
    In emerging markets alone: Strengthening Access to Finance for Women-owned SMEs in Developing Countries (International Finance Corporation, 2011), 3, http://www.ifc.org/wps/wcm/connect/a4774a004a3f66539f0f9f8969adcc27/G20_Women_Report.pdf?MOD=AJPERES.
    a recent survey . . . starting new ventures: Donna J. Kelley et al., *2013 United States Report: Global Entrepreneurship Monitor: National Entrepreneurial Assessment for the United States of America* (Babson College and Baruch College, 2014), 28, 39, www.babson.edu/Academics/centers/blank-center/global-research/gem/Documents/GEM%20USA%202013.pdf.

100 *"While philanthropy has always"*: Elizabeth Schaeffer Brown, "Can Women Lead the Social Enterprise Revolution?," *Forbes,* October 17, 2013, http://www.forbes.com/sites/yec/2013/10/17/can-women-lead-the-social-enterprise-revolution/.

101 *an unmet need of $260 billion: Access to Credit Among Micro, Small, and Medium Enterprises* (International Finance Corporation, 2013), 2, www.ifc.org/wps/wcm/connect/1f2c968041689903950bb79e78015671/AccessCreditMSME-Brochure-Final.pdf?MOD=AJPERES.
    In the United States, 72 percent: Alicia Robb et al., *Sources of Economic Hope: Women's Entrepreneurship* (Ewing Marion Kauffman Foundation, 2014), 4, 10–11, http://www.kauffman.org/~/media/kauffman_org/research%20reports%20and%20covers/2014/11/sources_of_economic_hope_womens_entrepreneurship.pdf.

102 *women received only 4.4 percent:* Kenneth Temkin et al., *Competitive and Special Competitive Opportunity Gap Analysis of the 7(A) and 504 Programs* (Urban Institute, 2008), 13, http://www.urban.org/UploadedPDF/411596_504_gap_analysis.pdf.
    In 2010, the year she was: Jeffrey Sohl, *The Angel Investor Market in 2010: A Market on the Rebound* (Center for Venture Research, 2011), http://www.unh.edu/news/docs/2010angelanalysis.pdf.

103 *launched a $100 million:* "The Coca-Cola Company and IFC Announce

Initiative to Support Women Entrepreneurs Across Emerging Markets," press release, March 11, 2013, http://www.coca-colacompany.com/press-center/press-releases/the-coca-cola-company-and-ifc-announce-initiative-to-support-women-entrepreneurs-across-emerging-markets#TCCC.

In 2013, the IFC also issued: Anna Yukhananov, "First Women's Bond from World Bank Raises $165 Million," Reuters, November 6, 2013, http://www.reuters.com/article/2013/11/06/worldbank-women-bond-idUSL2N0I R1IN20131106.

104 *A Lagos businesswoman:* "10,000 Women: Meet the Women: Ayodeji, Lagos, Nigeria," Goldman Sachs, accessed March 9, 2015, http://www.goldmansachs.com/citizenship/10000women/meet-the-women-profiles/ayodeji-profile.html.

Ayodeji was not alone: Candida G. Brush et al., *Investing in the Power of Women: Progress Report on the Goldman Sachs 10,000 Women Initiative* (Babson College, 2014), 2–3, http://www.goldmansachs.com/citizenship/10000women/news-and-events/10kw-progress-report/progress-report-full.pdf.

In March of 2014, Goldman Sachs: "Goldman Sachs 10,000 Women, IFC to Raise up to $600 Million to Support Women Entrepreneurs," press release, Goldman Sachs, March 5, 2014, http://www.goldmansachs.com/citizenship/10000women/news-and-events/10000women-ifc.html.

Because Ant Credit: "IFC, Ant Financial Services Group and Goldman Sachs 10,000 Women Launch First Internet-based Gender-Finance Program in China to Boost Women Entrepreneurship," press release, International Finance Corporation, January 27, 2015, http://ifcextapps.ifc.org/IFCExt/Pressroom/IFCPressRoom.nsf/0/5DFDA58BCBFE71B685257DDA00303B14?opendocument.

105 *One telling statistic . . . generate only about a third: The 2014 State of Women-owned Businesses Report.*

106 *A 2014 survey of* Inc. *magazine's . . . Even the twenty-five largest: Sources of Economic Hope: Women's Entrepreneurship,* 10–11.

107 *"We think as women":* Claire Cain Miller, "Two of Venture Capital's Senior Women Start a New Firm," *New York Times,* February 5, 2014, http://bits.blogs.nytimes.com/2014/02/05/two-of-venture-capitals-senior-women-start-a-new-firm/.

Founded in 1999 by Molly Ashby: Ryan Dezember, "The Buyout Brain Behind Annie's IPO," *Wall Street Journal,* April 13, 2012, www.wsj.com/articles/SB10001424052702303624004577339743538261650.

9. Unfinished Business

113 *"It is a violation of human rights":* "Hillary Rodham Clinton Remarks to the UN 4th World Conference on Women Plenary Session," Beijing, China, September 5, 1995, United Nations, accessed May 21, 2015, http://www.un.org/esa/gopher-data/conf/fwcw/conf/gov/950905175653.txt.

115 *In some countries . . . In fifteen countries: Women, Business and the Law, 2014:*
Removing Restrictions to Enhance Gender Equality (International Bank for
Reconstruction and Development and World Bank, 2013), accessed March 3,
2015, http://wbl.worldbank.org/~/media/FPDKM/WBL/Documents/
Reports/2014/Women-Business-and-the-Law-2014-FullReport.pdf.
In the United States, even though: Women in the Labor Force: A Databook (Bu-
reau of Labor Statistics, 2014), http://www.bls.gov/opub/reports/cps/women
-in-the-labor-force-a-databook-2014.pdf.
The gender pay gap: Michelle Budig, *The Fatherhood Bonus and the Motherhood Penalty: Parenthood and the Gender Gap in Pay* (Third Way Next, 2014),
21, http://content.thirdway.org/publications/853/NEXT_-_Fatherhood
_Motherhood.pdf.
Progress on closing the pay gap . . . The cumulative losses: "Fact Sheet: The
Wage Gap Is Stagnant for Nearly a Decade" (National Women's Law Center,
2014), www.nwlc.org/sites/default/files/pdfs/fact_sheet_wage_gap_is
_stagnant_2013.pdf.

116 *The United States is one: Maternity and Paternity at Work: Law and Practice
Across the World* (International Labour Organization, 2014), 16, http://www
.ilo.org/wcmsp5/groups/public/---dgreports/---dcomm/---publ/documents/
publication/wcms_242615.pdf.
Unsurprisingly, the lack of governmental support: Francine D. Blau and
Lawrence M. Kahn, "Female Labor Supply: Why Is the US Falling Behind?,"
Institute for the Study of Labor Discussion Paper No. 7140 (2013), http://ftp.iza
.org/dp7140.pdf, using data from OECD online employment database, http://
www.oecd.org/els/employmentpoliciesanddata/onlineoecdemploymentdata
base.htm.
These outdated systems: Sandra Bem, *The Lenses of Gender: Transforming the
Debate on Sexual Inequality* (Yale University Press, 1994), 184–91.
Today, roughly 60 percent: Calculated from number of families with both
parents employed out of total number of married-couple families. "Table 4.
Families with Own Children: Employment Status of Parents by Age of Youngest Child and Family Type, 2013–2014 Annual Averages," news release, Bureau
of Labor Statistics, April 23, 2014, www.bls.gov/news.release/famee.t04.htm.
Nearly a third: Calculated from number of families maintained by mother out
of total number of families maintained by single parent (mother or father).
"Table 4. Families with Own Children."

117 *women performed twice as much:* Nancy Folbre, *For Love and Money: Care
Provision in the United States* (Russell Sage Foundation, 2012), as cited in
Riane Eisler and Kimberly Otis, "Unpaid and Undervalued Care Work Keeps
Women on the Brink," *Shriver Report,* January 22, 2014, http://shriverreport
.org/unpaid-and-undervalued-care-work-keeps-women-on-the-brink/#_edn2.
Taken together, women's and men's: Benjamin Bridgman et al., "Accounting
for Household Production in the National Accounts, 1965–2010," *Survey of*

Current Business 92 (2012), 23–24, http://www.bea.gov/scb/pdf/2012/05%20 May/0512_household.pdf.

Working mothers are more: On Pay Gap, Millennial Women Near Parity—For Now: Despite Gains, Many See Roadblocks Ahead (Pew Research Center, 2013), 3, http://www.pewsocialtrends.org/files/2013/12/gender-and-work_final.pdf.

"pension crediting for caregivers . . . They improve pension adequacy": Elaine Fultz, *Pension Crediting for Caregivers: Policies in Finland, France, Germany, Sweden, the United Kingdom, Canada, and Japan* (Institute for Women's Policy Research, 2011), iii, 1, http://www.iwpr.org/publications/pubs/pension -crediting-for-caregivers-policies-in-finland-france-germany-sweden-the- united-kingdom-canada-and-japan.

In 2013, the cost of child care: Parents and the High Cost of Child Care, 2013 Report (Child Care Aware of America, 2013), 13, usa.childcareaware.org/sites/ default/files/Cost%20of%20Care%202013%20110613.pdf.

And for too many others: Characteristics of Minimum-Wage Workers, 2013 (Bureau of Labor Statistics, 2014), 4, http://www.bls.gov/cps/minwage2013 .pdf.

118 *"Arguably the best child care"*: Jonathan Cohn, "The Hell of American Day Care," *New Republic*, April 15, 2013, http://www.newrepublic.com/ article/112892/hell-american-day-care.

A 2011 report by: Lynda Laughlin, *Maternity Leave and Employment Patterns of First-Time Mothers, 1961–2008* (U.S. Department of Commerce and U.S. Census Bureau, 2011), 9, https://www.census.gov/prod/2011pubs/p70-128.pdf.

a recent survey of nearly seven: Robin J. Ely et al., "Rethink What You 'Know' about High-Achieving Women," *Harvard Business Review*, December 2014, https://hbr.org/2014/12/rethink-what-you-know-about-high-achieving-women.

119 *When Deloitte launched*: Kristin Schepici, "Lessons Learned: Deloitte's Women's Initiative Comes Full Circle," Linkage Leadership Insights (blog), August 24, 2011, mylinkage.com/blog/paul-silverglate-on-deloittes-womens -initiatives/.

Mike Cook: Ely et al., "Rethink What You 'Know' about High-Achieving Women."

Shaun Budnik: "Re-entry Program Targets Professional Women," Accounting Web, May 16, 2006, http://www.accountingweb.com/topic/education-careers/ re-entry-programs-target-professional-women.

120 *"Returning professionals offer"*: Carol Fishman Cohen, "The 40-Year-Old Intern," *Harvard Business Review*, November 2012, https://hbr.org/2012/11/the -40-year-old-intern.

At Vodafone, the global: "Vodafone Pioneers Global Maternity Policy Across 30 Countries," news release, Vodafone, March 6, 2015, www.vodafone.com/ content/index/media/vodafone-group-releases/2015/global-maternity-policy .html.

The company commissioned: Jena McGregor, "An Unusual New Policy for

Working Mothers," *Washington Post,* March 6, 2015, www.washingtonpost
.com/blogs/on-leadership/wp/2015/03/06/an-unusual-new-policy-for-working
-mothers/.

In March 2015, Vodafone: "Vodafone Pioneers Global Maternity Policy."

By contrast, professions: Claudia Goldin and Lawrence F. Katz, "The Cost of
Workplace Flexibility for High-powered Professionals," *Annals of the American Academy of Political and Social Science* 638 (2011), 45–67, scholar.harvard
.edu/files/goldin/files/the_cost_of_workplace_flexibility_for_high-powered_
professionals.pdf; Goldin, "A Grand Gender Convergence," 1091–1119.

121 *On October 25, 2010:* Janet Elise Johnson, "The Most Feminist Place in the
World," *Nation,* February 3, 2011, http://www.thenation.com/article/158279/
most-feminist-place-world.

In 2013, fifty years after: "The Wage Gap Is Stagnant for Nearly a Decade."

median salary of $39,157: Carmen DeNavas-Walt and Bernadette D. Proctor,
Income and Poverty in the United States: 2013 (U.S. Census Bureau, 2014), 10,
https://www.census.gov/content/dam/Census/library/publications/2014/demo/
p60-249.pdf.

Although slightly more women: David Wessel, "The Glass Ceiling Is Getting
Thinner," *Wall Street Journal,* October 1, 2014, http://blogs.wsj.com/
economics/2014/10/01/the-glass-ceiling-is-getting-thinner/.

the overall gap has barely . . . Average weekly earnings: "The Wage Gap Is Stagnant for Nearly a Decade."

The pay gap widens for women of color: "Median Usual Weekly Earnings of
Full-time Wage and Salary Workers by Selected Characteristics, Annual Averages," news release, Bureau of Labor Statistics, last modified January 21, 2015,
accessed March 3, 2015, http://www.bls.gov/news.release/wkyeng.t07.htm;
"The Wage Gap Is Stagnant for Nearly a Decade."

$466 for a family of four: Calculated using 2015 Poverty Guidelines, Office of
the Assistant Secretary for Planning and Evaluation, accessed May 19, 2015,
aspe.hhs.gov/poverty/15poverty.cfm.

The gap also widens for mothers: Budig, *The Fatherhood Bonus and the Motherhood Penalty,* 21.

Women were the sole: Wendy Wang et al., *Breadwinner Moms: Mothers Are
the Sole or Primary Provider in Four-in-Ten Households with Children; Public
Conflicted about Growing Trend* (Pew Research Center, 2013), 1, http://www
.pewsocialtrends.org/files/2013/05/Breadwinner_moms_final.pdf.

122 *That the women were Korean:* "How Action Figure Katherine Chon Helps
Fight Human Trafficking," *Women's Health,* December 12, 2006, http://www
.womenshealthmag.com/life/fighting-for-human-rights.

123 *In the United States, one estimate:* *Costs of Intimate Partner Violence Against
Women in the United States* (Centers for Disease Control and Prevention,
2003), citing unpublished data from 1995, http://www.cdc.gov/violencepreven
tion/pdf/IPVBook-a.pdf.

124 *The incidence of intimate partner:* Shannan Catalano, *Intimate Partner Violence, 1993–2010* (U.S. Department of Justice, 2012), 2, www.bjs.gov/content/pub/pdf/ipv9310.pdf.

In its first six years: Kathryn Andersen Clark et al., "Cost-Benefit Analysis of the Violence Against Women Act of 1994," *Violence Against Women* 8, no. 4 (2002), 417–28, citing abstract, https://www.ncjrs.gov/App/Publications/abstract.aspx?ID=194590.

Despite the progress: M. C. Black et al., *National Intimate Partner and Sexual Violence Survey: 2010 Summary Report* (National Center for Injury Prevention and Control, and Centers for Disease Control and Prevention, 2011), 1–2, www.cdc.gov/ViolencePrevention/pdf/NISVS_Report2010-a.pdf.

125 *The Department of Defense: Department of Defense Annual Report on Sexual Assault in the Military: Fiscal Year 2014* (Department of Defense, 2015), 8, http://sapr.mil/public/docs/reports/FY14_Annual/FY14_DoD_SAPRO_Annual_Report_on_Sexual_Assault.pdf.

And while across the globe: Global and Regional Estimates of Violence Against Women: Prevalence and Health Effects of Intimate Partner Violence and Nonpartner Sexual Violence (World Health Organization, 2013), 2, http://apps.who.int/iris/bitstream/10665/85239/1/9789241564625_eng.pdf.

127 *In Pakistan:* Mukhtar Mai, *Mukhtar Mai: In the Name of Honor* (Washington Square Press, 2006).

estimated to be 41 percent: "Child Marriage Around the World: Ethiopia," *Girls Not Brides,* accessed May 7, 2015, http://www.girlsnotbrides.org/child-marriage/ethiopia/.

In Niger: "Child Marriage Around the World: Niger," *Girls Not Brides,* accessed March 3, 2015, http://www.girlsnotbrides.org/child-marriage/niger/.

In Chad and the Central African Republic: "Child Marriage Around the World," *Girls Not Brides,* accessed March 3, 2015, http://www.girlsnotbrides.org/where-does-it-happen/.

According to the UNFPA: Marrying Too Young: Ending Child Marriage (UNFPA, 2012), 10, http://www.unfpa.org/sites/default/files/jahia-publications/documents/publications/2012/ChildMarriage_2_chapter1.pdf.

128 *Swan Paik:* Swan Paik and Julia Taylor Kennedy, "The Girl Effect: An Innovation Kitchen," *Policy Innovations,* August 30, 2011, http://www.policyinnovations.org/ideas/audio/data/000617.

The program resulted in: Agnes R. Quisumbing and Chiara Kovarik, *Investments in Adolescent Girls' Physical and Financial Assets* (UK Department for International Development and Girl Hub, 2013), 22, http://www.girleffect.org/media/1133/investing-in-adolescent-girls-physical-and-financial-assets.pdf.

129 *Malicounda Bambara:* Aimee Molloy, *However Long the Night: Molly Melching's Journey to Help Millions of African Women and Girls Triumph* (Harper Collins, 2013), 127–29.

Since Tostan began its work: "Our Impact," Tostan, accessed March 3, 2015, http://www.tostan.org/.

One village chief: Jesse Ellison, "Molly Melching: Enlist the Men!," *Daily Beast,* March 10, 2012, http://www.thedailybeast.com/articles/2012/03/10/molly -melching-enlist-the-men.html.

In Somalia, Dr. Hawa Abdi: Eliza Griswold, "Dr. Hawa Abdi and Her Daughters: The Saints of Somalia," *Glamour,* November 2010, http://www.glamour .com/inspired/women-of-the-year/2010/dr-hawa-abdi-and-her-daughters.

In 1983, Dr. Hawa: Dr. Hawa Abdi and Sarah J. Robbins, *Keeping Hope Alive: One Woman: 90,000 Lives Changed* (Grand Central Publishing, 2013).

130 *In 2010, members of the militia:* Mohammed Ibrahim and Jeffrey Gettleman, "Under Siege in War-Torn Somalia, a Doctor Holds Her Ground," *New York Times,* January 7, 2011, http://www.nytimes.com/2011/01/08/world/ africa/08somalia.html; Nicholas Kristof, "Heroic, Female and Muslim," *New York Times,* December 15, 2010, http://www.nytimes.com/2010/12/16/ opinion/16kristof.html.

131 *They comprise more than three-fourths:* "Protecting Women in Emergency Situations," UNFPA, accessed May 22, 2015, http://www.unfpa.org/resources/ protecting-women-emergency-situations.

targets of mass rape: Annabelle Timsit, "Protecting and Empowering Women and Girls in Situations of Crisis and Conflict," Georgetown Institute for Women, Peace and Security (blog), March 9, 2015, http://www.unfpa.org/resources/ protecting-women-emergency-situations.

132 *William reminded the members:* "Foreign Secretary and UN Special Envoy Urge UN to Tackle Sexual Violence in Conflict," press release, UK Foreign and Commonwealth Office and the Rt. Hon. William Hague, MP, June 24, 2013, https://www.gov.uk/government/news/foreign-secretary-and-un-special -envoy-to-urge-un-to-tackle-sexual-violence-in-conflict.

133 *It was the first time:* Security Council Resolution 1325, October 31, 2000, S/RES/1325, http://www.un.org/en/ga/search/view_doc.asp?symbol=S/ RES/1325(2000).

134 *Resolution 1820:* Security Council Resolution 1820, June 19, 2008, S/RES/1820, http://www.un.org/en/ga/search/view_doc.asp?symbol=S/RES/1820(2008). *Resolution 1888:* Security Council Resolution 1888, September 30, 2009, S/RES/1888, http://www.un.org/en/ga/search/view_doc.asp?symbol=S/ RES/1888(2009).

By one estimate, over: Pablo Castillo Diaz et al., *Women's Participation in Peace Negotiations: Connections Between Presence and Influence* (UNIFEM, 2012), 3, http://www.unwomen.org/~/media/headquarters/attachments/ sections/library/publications/2012/10/wpssourcebook-03a-womenpeace negotiations-en.pdf.

Unsurprisingly, about half: Donor Aid Strategies in Post–Peace Settlement

Environments (International Alert, 2006), 6, http://international-alert.org/sites/default/files/publications/Donor_Aid_Strategies_in_Post_Peace_settlement_environments.pdf.

10. Levers for Change: Technology and Education

136 *In the northeast of the country:* "Education for All Global Monitoring Report Fact Sheet: Education in Kenya" (UNESCO, 2012), 1, http://www.unesco.org/new/fileadmin/MULTIMEDIA/HQ/ED/pdf/EDUCATION_IN_KENYA_A_FACT_SHEET.pdf.
According to UNESCO: "Kenya Country Profile," UNESCO Institute for Statistics, accessed March 22, 2015, www.uis.unesco.org/DataCentre/Pages/country-profile.aspx?code=KEN&regioncode=40540.

137 *"Investment in the education":* Lawrence H. Summers, "Investing in *All* the People," Development Economics Working Paper, World Bank, 1992, www-wds.worldbank.org/servlet/WDSContentServer/WDSP/IB/1992/05/01/000009265_3961003011714/Rendered/PDF/multi_page.pdf.
the gender gap in education: Global Gender Gap Report, 2014 (World Economic Forum, 2014), 14, www3.weforum.org/docs/GGGR14/GGGR_Complete Report_2014.pdf.

138 *"Without education, there will":* Associated Press, "Malala Yousafzai Donates Prize Money to Rebuild Gaza School," *New York Times,* October 30, 2014, http://www.nytimes.com/2014/10/31/world/middleeast/malala-yousafzai-nobel-gaza-school.html.
Forty-four percent: Thomas Bisika et al., "Gender-Violence and Education in Malawi: A Study of Violence Against Girls as an Obstruction to Universal Primary School Education," *Journal of Gender Studies* 18, no. 3 (2009), 287–94, library.unesco-iicba.org/English/Girls%20Education/All%20Articles/Violence%20and%20Conflict/Gender%20violence-education%20in%20Malawi.pdf.
In Zimbabwe, an astonishing: Fiona Leach et al., "Preliminary Investigation of the Abuse of Girls in Zimbabwean Junior Secondary Schools," Education Research Paper 39 (Department for International Development, 2000), 42, https://www.sussex.ac.uk/webteam/gateway/file.php?name=preliminary-investigation-of-the-abuse-of-girls-in-zimbabwean-schools-paper-39.pdf&site=320.
A 2012 survey by Cornell: "They Are Destroying Our Futures": Sexual Violence Against Girls in Zambia's Schools (Avon Global Center for Women and Justice, 2012), 1, scholarship.law.cornell.edu/cgi/viewcontent.cgi?article=1004&context=avon_clarke.

139 *girls would be forced:* Farouk Chothia, "Who Are Nigeria's Boko Haram Islamists?," BBC, May 4, 2015, http://www.bbc.com/news/world-africa-13809501.
as suicide bombers: Fred Barbash, "Reports: 10-Year-Old Girl Suicide Bomber

Kills at Least 16 in Nigeria," *Washington Post,* January 12, 2015, http://www
.washingtonpost.com/news/morning-mix/wp/2015/01/12/reports-10-year-old
-girl-suicide-bomber-kills-at-least-16-in-nigeria/.

kidnapped another 500: "Boko Haram Crisis: 'About 500' Nigerian Children
Missing," CNN, March 24, 2015, http://www.bbc.com/news/world
-africa-32044695.

reportedly killing 50: Joe Penney, "Boko Haram Kidnapped Hundreds in
Northern Nigeria Town: Residents," Reuters, March 24, 2015, http://www
.reuters.com/article/2015/03/24/us-violence-nigeria-kidnapping-idUSK
BN0MK22Y20150324.

In May 2015, reports emerged: Adam Nossiter, "Boko Haram Militants Raped
Hundreds of Female Captives in Nigeria," *New York Times*, May 18, 2015,
http://www.nytimes.com/2015/05/19/world/africa/boko-haram-militants
-raped-hundreds-of-female-captives-in-nigeria.html.

*In 2009, over 50 percent: Global Education Digest, 2011: Comparing Education
Statistics Across the World* (UNESCO Institute for Statistics, 2011), 11, 18–19,
http://www.uis.unesco.org/Library/Documents/global_education
_digest_2011_en.pdf.

*Only 23 percent of underserved: The Millennium Development Goals Report,
2014* (United Nations, 2014), 17, http://www.un.org/millenniumgoals/2014%20
MDG%20report/MDG%202014%20English%20web.pdf.

143 *One study estimated that Kenya . . . lifetime earnings equivalent:* Jad
Chaaban and Wendy Cunningham, "Measuring the Economic Gain of Invest-
ing in Girls: The Girl Effect Dividend," World Bank Policy Research Working
Paper 5753 (2011), http://www-wds.worldbank.org/external/default/WDS
ContentServer/IW3P/IB/2011/08/08/000158349_20110808092702/Rendered/
PDF/WPS5753.pdf.

145 *A 2012 study by the Girl:* Judy Schoenberg et al., *Generation STEM: What Girls
Say about Science, Technology, Engineering, and Math* (Girl Scouts Research
Institute, 2012), http://www.girlscouts.org/research/pdf/generation_stem
_full_report.pdf.

146 *stereotype threat:* Steven J. Spencer et al., "Stereotype Threat and Women's
Math Performance," *Journal of Experimental Social Psychology* 35, no. 1 (1999),
4–28, http://www.sciencedirect.com/science/article/pii/S0022103198913737.

earn more math and science: Brittany C. Cunningham et al., *Gender Differ-
ences in Science, Technology, Engineering, and Mathematics (STEM) Interest,
Credits Earned, and NAEP Performance in the 12th Grade* (U.S. Department of
Education, 2015), 7, nces.ed.gov/pubs2015/2015075.pdf.

perform better in those classes: Daniel Voyer and Susan D. Voyer, "Gender
Differences in Scholastic Achievement: A Meta-Analysis," *Psychological Bulletin* 140, no. 4 (2014), 1174–1204, www.apa.org/pubs/journals/releases/
bul-a0036620.pdf.

At the bachelor's degree: "Report: Snapshot Report — Degree Attainment" (Na-

tional Student Clearinghouse Research Center, 2015), http://nscresearchcenter
.org/wp-content/uploads/SnapshotReport15-DegreeAttainment.pdf.

As of 2013, women held: John Finamore and Beethika Khan, "Characteristics
of the College-Educated Population and the Science and Engineering Workforce in the United States" (National Science Foundation, 2015), 1, www.nsf.
gov/statistics/2015/nsf15317/nsf15317.pdf.

One 2007 study: Anne M. Perusek, "The Leaky Science and Engineering Pipeline: How Can We Retain More Women in Academia and Industry?," *Society
of Women Engineers National Survey about Engineering* (2008), 11,
societyofwomenengineers.swe.org/images/swemagazine/RetentionStudy
Compilation.pdf.

Role models matter: Catherine Riegle-Crumb and Chelsea Moore, "The Gender Gap in High School Physics: Considering the Context of Local Communities," *Social Science Quarterly* 95, no. 1 (2014), 253–68, http://onlinelibrary
.wiley.com/doi/10.1111/ssqu.12022/full.

Another survey found that only 4: "Women in STEM Research: Findings from
Recent myCollegeOptions® College Planning Study," press release, National
Research Center for College and University Admissions, June 27, 2014, www
.nrccua.org/cms/press-room/2014/39/Women-in-STEM-Research-Gender
-Gap-in-STEM-Majors-Career-Interests.

"Looking back, I had wonderful": Michael W. Richardson, "Carla Shatz: Shat-
tering the Glass Ceiling," *Society for Neuroscience*, May 16, 2012, www.brain
facts.org/About-Neuroscience/Meet-the-Researcher/Articles/2012/Carla-Shatz.

147 *"I had many offers of chairs":* Carol Ann Paul, "An Interview with Carla Shatz,
Harvard's First Female Neurobiology Chair," *Journal of Undergraduate Neuroscience Education* 3, no. 2 (2005), E4–E5, http://www.ncbi.nlm.nih.gov/pmc/
articles/PMC3592607/.

Online harassment: "Amanda Hess Wins February Sidney Award for 'The
Next Civil Rights Issue: Why Women Aren't Welcome on the Internet,'"
Sidney Hillman Foundation, February 2014, accessed March 9, 2015, http://
www.hillmanfoundation.org/thesidney/amanda-hess-wins-february-sidney
-award-%E2%80%9C-next-civil-rights-issue-why-women-aren%E2%80%99t
-welcome-/backstory.

148 *"who embodied the combination":* Walter Isaacson, *The Innovators: How a
Group of Hackers, Geniuses, and Geeks Created the Digital Revolution* (Simon
& Schuster, 2014), 5.

"system service girls": ComputerHistory, *Jean Bartik and the ENIAC Women*,
YouTube video, 6:09 minutes, November 10, 2010, https://www.youtube.com/
watch?v=aPweFhhXFvY.

all-purpose computing machine: Isaacson, *The Innovators*, 95–100.

"untold stories of women in science": Megan Smith and Jo Handelsman, "The
Untold Stories of Women in Science and Technology: Let's Write Them Per-
manently into History," White House (blog), December 11, 2014 (4:26 p.m.),

https://www.whitehouse.gov/blog/2014/12/11/untold-stories-women-science
-and-technology-lets-write-them-back-history.

149 *She insists that entry-level:* Katie Hafner, "Giving Women the Access Code,"
New York Times, April 2, 2012, www.nytimes.com/2012/04/03/science/giving
-women-the-access-code.html?_r=0.

In 2013, around 47 percent: Peter Burrows, "Harvey Mudd's Klawe Maps Way
to Woo Young Women into Tech," *Bloomberg,* August 7, 2014, http://www
.bloomberg.com/news/2014-08-07/harvey-mudd-s-klawe-maps-way-to-woo
-young-women-into-tech.html. See also *Bachelor's Degrees Awarded, by Sex
and Field, 2002–12* (National Science Foundation, 2014), www.nsf.gov/
statistics/wmpd/2013/pdf/tab5-1_updated_2014_05.pdf.

151 *$4.7 million in wages:* "Impact Dashboard, 2015 Q1" (SamaSource, 2015), http://
www.samasource.org/wp-content/uploads/2015/04/Q1-Dashboard.pdf.

"We must do more": "Remarks at Breakfast with Women Entrepreneurs Attending the Presidential Summit on Entrepreneurship," Washington, D.C.,
U.S. Department of State, April 28, 2010, accessed May 7, 2015, www.state.gov/
secretary/20092013clinton/rm/2010/04/140998.htm.

"Games like iCivics": Stephanie Chang, "Q&A: Supreme Court Justice Sandra
Day O'Connor," Amplify, May 10, 2013, http://www.amplify.com/viewpoints/
q-supreme-court-justice-sandra-day-oconnor.

seven million students: "Our Story," iCivics, accessed March 22, 2015, https://
www.icivics.org/our-story.

in all fifty states: Chang, "Q&A: Supreme Court Justice Sandra Day
O'Connor."

152 *Ring the Bell:* "About," Bell Bajao, accessed May 8, 2015, www.bellbajao.org/
home/about/.

living in poverty globally: Asli Demirguc-Kunt et al., *Measuring Financial Inclusion: The Global Findex Database* (World Bank, 2013), 1, http://siteresources
.worldbank.org/EXTGLOBALFIN/Resources/8519638-1332259343991/N9
gender.pdf.

Through cellphone banking: Christopher P. Beshouri and Jon Gravråk, "Cap-
turing the Promise of Mobile Banking in Emerging Markets," McKinsey &
Company, February 2010, http://www.mckinsey.com/insights/telecommunica
tions/capturing_the_promise_of_mobile_banking_in_emerging_markets.

153 *In its 2015 annual letter:* Bill and Melinda Gates, *2015 Gates Annual Letter:
Our Big Bet for the Future* (Bill and Melinda Gates Foundation, 2015), 17–19,
http://al2015.gatesnotesazure.com/assets/media/documents/2015_Gates_An-
nual_Letter_EN.pdf.

Research by the Cherie Blair: Women and Mobile: A Global Opportunity (Cherie Blair Foundation for Women and GSMA, 2010), 6, 22, http://www.gsma
.com/mobilefordevelopment/wp-content/uploads/2013/01/GSMA_Women_
and_Mobile-A_Global_Opportunity.pdf.

155 *when that country is Myanmar:* Cyn-Young Park et al., *Myanmar in Transition:*

Opportunities and Challenges (Asian Development Bank, 2012), 3–4, 8, 24, www.adb.org/sites/default/files/publication/29942/myanmar-transition.pdf.
A 2010 report by the Cherie Blair: Women and Mobile: A Global Opportunity, 7.
200 deaths per 100,000: "Maternal Mortality Remains a Threat to Myanmar Mums," UNRIC, January 8, 2014, www.unric.org/en/latest-un-buzz/28957-maternal-mortality-remains-a-threat-to-myanmar-mums.
historically, women are: "UNESCO/IGU Workshop on Women in Engineering in Africa and the Arab States," summary record (UNESCO, 2013), 32, http://members.igu.org/old/IGU%20Events/other-igu-events/unesco-igu-workshop-on-women-in-engineering/transcript-igu-unesco-women-in-engineering_stm.pdf.

156   *"The Internet gender gap . . . nearly 35 percent*: Yana Watson Kakar et al., *Women and the Web: Bridging the Internet Gap and Creating New Global Opportunities in Low and Middle-Income Countries* (Intel, 2013), 4, http://www.intel.com/content/dam/www/public/us/en/documents/pdf/women-and-the-web.pdf.

11. Media Matters

161   *"In the nineteenth century"*: Nicholas D. Kristof and Sheryl WuDunn, *Half the Sky: Turning Oppression into Opportunity for Women Worldwide* (First Vintage Books, 2010), xvii.

164   *three hundred million*: Lily Rothman, "Yang Lan, the 'Oprah of China,' Expands Her Reach," *Time*, June 23, 2014, http://time.com/2907444/yang-lan-the-oprah-of-china-expands-her-reach/.
Lan Yang is actively: Kristi Heim, "In Person: Yang Lan Nurtures Philanthropy among China's Newly Wealthy," *Seattle Times*, July 24, 2011, http://seattletimes.com/html/businesstechnology/2015711627_inpersonyang25.html.

165   *"History until the 20th century"*: Rebecca Keegan, "Meryl Streep's Next Project: A National Women's History Museum," *Los Angeles Times*, December 28, 2011, http://latimesblogs.latimes.com/movies/2011/12/meryl-streeps-next-project-a-national-womens-history-museum.html.
"the first periodical ever". . . Mail from readers: Abigail Pogrebin, "How Do You Spell Ms.," *New York*, October 30, 2011, http://nymag.com/news/features/ms-magazine-2011-11/.

166   *"We need to move"*: Mary Harrison, "Steinem Outlines Future of Feminism, Activism," *Stanford Daily*, January 27, 2012, http://www.stanforddaily.com/2012/01/27/steinem-outlines-future-of-feminism-activism-myths/.
By one analysis, it will take: "Women's Share of Seats in Congress, 1960–2013, with Projection for Political Parity in 2121" (Institute for Women's Policy Research, 2013), http://www.iwpr.org/publications/pubs/women2019s-share-of-seats-in-congress-1960-2013-with-projection-for-political-parity-in-2121.

167   *young women who've grown up*: Max M. Houck, "Is Forensic Science a Gateway

for Women in Science?," *Forensic Science Policy and Management* 1, no. 1 (2009), 65–69, http://www.tandfonline.com/doi/full/10.1080/19409040802629744# .VV6wxcbkxwQ.

"Women are the future": Dena Potter, "'CSI Effect' Draws More Women to Forensics," NBC News, August 17, 2008, http://www.nbcnews.com/id/26219249/ ns/technology_and_science-science/t/csi-effect-draws-more-women-foren sics/#.VSg6JZTF-tt.

a 2012 analysis of gender stereotypes: Research from Geena Davis Institute on Gender in Media conducted by Stacy L. Smith et al., *Gender Roles and Occupations: A Look at Character Attributes and Job-Related Aspirations in Film and Television* (Geena Davis Institute on Gender in Media, 2012), 3, http://seejane .org/wp-content/uploads/full-study-gender-roles-and-occupations-v2.pdf.

A 2014 global report showed: Research from Geena Davis Institute on Gender in Media conducted by Stacy L. Smith, Marc Choueiti, and Dr. Katherine Pieper, *Gender Bias Without Borders: An Investigation of Female Characters in Popular Films Across 11 Countries* (Geena Davis Institute on Gender in Media, 2014), 5, http://seejane.org/wp-content/uploads/gender-bias-without-borders -executive-summary.pdf.

Only 17 percent of actors: Research from Geena Davis Institute on Gender in Media conducted by Stacy L. Smith and Crystal Allene Cook, *Gender Stereotypes: An Analysis of Popular Films and TV* (Geena Davis Institute on Gender in Media, 2008), 1, http://seejane.org/wp-content/uploads/GDIGM_Gender_ Stereotypes.pdf.

168 *"media diet"*: Andrew Phelps, "Ethan Zuckerman Wants You to Eat Your (News) Vegetables — Or at Least Have Better Information," *Nieman Lab,* November 8, 2011, http://www.niemanlab.org/2011/11/ethan-zuckerman-wants -you-to-eat-your-news-vegetables-or-at-least-have-better-information/.

"messages and images": Wendy Spettigue and Katherine A. Henderson, "Eating Disorders and the Role of the Media," *Canadian Child and Adolescent Psychiatry Review* 13, no. 1 (February 2004), 16–18, http://www.ncbi.nlm.nih .gov/pmc/articles/PMC2533817/pdf/0130016.pdf.

Unfortunately, the pernicious effects: "The Media and Entertainment Industry in the United States," SelectUSA, U.S. Department of Commerce, accessed March 9, 2015, http://selectusa.commerce.gov/industry-snapshots/media -entertainment-industry-united-states.

169 *The institute sponsored the largest:* Research from Geena Davis Institute on Gender in Media conducted by Stacy L. Smith and Marc Choueiti, *Gender Disparity On-Screen and Behind the Camera in Family Films* (Geena Davis Institute on Gender in Media, 2010), 1, seejane.org/wp-content/uploads/key -findings-gender-disparity-family-films-2013.pdf.

"Bechdel test": Neda Ulaby, "The 'Bechdel Rule,' Defining Pop-Culture Character," NPR, September 2, 2008, http://www.npr.org/templates/story/story .php?storyId=94202522.

170 *Furthermore, FiveThirtyEight found:* Walt Hickey, "The Dollar-and-Cents Case Against Hollywood's Exclusion of Women," *FiveThirtyEight*, April 1, 2014, http://fivethirtyeight.com/features/the-dollar-and-cents-case-against-hollywoods-exclusion-of-women/.

12. Moments in History: Our Moment Is Now

172 *In 1848, Charlotte Woodward:* "Charlotte Woodward," National Park Service, accessed March 27, 2015, http://www.nps.gov/wori/learn/historyculture/charlotte-woodward.htm.
Earlier that month: Nancy F. Cott, ed., *No Small Courage: A History of Women in the United States* (Oxford University Press, 2000), 231–43.

173 *"There are few facts":* Philip S. Foner, ed., *Frederick Douglass: Selected Speeches and Writings* (Lawrence Hill Books, 1999), 709.

174 *"A woman is nobody . . . demoralize and degrade":* Elizabeth Cady Stanton et al., eds., *History of Woman Suffrage, Vol. 1, 1848–1861* (Susan B. Anthony, 1889–1922), 803–4.
"The most shocking and unnatural": Oneida Whig, August 1, 1848, from Library of Congress, accessed May 10, 2015, http://www.loc.gov/exhibits/treasures/images/vc006199.jpg.
a fourteen-year-old girl: Leili Anvar, *Malak Jân Nemati: Life Isn't Short, but Time Is Limited* (Arpeggio Press, 2012).

175 *Malak Jân's father:* Hadj Nematollah (1871–1920), was a charismatic mystic and prominent leader with a considerable following in his region. In the 1830s his forefathers settled in the village of Jeyhounabad, in western Iran. As landowners, the family was recognized for its nobility and courage, governing the affairs of the village and defending it from insurgents. For more information on the life and work of Hadj Nematollah, see *Encyclopaedia Iranica*, Volume XIV; Jean During, *The Spirit of Sounds: The Unique Art of Ostad Elahi* (Cornwall Books, 2003), 23; Anvar, *Malak Jân Nemati*, 21–22.

176 *"Though hardly leaving her native":* Anvar, *Malak Jân Nemati*, 59.

177 *"The stunning contrast between":* Ibid., 60.
"By facilitating the emancipation": "Malak Jân: An Enduring Legacy," Malak Jân, accessed March 27, 2015, http://www.malakjan.com/enduring_legacy.html.
"She was well aware": Anvar, *Malak Jân Nemati*, 63.
"the most comprehensive global": Beijing+20: Past, Present and Future: The Representation of Women and the United Nations System 1995–2030 (UN Women, 2015), 4, http://www.unwomen.org/~/media/headquarters/attachments/sections/library/publications/2015/representation%20of%20women%20in%20the%20un%20system%201995%20-%202030.pdf.
"When we empower women": Beijing Declaration and Platform for Action: Beijing+5 Political Declaration and Outcome (UN Women, 2000), 7, http://www

.unwomen.org/~/media/headquarters/attachments/sections/csw/pfa_e_fi
nal_web.pdf.

178 Full Participation Report: *The Full Participation Report: No Ceilings* (Clinton
Foundation and Bill and Melinda Gates Foundation, 2015), 4, http://noceilings
.org/report/report.pdf.
"Despite all this progress": "Transcript of Hillary Clinton's News Conference,"
Bloomberg, March 10, 2015, http://www.bloomberg.com/politics/
articles/2015-03-10/transcript-of-clinton-s-news-conference.

Appendix A

181 *"We mostly don't"*: Herminia Ibarra, "Six Ways to Grow Your Job," *Harvard
Business Review,* September 25, 2013, https://hbr.org/2013/09/six-ways-to-grow
-your-job/.

182 *"the power centers" . . . "Confidence is the stuff"*: Katty Kay and Claire Shipman,
*The Confidence Code: The Science and Art of Self-Assurance — What Women
Should Know* (HarperCollins, 2014), xiii, 50.

183 *B-phobia can deter:* Catherine Rampell, "Women Should Embrace the B's in
College to Make More Later," *Washington Post,* March 10, 2014, http://www
.washingtonpost.com/opinions/catherine-rampell-women-should-embrace
-the-bs-in-college-to-make-more-later/2014/03/10/1e15113a-a871-11e3-8d62
-419db477a0e6_story.html.

184 *In her book* The Up: Megan McArdle, *The Up Side of Down: Why Failing Well
Is the Key to Success* (Penguin Group, 2014), xiii, 3–7, 48–50, 250–51.

185 *disproportionate share of criticism:* See, e.g., Alice H. Eagly and Steven J.
Karau, "Role Congruity Theory of Prejudice Toward Female Leaders," *Psychological Review* 109, no. 3 (2002), 573–98, http://www.rci.rutgers.edu/~search1/
pdf/Eagley_Role_Conguity_Theory.pdf.

188 *Studies have found that people . . . rates of volunteerism:* Grimm, Spring, and
Dietz, "The Health Benefits of Volunteering."

189 *As Aaron Hurst notes:* Aaron Hurst, *The Purpose Economy* (Elevate USA,
2014).

192 *"kitchen cabinet"*: Bob Frisch, "Who Really Makes the Big Decisions in Your
Company?," *Harvard Business Review,* December 2011, https://hbr.org/2011/12/
who-really-makes-the-big-decisions-in-your-company.

194 *"a useful source"*: Tanya Menon and Leigh Thompson, "Envy at Work," *Harvard Business Review,* April 2010, https://hbr.org/2010/04/envy-at-work.

Index